American Mainline Religion

Wade Clark Roof
William McKinney

American Mainline Religion

Its Changing Shape and Future

Rutgers University Press

New Brunswick and London

Library of Congress Cataloging-in-Publication Data

Roof, Wade Clark.
    American mainline religion.

    Includes index.
    1. United States—Religion—1960–   . I. McKinney,
William, 1946–   . II. Title.
BR526.R655   1987   306′.6′0973   86–17853
ISBN 0–8135–1215–8
ISBN 0–8135–1216–6 (pbk.)
British Cataloging-in-Publication Information Available.

*To Terry Potter Roof
and Linda Roberts McKinney*

Contents

Figures

Tables

Acknowledgments

This book represents five years of collaborative research and writing on American religion. Since the early 1980s the two of us have been involved in several research projects inquiring into one aspect or another of mainline religious life, all valuable in themselves but none offering a broad picture of the contemporary situation. In this volume we have sought to pull the many strands of that work together into a general perspective on religious and cultural trends.

Our purpose in writing the book was to try to understand how and why the religious scene is changing and its likely future. One of us is a sociology professor in a state university, the other is a seminary professor and administrator. Together we have benefited from the mix of ideas arising out of theology, the social sciences, and the churches themselves. We hope the analysis has benefited as well, making for an empathetic, yet rigorous empirical approach to the subject.

Over the years our work has been supported and funded by the Spencer Foundation, Lilly Endowment, Inc., Hartford Seminary, the United Church Board for Homeland Ministries, and the University of Massachusetts. We are grateful to all these agencies and institutions and especially to Robert Wood Lynn, senior vice president for religion, Lilly Endowment, Inc., for his support and encouragement. The Rowny Foundation provided a lovely place to live and work in Santa Barbara, California, for one of us while on sabbatical leave to work on the project. Several colleagues and friends provided us with helpful comments along the way, particularly Jackson W. Carroll, Phillip E. Hammond, Armand Mauss, Robert S. Michaelsen, and David A. Roozen. Wayne Thompson, Sheila Ayres, and Jennifer Roof assisted in the research in various of its phases. To all of them we are deeply indebted. None of course are responsible for any errors of interpretation that might remain.

Several themes in this volume were anticipated in a number of essays published by one or both of us during these years: "America's

Voluntary Establishment: Mainline Religion in Transition," *Daedalus* 111 (1982); "Beyond *Protestant—Catholic—Jew*," *New Conversations* 6, no. 3 (Spring 1982); "A Social Profile of American Religious Groups," in *Yearbook of American and Canadian Churches*, ed. Constant H. Jacquet, Jr. (Nashville: Abingdon Press, 1982); "Denominational America and the New Religious Pluralism," *Annals of the American Academy of Political and Social Science* 480 (July 1985); and "Liberal Protestantism: A Socio-Demographic Perspective," in *Liberal Protestantism: Realities and Possibilities*, ed. Robert S. Michaelsen and Wade Clark Roof (New York: Pilgrim Press, 1986). The ideas and interpretations advanced in the pages that follow in part draw from and develop out of these earlier essays.

Finally, we appreciate the support and encouragement of Terry Potter Roof and Linda Roberts McKinney, to whom the book is dedicated.

American Mainline Religion

Introduction

"**W**e live in the description of a place and not in the place itself," Wallace Stevens wrote—in a poet's way of speaking, a profound sociological truth. But how do people live when the place itself is changing and when those who presumably should know what is going on cannot agree as to where the place is, or whether it is changing for the better or the worse?

The question is a good one for America's religious establishment today. Many people, both within and outside organized religion, are concerned about the current religious and spiritual climate of the nation. Journalists, scholars, commentators, religionists—all write about how the religious scene is in flux, but they hardly agree in their interpretation of what is happening. Many point to how the older orthodoxies and moral certitudes that once reigned in American life have lost their force; others see powerful new religious forces at work revitalizing the culture. Institutional religious trends are ambiguous: some indicators suggest a religious upswing at present; others point in the direction of a growing secularism and a decline in religion's influence. Not surprisingly, many members of churches and synagogues today find themselves confused about what is happening and about the future. More than confused, many feel buffeted about by forces, leaving them unsure, as the poet says, of the "description of a place" they now occupy.

The place of the religious institutions in American society is indeed changing, and at a fairly rapid pace. Since the 1960s the country has been caught up in a series of social and cultural shifts that have greatly altered the place of religion in the lives of many Americans. So massive and far-reaching have been the changes that the religious landscape is considerably different now than it was even as recently as twenty-five years ago. Many of the changes are well known, such as the rise of cults and charismatic gurus, popular movements of born-again Christianity, and grass-roots organizations such as Moral Majority, Inc.; others having to do with core values and outlook and the subtle shifting patterns of religion and culture are far less visible.

Two major developments leaving their imprint upon the period were the youth counterculture of the late 1960s and the evangelical revival of the mid-to-late 1970s. The two movements had little in common as to style and ideology—one arising out of the "fringes" and the other from the "bottom" of the socioreligious order, so to speak. Yet both mobilized deep sentiments and sharpened the edges faith presents to the world, and thus brought to the fore powerful religious impulses during a time of extraordinary ferment. Both challenged the religious establishment as well as modern secularity with which it is often comfortably allied. And both were expressions of a search for spirituality and inner truth, one drawing off Eastern themes and the other off older, more indigenous elements of the American religious heritage. Far from being superficial or inconsequential, they unleashed new energies and cultivated psychoreligious cultures that are having, and are likely to continue having for some time to come, a profound impact on the religious scene.

Gradually we are beginning to grasp the full force of these broader religious changes. Developments at the religious and cultural center are always slower to crystallize than those on the periphery, but in the 1980s the contours of a new, reshaped religious mainline are coming into sharper focus. What were once just rumblings on the "fringes" and at the "bottom" are now reverberations that have reached all the way to the "center." Just listing a few of the trends attracting much attention in recent years shows the depths of the changes now underway:

—The privileged Protestant mainline has fallen upon hard times and no longer enjoys the influence and power it once had.
—Conservative Protestants are flourishing and are now much more culture affirming than they used to be.
—Roman Catholic leadership has assumed a new position in the center and is articulating a social vision to its constituency and the public at large.
—American Jews seem to have experienced a shift in outlook— more concerned now with group interests and survival and less with assimilation.

—Black religionists are now holding up a more inclusive vision of America and are less prone to a separatist outlook.
—Secular humanism is identified as a growing and hostile force in relation to traditional religion and morality

As these examples suggest, the religious landscape in America in the 1980s is undergoing massive shifts. Far more than spiritual rumblings on the periphery and at the bottom, the religious establishment itself is caught up in a profound transformation. The shifts signify a new religiocultural order now in the making—a rearrangement of groups and forces, a realignment of power and influence, and a change of mood and outlook. Religious themes have taken on an enlivened presence in public life in recent years: many people are keenly aware of the many religious voices now heard speaking out on moral values and life-style issues, and many are concerned about the direction of the nation's future. Americans generally are now grappling seriously with issues of public faith and morality, more so than at any time in recent memory.

What are the dominant trends now shaping American religious life? What is the emerging new shape of religion in the United States? What does the nation's religious future hold? These are the questions that concern us in this volume, questions that have led us to a new "mapping" of religion in contemporary America. Such questions are difficult to answer, partly because we are still too close to this period of change. Time must pass before we can grasp fully all the implications. Yet because we believe the issues are important, we grapple with them in the pages that follow. "Observers of American religion regularly need to map the terrain," writes Martin E. Marty, "Its bewildering pluralism, they soon learn, resists a single or permanent outline."[1]

This mapping is a formidable task. As historian Philip Schaff observed more than a century ago, "The United States is a motley sampler of all church history."[2] In addition to all the religious divisions of the past, America has produced its own schisms and heresies in abundant numbers. In the *Encyclopedia of American Religions*, J. Gordon Melton compiles information on more than twelve hundred different groups of varied traditions now active in the United States.[3] Aside from sheer numbers and complexity, there is volatility as well: religion in this country is always changing. For all these reasons it is tempting for the person trying to make sense out of it all to simply assume that there are Protestants, Catholics, and Jews and let it go at that, which is what many pollsters and social analysts do. Or one might choose to describe in great detail and depth just one or a few of the hundreds of groups that make up the American religious scene, which is what ethnographers and historians often do. Both approaches are valid in themselves and yield insights, but neither is very satisfactory for our purposes.

Our concern is with "mainline religion"—admittedly a vague, somewhat value-laden designation, yet it focuses attention on the religious and cultural center. By *mainline* (or *mainstream* which is a frequently used synonym), we mean the dominant, culturally established faiths held by the majority of Americans. To focus on the center calls for a level of description and generality above that of ethnography while at the same time resisting simple categorization. For much of American history, mainline religion meant simply white Protestant, but as the boundaries of pluralism expanded mainline religion has come to mean more. Many groups— Protestant, Catholic, Jewish, white and nonwhite—that command the loyalities of large numbers of persons and help shape the normative faith and outlook of the populace lay claim to being in the mainline. Of interest to us is what is happening at this religious core, not so much among the marginal cults, sects, new religious movements, or even many of the smaller religious bodies in the country today.

Centripetal forces run deep in the American experience—that is, the tendency for beliefs, values, and normative styles to crystallize at the center. Sectarians over time often become more churchlike; fringe movements if they survive typically become more accommodating. Faith and culture are closely intertwined, making for some distinctive features of American religion. One is its secular, all-pervasive quality: more than a sacramental, an ecclesiastical, a dogmatic-confessional, or a transcendentally directed faith, religion in this country is directed toward the actual world in which people live. A second is its almost total acceptance of the social environment: Americans have traditionally viewed the state, the community, the family, and the marketplace as "God-given," as agencies of divine purpose in a world that is still taking shape. A third feature —especially evident in the religious mainline—is its dynamic, populist character: religious styles and institutions are inevitably influenced by the moods and sentiments of the people.

The reasons for focusing upon the mainline thus seem evident. Here popular religious impulses work themselves out. Here the dominant ethos of the country takes shape. Here large numbers of lives are influenced. Religious and cultural innovations often have their sources elsewhere, at the fringes or bottom, but inevitably, if the innovations are to have much influence, they must find their way to a larger public. Our concern is with this "vital center" of American life and the forces now reshaping it. What happens at the center is crucial—both for the religious establishment and for the nation's future. If the present is indeed a time of major shifts in the relations of religion and culture and changing, normative faiths, then it is imperative that we understand what is happening and what these changes might mean for the years ahead.

Our perspective draws upon both demographic and cultural analysis. Demographics play a great part in shaping the religious mainline: some groups are growing; others are losing members. Membership statistics, birth rates, age cohorts, and success in converting new members are all factors in describing the changing religious composition of the country and thus figure prominently in our analysis. We believe these data showing social and demographic trends are crucial for understanding the changing religious scene, and thus we highlight them even though to do so requires that we include many tables and figures in our text. All too often such data are overlooked by theologians as well as social scientists, which is unfortunate; for this very reason we seek to present these materials.

Of importance as well are social and cultural trends that are closely associated with religious changes. Obviously the demographics alone are insufficient for defining and describing what is the "mainline" of religion; religious establishments have power—social power, economic power, cultural power. Since the 1960s the realities of pluralism and privatism have done much to undermine old religious and cultural hegemonies. Pluralism has long been a recognized feature of American religious life, yet as we shall see, its impact upon the dominant order was especially felt in this period. Less obvious as a factor is the greater privatism of the modern era, or the tendency toward highly individualized religious psychology without the benefits of strong supportive attachments to believing communities. A major impetus in this direction in the post-1960s was the thrust toward greater personal fulfillment and quest for the ideal self. While the quest itself is as old as the American experience, social scientists and cultural historians are generally agreed that in the sixties and seventies this quest was pursued with particular intensity. It was pursued on a far wider scale than ever before, touching almost every sector of society. What William James called "the sphere of felicity"—the inner life of impulse and subjectivity—was deeply expanded and enriched. Viewed as healthy by some, and with alarm by others, we look upon this highly individualistic ethos favoring greater religious subjectivity and personal choice as having important implications for American religious life and for enlarging, perhaps permanently, the boundaries of moral and religious discourse in this country.

To tell the story of the changing face of religion in America is to pull together these strands—demographic, cultural, psychological. The past two decades are a watershed period of great significance precisely because of the broad scope of changes that interacted with one another to rock the old religious establishment. With an altered religious mainline has come an eclipse of old patterns of faith and culture, but also new religious possibilities and opportunities. Ours is a time of "disestablishment," when many of the older taken-for-granted realities have disappeared; in such times passions and energies often run strong. In our diagnosis and prognosis of the changing religious center, we have sought to combine rigorous analysis with as compassionate yet balanced a perspective as possible. We have tried to be "realists," while at the same time avoiding painting scenerios that are unduly pessimistic or superficially optimistic.

Certainly we are not as hopeful as some recent commentators— for example, Harvey Cox and William G. McLoughlin—who discern a profound religious awakening in the making and the return of the sacred.[4] There are of course some signs of a religious upswing, but so is there much evidence of a growing secularity which is perhaps even more important. At the same time, we do not write off the modern world as an age of rampant secularization and religious decline as do many scholars and intellectuals. We part company, for example, with Michael Harrington, who, as has others before him, speaks of "the politics at God's Funeral."[5] Secularization is, to be sure, a reality to reckon with, and we do so by looking at it as a corrosive influence upon organized religion, yet we do not view it as a force that is intrinsically and irreversibly antagonistic to religion. Modernity has brought about many changes in the realms of faith, but most of all it has created a situation that is open-ended and varied, somewhat unpredictable, and certainly one that defies simple and easy generalizations. As many commentators have said, Americans are deeply religious and deeply secular; for us the challenge is not in choosing one or the other of these labels but in sorting out the intricacies of the relations between them.

Our analysis begins with the recent broad changes in religion and culture in the United States. We describe in some detail in chapter 1 changes flowing from the 1960s—the nation's changing religious composition, declines in the liberal faiths, the evangelical and fundamentalist resurgence, and a growing secularism. Critically important are the erosion of a public faith, the polarization of American life, and the heightened religious individualism of our time. More generally, we explore the challenges to the mainline faiths and the vacuum in the culture created by the collapse of the middle.

In chapter 2 we examine the "new voluntarism" which now finds expression in American religion. This term refers to the greater choice in religious affiliation and the more privatized psychology of religious faith and identity, in keeping with the cultural mood of the sixties and seventies. The relation of these trends to basic demographic, social, and cultural changes of the post-1960s takes up much of the chapter. The implications of greater individualism and voluntarism for religious belonging are crucial for understanding what is now happening on the religious scene.

The major religious families comprising the religious mainline today are described in chapter 3. We compare the traditions by looking at their changing postures, behavioral styles, and communal bonds. Of particular concern are the levels of group attachments for members, some of the families being far more successful than others in creating a strong sense of community. Utilizing survey data, we provide descriptive information on the groups and their social and religious characteristics.

Chapter 4 looks at the classic "social sources of denominationalism" in this country. We explore several major historic social factors linked with religious groups—social class, ethnicity, race, and region—and examine the extent to which these factors still divide the religious communities. Major attention is given to the changing social bases of mainline religion in the contemporary United States. Continuity versus change is a concern in mapping the social location of the religious traditions today.

The demography of religious change is taken up in chapter 5. Here we examine factors of births, deaths, and religious switching, all of which bear directly on the size and growth potential of religious groups. Of interest are the social and cultural characteristics of switchers and the several "streams" of switching now reshaping the religious establishment. Greater voluntarism results in shifts from one faith to another, and shifts away from faith, and is a significant factor in the growth and decline of the various religious and cultural constituencies.

Current controversies over moral values and life-styles are discussed in chapter 6. Issues surrounding abortion, homosexuality, changing sexual norms, women's rights, racial attitudes, and civil liberties are all crucial in the religious establishment today. We look at the moral polarization in religion, the new alignments of the groups, and the changing boundaries of religious pluralism generally. Of much interest is the character of moral and religious rhetoric lying at the center of the divisions as well as the value conflicts in American society at present.

Finally, chapter 7 ponders the future shape of American religion. Based upon demographic projections and current religious trends we speculate about the changing composition of the religious mainline. We explore its weaknesses and strengths, its possible role in American life, and its changing institutional forms in the years ahead. Of concern are the nation's changing religious profile and a weakened public faith, both of which imply a different picture of religious pluralism for the future.

Chapter One

The Legacy of the Sixties

A Great Puritan Epoch can be seen as beginning in 1558 with the death of Mary Tudor, the last monarch to rule over an officially Roman Catholic England, and as ending in 1960 with the election of John Fitzgerald Kennedy, the first Roman Catholic president of the United States.

—SYDNEY E. AHLSTROM

The 1960s marks a turning point in American religious life. Future historians will have to judge how great a turning point it was, but we are convinced that during these years patterns of religion began to change in significant ways. The decade brought a shift of mood and widespread social and institutional dislocations. For young Americans especially it was a turbulent and at times traumatic period; the culture was deeply shaken—with repercussions felt in the mores and ethos, in life-styles and world views, and even at the profoundest ethical and spiritual levels. It was as if the old synthesis of religion and culture fell apart, or as historian Sydney E. Ahlstrom put it, a time when the "old foundations of national confidence, patriotic idealism, moral traditionalism, and even of historic Judaeo-Christian theism, were awash. Presuppositions that had held firm for centuries—even millenia—were being widely questioned."[1]

The breakup was especially evident on the fringes of the culture. The rise of new religious movements and spiritual experimentation of many kinds signaled deeply rooted shifts in outlook and beliefs. Early on, theologians on talk shows and the lecture circuit began proclaiming the "death of God" and mounting a movement to reconceptualize faith in radical, de-mythologized terms. The old supernatural language had reached a crisis point, at least within some theological and intellectual circles. Yet at the same time, ironically, new gods were being born in the most unexpected of places—the secular college campuses. At colleges and universities across the country, many new sects and cults emerged, with their members wearing strange garb, practicing ancient rituals, and speaking in esoteric tongues: Hare Krishnas, Zen Buddhists, Vedantists, Sufis, and scores of other "new religions." And the converts were disaffected middle-class youth who were looking for alternatives to the more established faiths. The spiritual ferment took many forms, including mystical cults, religious communes, the occult, the "Jesus people," Eastern spiritualists, and the human potential movement.

There were many signs of cultural change. Countercultural youth experimented not just with new religions but with alternative political, economic, family, and sexual styles. It was the Age of Aquarius and a time for "getting into" a range of experiential frames—from astrology to Zen. In Emile Durkheim's terms, these were "moments of effervescence," one of those periods when religious and cultural meanings become infused anew in the world and ways of perceiving and experiencing life are substantially altered.

Though far less visible, strains were beginning to be felt in the more established religious traditions as well. The Roman Catholic church was in the throes of a profound transition, brought on by Vatican Council II and its call for *aggiornamento*, or updating of the church in the face of modernity. Nowhere would the council's actions have greater consequences than in the United States, where pressures had long been mounting for a more democratized, lay-centered church. Its impact would be felt immediately, and for decades to come, within the church hierarchy and the larger Catholic community; virtually all aspects of parish church life—including the authority of the church itself—would be deeply affected. So abrupt and widespread were the changes that John Cogley spoke of the 1960s as "the most dramatic, critical ten years in American Catholic history."[2]

Protestantism was following a course that would climax in serious strains and reordering as well. The old Protestant establishment was in a state of decline and seriously confronting for the first time the reality of pluralism. Secular and religious alternatives presented themselves as never before, posing new challenges and an uncertain future for what had long been the nation's dominant cultural and religious tradition. For liberal Protestants, the older theological solutions had ceased to satisfy, amidst calls for a more radical theology; among the rank-and-file laypersons there was division over the church's involvement in social issues and growing signs of a "gathering storm in the churches."[3] With the civil rights movement, black churches became important centers of social protest and group solidarity. And by the end of the decade there was evidence of a resurgent conservative Protestantism and growing sentiment for a return to traditional values and beliefs, all of which led Martin E. Marty to comment upon the "seismic shift" occurring in the nation's religious landscape.[4]

More broadly, the old civil faith that once unified Americans around the celebration of national values and purpose was deemed by many to be hollow and deceitful. The traumatic events surrounding the assassination of a president, the civil rights struggle, an unpopular war in Vietnam, and the generational conflict all contributed to a sense of despair and disillusionment. In a real sense, the culture was in travail at its deepest moral and spiritual levels; national values and institutional patterns that had guided Americans for generations seemed to be in a state of flux. Nowhere was this travail more apparent than in the public opinion polls that regularly tapped the religious sensibilities of the land: churchgoing declined steadily year by year during the 1960s, and the proportion of Americans who thought religion was losing its influence grew as the decade progressed.[5] Terms such as *post-Protestant, postreligious*, and *secular city* found their way into common parlance. A change in the mood and outlook of the country was much in evidence.

Beyond *Protestant—Catholic—Jew*

The shift in mood becomes all the more evident when contrasted with the earlier religious climate of the 1950s. At midcentury indicators had pointed to good times for religion. Church membership statistics were up; interest in morality and religion seemed high. A popular, highly generalized version of religion prevailed: "He" was a best-selling lyric set to music; God was pictured as the "man upstairs"; motion pictures brought to the screen epic biblical dramas such as *The Ten Commandments* and *Ben Hur*; magazines held up religious figures as symbols of the American Way

of Life. The most symbolic figure of all was Pres. Dwight D. Eisenhower, who picked up the old theocratic language and spoke of God
and country in eloquent terms. Religion enjoyed a comfortable alliance with the culture and was seemingly all-pervasive and diffuse in
American life.

Perhaps the most insightful commentator at the time was Will
Herberg, whose *Protestant—Catholic—Jew* captured the generalized religious mood of the period. "The outstanding feature of the
religious situation in America today," wrote Herberg in 1955, "is
the pervasiveness of religious self-identification along the tripartite
scheme of Protestant, Catholic, Jew."[6] He pointed to the close ties
between religion and the American way of life and the forces pres-
suring Americans to belong to one or another of the three great religious communities. Group differences seemed to be on the decline
in a more homogenized and integrated culture. The central theme
was religious conformity, which was more pronounced, as he saw it,
among younger, "modern-minded" suburban dwellers. As Herberg
said:

> Not to be—that is, not to be a Protestant, a Catholic, or a Jew is
> somehow not to be an American. It may imply being foreign, as
> is the case when one professes oneself a Buddhist, a Muslim, or
> anything but a Protestant, Catholic, or Jew, even when one's
> Americanness is beyond question. Or it may imply being ob-
> scurely "un-American," as is the case with those who declare
> themselves atheists, agnostics, or even "humanists." . . .
> Americanness today entails identification as Protestant, Catho-
> lic, or Jew in a way and to a degree quite unprecedented in our
> history. To be a Protestant, a Catholic, or a Jew are today the al-
> ternative ways of being an American.[7]

But Herberg's thesis fails to ring true in America in the 1980s. If
the three great religious communities were the primary sources of
individual and social identity in the 1950s (which may have been
overstated then), this no longer holds. Something happened in the
1960s that moved the nation beyond this scheme of religiously
based core-culture affirmations. In the aftermath of that eventful decade, the range of alternatives had broadened and the pressures of religious conformity had weakened. "To be a Protestant, a Catholic,

or a Jew" simply conveyed less force of meaning than it had in the years before.

A New Pluralism

The profiles of Herberg's three great religious communities have changed significantly since he wrote. Most notable is the steady numerical decline of the Protestant majority. That majority is still intact, but its size has eroded over the past three decades —from 67 percent of the American population in 1952 to 57 percent at present, or a proportional loss of 15 percent. What Herberg said then is even more true now: "Protestantism in America today presents the anomaly of a strong majority group with a growing minority consciousness."[8]

Throughout this century Protestants have had to adapt to declines. Pressures of urbanization, immigration, and internal controversy over religion's accommodation to modernity in the early years all contributed to the erosion of Protestantism's cultural hegemony. More than simply a matter of declining numbers, there was a discernible shift in ethos. Historians date the beginnings of the Protestant establishment's decline to the 1920s and 1930s, but the "age of the WASP" did not really end in the minds of most Americans until the 1960s. During that decade, the nation elected, for the first time, a Roman Catholic president, and the Supreme Court rendered two crucial decisions, one mandating "one man one vote" and the other ruling public school prayer unconstitutional.[9] The Kennedy election was deeply symbolic of a new era, and the Court's decisions greatly undermined the old historic religious power base and the dominant culture. The message of the sixties rang loud in Protestant ears: pluralism in religious and cultural styles was here, and here to stay.

During these same years Catholics were gaining in numbers and influence. In the short space of thirty years, Catholics grew from 25 percent to 28 percent of the nation's population, increasing 12 percent. Benefiting from a high birth rate and immigration, Catholicism has grown proportionately almost as much as Protestantism has declined. The social basis of the religious community likewise shifted. After World War II Catholics made such spectacular gains in

TABLE 1-1

TRENDS IN RELIGIOUS PREFERENCE, 1952–1985

	1985	1952	Percentage Change
Protestant	57	67	− 15
Catholic	28	25	+ 12
Jewish	2	4	− 50
Other	4	1	+300
None	9	2	+350

Source: *Emerging Trends*, vol. 8, no. 2 (February 1986). Published by Princeton Religion Research Center.

education, occupational status, and income that by the 1970s their overall status levels were roughly equal to those of Protestants. With upward mobility and rapid assimilation, Catholics moved into the mainstream socially, culturally, and religiously. They have come to resemble other Americans in many respects: in social attitudes, child-rearing values, political party affiliation, and religious patterns. Young Catholics, especially now, attend worship services, join churches, and drop out of churches much the same as Protestants.

In contrast with Protestants and Catholics, the Jewish proportion of the population has declined since midcentury. A low birth rate and high levels of intermarriage have worked to keep its size small. In terms of power and influence, however, Jews are still a major religious and cultural community. In the larger context of America's religious groups, they are also something of a special case, both as a religious and an ethnic group. The latter makes for enduring communal bonds, a factor of no small significance in American religious life. Some of the most striking and, to some, alarming changes have to do with levels of religious commitment.

All three religious communities lost some of their most committed members during the 1960s. Throughout the period of public opinion polling up until the midsixties, roughly three-quarters of the American population reported they were church or synagogue members. But polls in the seventies and early eighties began to show distinct declines in religious membership, reaching a low of 67 percent in 1982. Eighty percent of Catholics are members of a congregation, as are 73 percent of Protestants and 45 percent of Jews.[10] These downward trends have in recent years given rise to concerns about "unchurched Americans" and the growing numbers of persons having little or no contact with organized religion.

Studies show that the "unchurched" are disproportionately young, male, white, well educated, nonsouthern, and frequent movers. They are less conformist on social issues and cultural attitudes and far more tolerant and open to change.[11] In profile characteristics they are the mirror image of those who are the most religiously committed—older persons, females, blacks, the lesser educated, southerners, and the geographically stable. So striking are the contrasts that the possibility of a growing cleavage between religious and secular America appeared more likely during the 1970s than at any time in the past quarter century. George Gallup, Jr., the nation's most prominent religious pollster, concluded after surveying the scene that the shape of the future depends, to a large degree, on the religious belief and practice of two key groups—the college educated, who include most of the opinion leaders in the society, and the young, who will set the tone for church and nation in the years ahead.[12]

As might be expected, the largest proportionate increases since the 1950s have come not in Herberg's three great religious communities but among those who classify themselves as "other" or "none." Today 4 percent of the population claim a faith outside the three major traditions, compared to about 1 percent in the early fifties; 9 percent identify as "none" (or nonaffiliated), which is seven points higher than before. Because the percentage base for these categories is small, the importance of the proportional changes should not be overdrawn. Still the figures are striking. A heterogeneous assortment of non-Judeo-Christian faiths now commands the loyalties of more Americans than does Judaism. This represents a sizable number of followers and practitioners falling outside the more conventional faiths. And the fact that almost 10 percent of Americans report themselves nonaffiliated is revealing on two counts: it points not only to a growing secularized sector of the population but also to the greater ease with which Americans "reject" a religious affiliation. The decline in religious membership since the early seventies (7 percent or 8 percent) about equals the current percentage expressing no religious preference.

Reflected in these figures are the large numbers of young, well-educated, middle-class youth who defected from the churches in the

late sixties and the seventies. This period witnessed a religious defection of unprecedented proportions that represented more than
the usual turning away of the young in the adolescent and early
adult years. Both the numbers and the scope of spiritual experimentation involved point to nothing less than a revolt against the established faiths. The polls give only hints of what happened to the
young defectors: some joined new religious movements, others
sought personal enlightenment through various spiritual therapies
and disciplines, but most simply "dropped out" of organized religion
altogether. A 1976 Gallup survey revealed that 4 percent of the adult
population professes involvement in Transcendental Meditation, 3
percent in yoga, 2 percent in mysticism, and 1 percent in Eastern religions.[13] Though small in percentages, these constituencies are
impressive. For example, the 4 percent participating in TM projects
to fully 6 million persons—about as many as those who identify
themselves as Presbyterians. Some church members also experimented with the new therapies, but by and large it was disaffected
youth who turned inward in these quests. Commitment to social
causes, which had inspired so much energy in the early sixties, gave
way to a greater concern with the self.

Out of all this ferment has come a vastly more pluralistic religious environment, even more than could have been envisioned just
a few decades ago. There are two Hindu temples on a single block in
Queens, a Moslem mosque rising in Allentown, Pennsylvania, and a
Buddhist temple in the shadow of the Mormon Tabernacle in Salt
Lake City, and the cofounder of Apple Computer talks freely of having his head shaved by an Indian baba in the Himalayas.[14] The
boundaries of what is popularly regarded as "conventional" in religion have expanded. Earlier lines between normative faith and de-
viant belief, between those loyal to the Judeo-Christian faiths
and those opposed or indifferent to them, have been redrawn to include faiths as "foreign" as Buddhism and Islam; even atheism, ag-
nosticism, and humanism, once truly in the outer limits, are now
more acceptable. Extraordinary religion has in time become quite
ordinary.

The Plight of the Liberal Churches

Of all the postsixties religious changes, none was
better documented than the membership declines of the liberal,

mainline Protestant churches. Beginning about 1965, many well-established Protestant churches not only stopped growing, but actually began reporting significant membership losses. Denominations with records of sustained growth and prosperity, some dating to colonial times, experienced their first major downturns. Many of them continue to lose members twenty years later.

As early as 1972, Dean M. Kelley, in *Why Conservative Churches Are Growing*, called attention to what was happening to these churches. This book described the shifting balance of power, and its title might just as well been "Why Liberal Churches Are Declining." Kelley postulated that churches were growing, or declining, in proportion to their position on what he called "the Exclusivist-Ecumenical Gradient." Grouping the churches from the top, he listed the following as the most exclusivist and antiecumenical:

Black Muslims
Jehovah's Witnesses
Evangelicals and Pentecostals
Orthodox Jews
Churches of Christ
Latter-Day Saints (Mormons)
Seventh-Day Adventists
Church of God
Church of Christ, Scientist

Next were larger religious communities of somewhat ambiguous status—less exclusivist but intact enough to provide a distinctive identity for their members:

Southern Baptist Convention
Lutheran Church—Missouri Synod
American Lutheran Church
Roman Catholic Church
Conservative Jews
Russian Orthodox
Greek Orthodox

Finally, there were the churches more typically mainstream:

Southern Presbyterian Church
Reformed Church in America

Episcopal Church
American Baptist Convention
United Presbyterian Church
United Methodist Church
United Church of Christ
Reform Jews
Ethical Culture Society
Unitarian-Universalists

Kelley went on to suggest an interpretation: "Other things being equal, bodies low on the list will tend to diminish in numbers while those high on the list will tend to increase."[15] Those groups closely identified with the mainstream culture were in trouble, but those most distanced from it enjoyed continuing vitality and growth.

For the most part, Kelley's interpretation holds. Even if his explanation for why growth stopped is unconvincing, his scheme is descriptively accurate. The large ecumenical bodies most comfortably allied with the culture were losing members. To cite some prominent examples, the Episcopal Church, the United Presbyterian Church, the United Methodist Church, the Christian Church (Disciples of Christ), and the United Church of Christ all reported losses beginning in the midsixties. They all lost members during the sixties and seventies—some by as much as 10 percent or more per decade. By the end of the 1970s, Lutherans and the Reformed Church in America had joined the list of mainline bodies with net membership losses.[16] For all these churches, those losses represented an abrupt and dramatic turnaround in their privileged status and respectability: churches seemingly as American as apple pie and the Fourth of July suddenly fell upon hard times. As many as ten of the largest Protestant denominations were in the throes of what can only be described as a serious religious depression.

Careful analysis of membership trends shows that the churches hardest hit were those highest in socioeconomic status, those stressing individualism and pluralism in belief, and those most affirming of American culture.[17] All three are features of liberal Protestantism. Identification with the American Way especially lies at the core of this tradition. For the period between 1965 and 1975, the correlation between identification with the culture and membership decline is a staggering .97! Almost all of the churches that retained distance from the culture by encouraging distinctive life-styles and beliefs grew; those most immersed in the culture and only vaguely identifiable in terms of their own features suffered declines.

More than just membership losses, the churches experienced declines in religious participation and institutional support. Attendance at worship services dropped steadily throughout the sixties and well into the seventies, especially for such mainline Protestant denominations as the Methodists, Lutherans, Presbyterians, and Episcopalians. Religious giving in relation to inflation declined; new church construction slumped. Like other "establishment" institutions of the late sixties and early seventies, the liberal Protestant mainline suffered from a loss of vigor and vision.

Though liberal Protestantism was the hardest hit, Catholicism hardly escaped the strains and tensions. Catholic membership grew in this period but at a slowing rate. More noticeable were the declines in religious participation, from 74 percent attending mass weekly in 1958 to 51 percent in 1982.[18] Declines in mass attendance were most pronounced for young, upwardly mobile Catholics. Rising socioeconomic levels and rapid assimilation into American life in the years after World War II led many Catholics to discard much of their immigrant heritage, and Vatican II brought about a new climate of lay participation and freedom, inspiring greater religious individualism and choice. The culture at large was caught up in value changes that cut across social and religious group lines. Catholics joined the ranks of the mainline and in so doing took on both the burdens and the glory of identifying with the dominant culture.

In this period the term *mainline* was used increasingly to describe what was happening in religion. At first the term was used to distinguish the established faiths from the esoteric cults, and later from the more militant evangelical and fundamentalist groups. Not just many Protestants were considered "mainline," but Catholics and Jews (other than Orthodox) as well—the very groups that Herberg had identified in the fifties as embodying the American Way of Life. Once this core culture had been a source of meaning and solidarity, but by the late sixties and early seventies it had broken down. No longer were people finding the sense of identity, either personal or collective, that they had obtained earlier from their religious belonging.

Martin E. Marty summed up the situation of
the mainline churches:

> [M]ainline churches always have the advantage that in years in
> which the official culture is secure and expansive, they are well
> off . . . [but they] suffer in times of cultural crisis and disintegra-
> tion, when they receive blame for what goes wrong in society
> but are bypassed when people look for new ways to achieve so-
> cial identity and location. So they looked as good in the 1950s as
> they looked bad by the 1970s.[19]

In retrospect, it is clear that the established institutions had enjoyed an almost artificial prosperity in the fifties—churches grew in
record numbers and in popularity. It is also clear that these faiths
had become something of a "culture-religion," very much captive to
middle-class values and somewhat lacking in their ability to sustain
a strong transcendent vision. So wedded were the liberal, mainline
churches to the dominant culture that their beliefs, values, and behavior were virtually indistinguishable from the culture. Theological constructions sought to restore traditional faith, but with limited success. Protestant neo-orthodoxy had managed, as Ahlstrom
said,[20] to place a "layer of dogmatic asphalt" over what had become
a rather bland and not very inspiring culture-faith. Such maneu-
vering could not ward off for long the impending crisis. The old liberal synthesis of religion and culture was itself in crisis, and unable
any longer to forge a meaningful vision of modern life.

Several aspects of the situation suggest a broadly based cultural
shift for the mainline faiths. One was the simple matter of timing.
The drop in membership and related declines came at about the
same time for all the affected churches, the mid-1960s. Whatever
brought about the changes cut across traditions and had its origins
broadly based in the culture. Second, the churches all experienced
decreasing numbers of new members. There was no massive exodus
of old members from these institutions. Rather, after the midsixties
fewer young persons were joining the mainline churches, and fewer
still chose to become active participants and faithful supporters.
Youth growing up in church families were not remaining within the
fold as they once did. There were simply too few recruits to keep the
membership rolls of the old established churches constant, much
less growing.

Conservative Growth

Not all churches were declining. Protestant evangelicalism and fundamentalism, neo-Pentecostalism, and some splinter faiths were flourishing. All of them conservative, they grew at rates often exceeding the nation's population growth rate. Among the growing denominations were the Seventh-Day Adventists, the Church of the Nazarene, Jehovah's Witnesses, the Salvation Army, the Mormons, the Assemblies of God, and various Pentecostal and holiness bodies. Theologically they were far more diverse than might appear, but they had one thing in common—they clustered together at the exclusivist end of Kelley's gradient. They were "identifiable" religiously and culturally, known for their distinctive beliefs and moral teachings; they offered an experiential faith centered around belief in salvation through personal commitment to Christ. Most of the rapidly growing groups had small memberships, a major exception being the Southern Baptist Convention, which in 1967 surpassed the Methodists to become the nation's largest Protestant denomination. Southern Baptists have continued to grow, often setting new records of Sunbelt prosperity and affluence. Aside from church membership, other signs pointed to a conservative religious resurgence: rising Sunday school enrollments, increasing campus ministries, book publishing and use of the religious media, and founding of independent Christian schools.[21]

Judging from public opinion polls, there was a popular turn toward experiential religion. Persons claiming that religion was "increasing its influence on American life" tripled from 1970 to 1978, rising from 14 percent to 44 percent.[22] A widely reported Gallup poll in the summer of 1976 claimed that one out of every three persons (34 percent) had been "born again"; this poll was one of a set of religious indicators that led George Gallup, Jr., to suggest that the country was in an "early stage of a profound religious revival."[23] Using a more rigorous definition—identifying as evangelicals those who (1) describe themselves as "born-again Christians," (2) have encouraged other people to believe in Jesus Christ, and (3) believe in literal interpretation of the Bible—Gallup estimated there were 35 million adult evangelicals in the United States. Since 1976 the proportion of the population meeting all three of Gallup's evangelical criteria has risen from 18 percent to 22 percent. Another widely acclaimed poll—*The Impact of Belief*, commissioned by the Connecticut Mutual Life Insurance Company in 1981—foresaw a groundswell of traditional belief and went so far as to claim that religion had become "a stronger determinant of our values than whether we are rich or poor, young or old, male or female, black or white, liberal or conservative."[24]

The conservative tide spilled over into traditions other than evangelical Protestantism. Within the Jewish community there was spiritual renewal, albeit on a lesser scale best reflected in the growth of Orthodox Judaism during this period.[25] Rejecting what many regarded as the lax observance and permissiveness of many synagogues, some Jews found within the more orthodox expressions of faith and ritual a stronger religious and cultural identity. They rediscovered their "roots" in the traditional Jewish heritage, often at the expense of Reform and Conservative congregations. Similarly, among Catholics much sentiment surfaced favoring a return to traditional values and morality and concerned with placing some limits on the changes brought about by Vatican II. On issues of priestly celibacy, the role of women in the church, abortion, and birth control, many Catholics have continued to follow the teachings of the church. After his election in 1978, Pope John Paul II's defense of doctrine and discipline especially inspired many conservatives in the church to hold firm in the faith.

Much of conservative religion's visibility is due to the media, especially the so-called electronic church and its vast network of religious programming and popular television preachers. Ironically, a cadre of televangelists use the latest marketing techniques and the most sophisticated electronic media to attack modernity and secularism, and do so by proclaiming the "old-time" religion as the answer to the nation's ills. By 1980, expenditures for religious television programming, most of which was concentrated among evangelicals, had risen to $600 million annually, up from $50 million in 1970. Oral Roberts received $60 million, Pat Robertson $58 million, Jim Bakker $51 million, and Jerry Falwell $50 million.[26] And evangelical Christians were by far the greatest viewers of these programs. Fears were raised in many quarters that the media was undermining the churches, but such fears were largely ill founded. A major study commissioned by the National Council of Churches concluded that the religious media did not really siphon off members from their lo-

cal churches, but instead often reinforced church and synagogue loyalties.[27] The electronic church was a powerful instrument, but was
unlikely to be a serious competitor with the local congregation.

Gauging the extent or long-term impact of this religious upswing
is difficult. Even if one questions any genuine return to "old-time"
religion, certainly it cannot be dismissed as a marginal phenomenon. Evangelical loyalties are proclaimed by the past three presi-
dents of the United States and one after another entertainer, athlete,
and beauty queen. The religious movement expresses itself in Christian "Yellow Pages," cable television networks, and bumper stick-
ers. It gives rise to best-selling books on "possibility-thinking,"
Christian economics, and advice about cosmetics, charm, and becoming *The Total Woman*.[28] It inspires right-wing political causes
and moral crusades, raising concerns about a "born-again" vote in
local and national politics.[29] But what is most striking about the
new religious conservatism is not its numerical growth—for evangelical and fundamentalist churches have been gaining on the liberal churches throughout this century—but rather its changing cultural ethos. At one time old-style evangelicalism was passive and
withdrawn, but by the mid-1980s it had emerged as a more aggres-
sive and culture-affirming force in the nation. Being born again became more fashionable and was on its way toward becoming a shaping influence upon contemporary American life.

Collapse of the Middle

In the sixties and seventies, then, religion was flourishing on the right and left fringes but languishing in the center.
There was much experimentation with "new religions" and various
quasi-religious and spiritual therapies. Many young, well-educated
persons of middle-class background turned to mystical faiths and
meditation techniques, out of rebellion against old authorities and
in pursuit of their own spiritual quests. In a world that seemed to
have lost direction, an inward turn in search of self-enlightenment
seemed the way to go. At the other extreme, conservative faiths
seeking to restore customary ways of believing and behaving were
prospering as well. A new surge of experiential faith swept the country as many sought to reestablish some kind of external authority to

belief and morality. Over against the new faiths of the young were the old faiths of the fathers. But those in the middle—the more liberal, culturally accommodating versions of Protestant, Catholic, and Jewish faith—were in a state of collapse. Pulled from all sides, the liberal religious center was unable to hold. Gaps had widened between religious and secular world views and between those in pursuit of self and inner truth and those who sought to restore a more theocentric and traditional religious order.

The growing tensions at the center reached deep into the fabric of American life. Commentators ever since Alexis de Tocqueville in the 1830s have observed a paradoxical quality about America: it is at once the most religious and the most secular of nations. Thus as Herberg had argued in the fifties, there were secular reasons for the heightened religiosity of that period. And now, in a time of religious depression, it was also apparent that the sources of religious change lay deep in the social and cultural experiences of the post-1960s. "Disestablishments" of religion, no less than their establishments, have social roots and follow from the ebbs and flows of popular sentiment.

With the breakup of the old synthesis, there are profound ramifications for religion and culture. These include (1) a weakened public faith, (2) an expanded moral and cultural pluralism, and (3) greater religious individualism.

Faith and Public Purpose

The mainline churches over the years have served as bridging institutions, as "trustees" of the society's values. Stressing nurture as well as conversion, and public as well as private faith, they have played an important role as a culture-shaping force; by linking the fate of individuals and congregations with that of the country, they helped create a sense of moral community and national unity. In actual practice they have engaged in what Benjamin Franklin described as "publick religion": the interpretation of American life in relation to a transcendent order. This has meant reflecting critically upon national and group experience from the vantage point of the Judeo-Christian heritage and articulating an inclusive vision of public order and societal well-being. Norms of civility and responsible concern for all people, religious or not, are in keeping with this tradition.

This bridge between religion and culture was unusually strong in the 1950s. A vital synthesis of beliefs, values, and national ideals existed, sustained by a cold war ideology and close links between civic piety, national visions, and self-understanding. There was at the time a widespread consensus that personal religious faith was an essential component of patriotic commitment. Religion and Americanism were brought together to an unusual degree, the two reinforcing one another. Out of this unity came meaning and belonging, a sense of identity and direction. To be sure, the religiosity was of a highly generalized sort, and there was as Herberg said much "faith in faith," yet it thrived by being so closely attuned to the temper of the times.

In any period this mix of myth, belief, and symbol is essential in linking personal and public faith. To a remarkable degree, Americans find it possible to fuse their faiths as members of a particular religious body and as loyal citizens of the commonwealth. Not that tensions between God and country are ever fully resolved, for they seldom are, as many examples of sectarian intolerance past and present amply illustrate. But for the vast majority the theologies of church and republic blend together in a country that G. K. Chesterton once described as "a nation with the soul of a church."[30] As Lowell Streiker and Gerald Strober observe, the operative faiths of Americans weave together three important strands: (1) the personal piety of the revivalistic heritage; (2) civil religion, or dedication to the traditions, symbols, and destiny of the nation; and (3) the liberal tradition of optimism and belief in progress and rationality.[31] Though they are distinctly different sets of values and symbols, they have readily combined as sources of individual motivation and national self-understanding.

No one said it better than Will Herberg:

> If the American Way of Life had to be defined in one word, "democracy" would undoubtedly be the word, but democracy in a peculiarly American sense. On its political side, it means the Constitution; on its economic side, "free enterprise"; on its social side, an equalitarianism which is not only compatible

with but indeed actually implies vigorous economic competition and high mobility.

The American Way of Life is individualistic, dynamic, pragmatic. It affirms the supreme value and dignity of the individual; it stresses incessant activity on his part. . . . The American Way of Life is humanitarian, "forward looking," optimistic. . . . The American believes in progress, in self-improvement, and quite fanatically in education. But above all, the American is idealistic, Americans tend to be moralistic: they are inclined to see all issues as plain and simple, black and white, issues of morality.[32]

But by the late sixties this synthesis of religious and utilitarian cultural faith was in deep trouble. A growing sense of discontinuity between ideals and realities became evident during the Johnson administration, when the country was beleaguered with the domestic issues of civil rights, urban rioting, and crime. There was a feeling of inner contradiction and an awareness of social problems for which there were no easy solutions. America, for all its might and technological prowess, seemed unable to deal with its own domestic life. The single most important catalyst of tension was the Vietnam War, which would come to be seen as morally ambiguous if not immoral by a majority of the population. The war produced an estrangement for the young, both for those opposing it and for those fighting in it. Then came the Watergate scandal, which further undermined confidence in the nation and its leadership. By that time the old civil faith embodying national ideals and messianic conceptions of America as an instrument of divine purpose had lost much of its force.

Public faith fell upon hard times. Values that had previously been so important—patriotism, conformity, capitalism, hard work, success, familism—failed to inspire. And worse, the discontinuities of the period made clear just how cut off the nation had become from its old Puritan heritage of a covenant and a shared biblical morality. That the covenant linking God and nation was "broken" was one thing, but more telling was that many Americans did not really grasp what was broken. In a more secular age, fewer Americans understood the heritage or were able to discern a transcendent ethical vision for the nation. Robert Bellah put it tersely in *The Broken*

Covenant: "Today the American civil religion is an empty and broken shell."[33]

Those faiths positioned at the center felt most acutely the strains. By virtue of their heritage, such faiths have a particular role in conveying broadly shared moral values. As Bellah observes, the "soft structures" that deal with human motivation—the churches, the schools, the family—were all deeply affected by the upheavals, especially in "their capability to transmit patterns of conscience and ethical values."[34] The bridge between public and private faith collapsed, and liberal optimism and belief in utilitarian progress and rationality faltered. The result was a de-centering of American culture and a weakening of the commitments that had once galvanized great numbers of Americans into a common creed.

The 1960s, thus, gave rise to a series of precipitating events that led to the collapse of the old cultural faith. Tensions ran deep and had been building for a long time. Herberg himself had expressed concern about the secular aspects of the piety in the 1950s and had called for a "prophetic faith" to turn the country around. As Daniel Bell has argued, modern capitalism brought with it jarring disjunctions between the public and the private and between the public and the political realms of American life.[35] In an age of managerial capitalism, more and more Americans worked in large, corporate structures; economic and political bureaucracies dominated the public sphere. Not only were religious institutions largely removed from these secular, deeply utilitarian structures, but the very notion of a mainstream set of values had become problematic. With greater institutional differentiation and societal complexity, the churches had come to have little persuasive power over the bureaucratic giants. Increasingly the public sector was governed by a largely unrestricted interplay of economic forces, which seemed impervious to individual religious and altruistic motives. Indeed, in a world of huge economic conglomerates and multinational corporations, it appeared unlikely that religion could sustain any deep consensus of faith and values.

Moral and Cultural Pluralism

With greater secularity and rationality has come more diversity in moral values and life-styles. Disputes over moral and ideological issues intensified across a wide spectrum—abortion, the Equal Rights Amendment, women's issues, gay rights, plus a miscellany of environmental and consumer concerns. A more broadly shared bourgeois morality gave way to passioned and sharply differentiated moral positions. Brought on less by the diversity per se than by the depth of emotions aroused, complex and personal issues lie at the center of the new religious debates. Moral rhetoric was changing as it became more centered upon life-style choices and the struggles of individuals to be ethically responsible in their own lives.

As a result, moral and religious attitudes have crystallized around one of two camps: moral traditionalists versus those advocating a more libertarian, freewill position. The aggressively conservative ideology of the Religious Right clashes on one issue after another with what it unceasingly labels "secular humanism". Views are most polarized around two key social institutions: the family and the school.

At the center of the controversy are family and gender role issues, most notably, abortion and women's rights. Throughout the 1970s "profamily" leaders crusaded for a return to traditional roles for men and women and actively opposed extending legal rights and protections to women and homosexuals. The polls showed that evangelicals and fundamentalists were far more inclined than mainliners to favor a ban on abortion, to oppose the ERA, and to be against the hiring of homosexuals as teachers in public schools; on at least one of these issues, abortion, a 1981 poll indicated that the differences between evangelicals and nonevangelicals were wider than those between Protestants and Catholics.[36] Likewise many people are concerned with the public schools and how they deal with these issues. Leaders of the "profamily" movement accuse the schools of eroding the morality of children by teaching evolution and sex education, by using "humanist" textbooks, and by not mandating school prayer. At present there is widespread support for a constitutional amendment permitting prayer in the schools, and the public appears to be about equally divided on whether evolution or creationism should be taught in the classroom.

A resurgent old-time religion responds to a hunger for a certainty, for moral absolutism, and for wholeness of faith and experience.

Over against the calmer, more liberal voices, the noisier, and at times militantly antimodernist and tribalist, rhetoric of the conservatives evokes passionate emotions. Hard-core fundamentalists of the Religious Right identify America as the world's bulwark against godless communism and promise to restore the nation's role as defender of laissez-faire economics and democracy; calling for a return of traditional values, fundamentalists and evangelicals argue that moral degeneracy and court decisions, especially those against school prayer and Bible reading and in support of abortion, have undercut the nation's divinely sanctioned mission. Fervently and determinedly they seek to turn the country around and to restore a "Christian America."

Religious forces have responded, of course, to counterreligious trends. Secular themes not only shape much of modern life, but they define many of the issues to which the religious powers respond. The secular humanistic culture moulds the dominant ethos with its implicit values of individualism, freedom of belief, openness, and tolerance. These values pervade the rational economic and technological sectors of the society and increasingly the private moral and religious realms as well. Secularists push for greater cognitive and normative openness, insisting that individuals are fully capable of choosing for themselves what to believe and how to make moral choices. By and large more accommodating than dogmatic, secular ideology has taken on a more distinct presence in American life in recent decades. It is characterized less by ideological fervor than by a concern to protect a libertarian, freewill stance; its posture is less that of a militant and unyielding force than one of indifference in encounters with traditional religious beliefs and values.

Most important, the secularism of the post-1960s has lifted up anew the fact of pluralism—namely moral and life-style pluralism. Of course America has a long history of religious pluralism; its system of denominational pluralism emerged as an appropriate institutional form for religion in a voluntary order. Such a system historically has assumed a shared morality, or at least a common biblically based framework of values and moral ideals, as a basis for ethical reflection. Today such assumptions are questionable. With an expanded moral pluralism (as distinct from religious pluralism), this framework is itself challenged and often fails to contain issues and controversies. Both the boundaries of discourse and the terms of logic have widened, all of which has given rise to new meanings and possibilities for pluralism in contemporary America.

Religious Individualism

Another product of the period is greater religious individualism. With less conformity in faith and morality, Americans today enjoy a great deal of freedom to believe as they wish and to pursue spiritual quests as they please. Those persons most exposed to modernity, especially the young, the better educated, and the middle classes, enjoy this freedom. Choice and taste are themselves crucial factors.

Choice and taste are, of course, key traits of middle-class individualism in the United States. No other sector of the society enjoys as much opportunity to pursue its own preferences. For middle-class Americans, a rational and calculating attitude is an essential ingredient in approaching various aspects of their lives. The rationality of means and satisfaction of individual wants are dominant motifs in a culture so deeply influenced by the "Protestant ethic" heritage. Modern life rests upon a high degree of personal initiative and individual autonomy, often at the expense of social commitments and communal bonds. Utilitarian aspects of individualism encourage the pursuit of self-interest and personal achievement and hold up these values as taking primacy over group loyalties.

Various commentators and critics have pointed to a more expressive individualism that seems to have emerged in recent decades. This new culture is described by many labels—the therapeutic sensibility, the culture of narcissism, the pursuit of self-fulfillment, and civic privatism.[37] Whatever its characterization, the culture thrives upon individuality as a key value. The pursuit of a free, gratified, and unalienated self is seen as not only desirable, but essential to personal fulfillment. Normative matters are treated as open to choice and taste and often as an extension of the self. "Finding oneself" thus is now a central quest for many Americans, opening up a plethora of possible identities and allowing many new figures— spiritual gurus and secular therapists—to rise to the role of cultural heros.

In this climate of expressive individualism, religion tends to become "privatized," or more anchored in the personal realms. Custom and tradition play less of a role in shaping what an individual believes; religious feelings and meanings become, or can become, more a matter of choice and preference. Privatized faith is subjective, often concerned more with style than with substance, and more with sensibility and taste than with shared meanings and shared realities. Put simply, religious pluralism in the modern context is further individualized: each person has a different "version" of religious reality.

This trend is significant for both religion and the larger culture. By virtue of their heritage, Americans are individualists in their religious beliefs and practices, but also conformists sensitive to prevailing cultural norms and opinions. Historically much of the paradoxical quality of American religion has been its double-faced character—personal yet public, individualist yet collectivist. But recent developments have served to further uncouple these two aspects of faith. The sensitive balance between them has shifted in the direction of a less socially restrained, more personally expressive mode of religiosity. Commitment to self has grown at the expense of community, disrupting especially loyalties to traditional religious institutions.

A Third Disestablishment?

As a result of all these trends, religion has lost force as an integrative influence in America. While much religious rhetoric is heard in the public sector, by and large it is a rhetoric lacking in any broad consensus. With the collapse of the religious and cultural middle, the result is what Richard John Neuhaus has called the "naked public square"[38]—the effective elimination of religious values and symbols from the conduct of public discourse.

Even civil religious rhetoric, presumably the most unifying of religious themes, lacks substance and has become more divisive than integrative. While such discourse uses the culturally resonant language of cohesion, recent efforts to articulate a sense of national purpose—whether cast as traditional values of God and country by Jerry Falwell and his colleagues on the religious Right, as prophetic concern for the poor and the dispossessed by Jesse Jackson and his

campaign for democratic inclusion and justice, or as the moral supe-
riority of democratic capitalism by neoconservative supply-siders
—all reflect a fractured interpretation, more a legitimation of inter-
est-group politics than an overarching canopy of national meaning.
America seems more and more to resemble an uneasy coexistence of
splinter groups differing across race, gender, class, and, of course, religious ideology. Perhaps in Richard Merelman's terms, American
culture has become too "loosely bounded" to support a single and
coherent civil religion.[39]

This breakdown in the national religious culture may be the most
important "contribution" of the 1960s, for it altered significantly
the normative basis of American religious pluralism. Pluralism encourages, indeed it requires, norms of tolerance and acceptance—
what John Murray Cuddihy calls the "religion of civility," a stance
of being religiously inoffensive, of being sensitive to religious differences in a pluralist context. An emphasis upon "good taste" and
tolerance is essential to the larger religious unity. Pluralism forces
upon each group, no matter what its heritage, the status of "denomination"—that is, each group has to accept coexistence with others
and must give up claims of authority over them. Catholics and Jews
thus have become "denominationalized" as they have accepted
norms of freedom and tolerance in keeping with pluralism, and have
modified their teachings and practices. Over time they have adjusted to the realities of voluntarism, though not always without
theological ordeal or institutional trauma.

As Cuddihy says:

> Immigrants arrive with their sects, shuls, and churches.
> America then teaches them to be discreet. It does so by means
> of its unique creation: the denomination, or better many de-
> nominations. This is known as "pluralism." America tames re-
> ligious sects up into denominations bringing them into the re-
> spectable middle class. America also tames churches down into
> denominations (The American Catholic Church is one of its re-
> cent converts and now bears the humble civil demeanor of an
> American denomination.).[40]

The point is that centripetal forces in American religion propel
—"taming" up or down—toward some inclusive culture of non-
offensiveness. Those elements of religious traditions that are extra-

neous or monopolistic are expelled in favor of values, beliefs, and principles that allow a positive assent to pluralism. All claims to uniqueness, whether they be Roman Catholic (the "one true church"), Jewish ("the chosen people"), or Protestant fundamentalist ("only Jesus saves"), are viewed as at odds with a pluralism that encourages rationality, tolerance, and civility. No doubt this accounts for why pluralism has succeeded so well in this country. The United States has avoided serious intergroup hostilities and conflict for a simple reason: particular religiousness has tended to give way to more unifying expressions of faith.

But harmony and coexistence were only possible given a unifying religious culture. Pluralism did not pose much of a problem throughout the period of the nation's history when a core of religiously grounded moral values could be taken for granted. Insofar as such values were widely accepted, they provided a practical basis for social life. So long as Americans shared a consensus of moral ideas and values, they could differ in religious views without posing a serious threat to the public order. The great accomplishment of nineteenth-century group pluralism in America, as Tocqueville observed, was a rich civic culture that drew off the resources of the religious traditions. Tocqueville was struck by the ways the voluntary religious spirit in America helped rechannel individualistic and group interests into concerns coinciding with the general welfare of the society—what he described as "self-interest properly understood." Thus he drew attention to religion's creative force upon the culture in the early nineteenth century.

Throughout the nineteenth century, and well into the early decades of the twentieth, the white Anglo-Saxon Protestant (WASP) culture dominated the religious establishment. For a hundred years or more, Americans made very little of pluralism; in self-perception if not in fact, the United States was a white country in which Protestant Christianity set the norms of religious observance and moral conduct. WASP influence shaped much of the public life. Catholics, Eastern Orthodox, Jews, and blacks often experienced prejudice and discrimination at the hands of a religious majority that viewed its identity as the same as the nation's. The dominant religious tradition provided the symbolism and mythology that shaped the nation's folklore, literature, theater, art, and music. The "Protestant ethic" left its stamp on public institutions and business creeds and on the ways Americans raised their children and styled their personal lives. In racial stock, creed, and cultural heritage, it was a narrow vision of America, yet one that was sustained for a considerable period in the name of "Righteous Empire" and "Christian America."

The breakdown of this order came in the twentieth century in two historic phases: one during the 1920s and 1930s, and the second since the 1960s. After World War I the old WASP order confronted a growing pluralism. Americans began to take pluralism more seriously in the sense of expanding the boundaries to include more *religious* groups. The old era of the Protestant cultural hegemony was drawing to an end—what Robert T. Handy speaks of as a "second disestablishment."[41] Having long been legally disestablished, Protestantism was forced to accommodate other faiths—to accept the fact that the United States was a "Protestant-Catholic-Jewish" country.

Beginning in this earlier period, norms of pluralism expanded to include growing numbers of non-Protestant immigrants of diverse origins. Along with changes in the religious composition of the society, the normative matrix shifted in the direction of greater tolerance and acceptance of religious pluralism. Levels of trust and acceptance improved, broadening the boundaries of moral community and upgrading the basis of unity. Community was possible only by repressing absolutistic tendencies within the particular faiths and by stressing instead the more inclusive, more universal elements of national faith. Civic piety played a critical part in upholding tolerance of differing faiths and in sustaining a sense of *E pluribus unum*, so essential to the survival of a genuine religiously pluralist order.

Yet as we have seen, not until the 1960s did the realities of an expanded pluralism became apparent. It took that turbulent decade to expose the moral crisis emerging with pluralism and its implicit secularity. With the decline of liberal optimism and confidence that had sustained decades of civic piety, the linkage between religion and culture was greatly altered. The youth counterculture of the period was a "breaking point" exposing the tensions and contradictions in the larger culture, and in turn provoking great concerns and reactions on the part of traditionalists who found the moral chaos so threatening.

Why were events at the time so unsettling? James Davidson

Hunter, in *American Evangelicalism*, offers a clue.[42] Evangelical and fundamentalist Protestantism had been largely cut off from the mainstream of public life since the 1920s. Though religious conservatives had lost control over many of the Protestant churches and their seminaries in the earlier years, still, as Hunter points out, they believed that on moral matters their views were widely shared in the society. On matters such as premarital chastity, marital fidelity, the undesirability of divorce, and traditional understandings of family life and gender roles there seemed to be a broadly based normative consensus. But not so after the 1960s. During that turbulent decade the realities of a changing world broke through. The counterculturalists flaunted their rejection of the older moral values, and everywhere it seemed there were signs of breakdown in the way Americans had lived. Increasing rates of divorce, permissive sexual mores, divergent life-styles, changing gender roles, the perceived collapse of the family, more openly expressed homosexuality, and the availability of abortion on demand all posed a challenge of unprecedented proportions to religious traditionalists. The fact that the liberal, mainline churches were in a state of decline, that civil religion was in a shambles, and that secular humanism seemed to be growing in its public influence only contributed to an aroused militancy and conviction that conservatives must "go public" with their concerns.

These developments have all brought about a new situation for American religious pluralism. Lacking a common religious culture, groups now contend with one another for power and influence. Groups that felt alienated from the mainstream or that had never really consented to the pressures of pluralism are now launching crusades to reform the country. Not all faiths had been brought into the "religion of civility," and indeed its leveling effect has the potential of arousing strong authoritarian impulses. Less tolerant, more zealous, and fanatically committed—in short, "uncivil"—the resurgent forces of fundamentalism and conservative evangelicalism have claimed a different version of America. In their eyes America is still a "Protestant Christian" nation, but one now threatened by moral breakdown and secularity.

The truth is that religion has lost much of its great binding power on the society. The greater religious individualism of the 1960s and 1970s diminished possibilities of a common universe of religious meanings and eroded many of the support structures for religion. Earlier in the 1960s, Peter Berger envisioned this outcome as a result of the privatizing trends of modern life:

> privatized religion is a matter of "choice" or "preference" of the individual or the nuclear family, *ipso facto* lacking in common, binding quality. Such private religiosity, however "real" it may be to the individuals who adopt it, cannot any longer fulfill the classical task of religion, that of constructing a common world within which all of social life receives ultimate meaning binding on everybody.[43]

By the 1980s there was little question that the social and religious order was deeply fragmented. The forces of habit and custom had diminished, and so had many of the bonds holding Americans together. Religion manifested itself as "private virtue" and "public rhetoric," but this was symptomatic of the loss of shared norms. As Berger said, "insofar as religion is common it lacks 'reality,' and insofar as it is 'real' it lacks commonality."[44] Pluralism had taken new shape, more widespread, diverse, and variegated than at any earlier period in American history.

Thus religion confronts another and far more serious challenge today. With a weakened religious culture and greater individualism, religion now faces what may be thought of as a "third disestablishment": an expanded pluralism in which there is less of a religiously grounded moral basis for the society. The normative basis of pluralism appears to have shifted as the unity of religious and cultural values has dissolved. Lacking a commonly accepted faith and morality, now religious groups find themselves contending with one another to become the shaping cultural influences. The challenge is no longer to accommodate new and different religious groups, but rather to adjust to a broader pluralism of religious and secular ideologies. Civility, or style of religious affirmation, is no longer so much the issue as is the very character of the *civitas* itself.

We are discovering that pluralism as it is known today—moral, ideological, deeply individualistic—is not without its dangers. From the very beginnings the American system of religious pluralism has rested upon maintaining a precarious balance between two extremes: on the one hand, the possibility of secular indifference and moral crisis, and on the other hand, the threat of reactionary sectarianism. One threatens to erode the common religious faith that binds Americans into a moral and civic order, and the other threatens to disrupt the pluralism by means of narrow, dogmatic efforts at restoring unity on its own terms. If the former risks a loss of coherence, the latter raises the specter that some group waving the banner of righteousness will try to impose a new unity upon the nation. These tensions have surfaced anew in the 1980s, but this time under conditions of an expanded pluralism.

What kind of rapprochement between religion and secularity we can expect for the future is very much an open question. An old religious order has passed; the new pluralism now faces unprecedented challenges. We attempt to map this changing scene, but first we must examine the trends toward greater religious individualism and their effects on the character of religious belonging. Greater privatization of faith is a central theme in the post-1960s era and one that bears directly on the religious climate for the future.

Chapter Two

The New Voluntarism

*Voluntarism is so obvious a principle, as it is exhib-
ited in American churches, that its significance is
overlooked, but it is one of the revolutionary principles adopted by modern ecclesiastical organizations.*

—HENRY K. ROWE

O f all the recent religious changes in America, few are more significant, or more subtle, than the enhanced religious individu-
alism of our time. Americans generally hold a respectful attitude
toward religion, but also they increasingly regard it as a matter of
personal choice or preference. Today choice means more than simply having an option among religious alternatives; it involves religion as an option itself and opportunity to draw selectively off a variety of traditions in the pursuit of the self. Radically individualistic
religion presumes an autonomous believer, one who is on a spiritual
journey, on his or her own quest, and often with little involvement
in or connection with a particular religious community. Questions
of authority, discipline, practice, and common life often seem foreign, or at least secondary. Foremost is the individual's choice of
whether to pursue a "religious matter"; then come whatever commitments of a personal or communal sort, if any, a person may
choose to make.

Examples of religious individualism abound in contemporary
America. Consider the following three:

Item: Who Is a Good Christian?

The question of who is a good Christian arose in a
sharp and pointed way during the presidential campaign of 1984. Re-

call that Geraldine Ferraro, the Democratic candidate for vice president, first raised the question; and soon the president responded with his carefully chosen words:

> GERALDINE FERRARO: the president walks around calling himself a good Christian, but I don't for one minute believe it because his policies are so terribly unfair. They are discriminatory and they hurt a lot of people.
>
> PRESIDENT REAGAN: The minute I heard she'd made that statement, I turned the other cheek.

Seldom in the heat of campaign rhetoric have such gibes been made about a candidate's faith. As it turned out, the vice-presidential nominee's own faith came under scrutiny as attacks mounted on her views on abortion. Catholic bishops took issue with Ferraro and questioned how in good conscience a Catholic could vote for a candidate who supported the policies she endorsed.[1]

This exchange illustrates the highly "individualized" character of religious belief and practice in modern America. Moral concerns were at the heart of the controversy: administration policies and views on abortion, not religious dogma or articles of faith, are what mattered. Involvement within a religious institution seemed not to matter much: Geraldine Ferraro was a regular communicant of a Catholic parish, but that fact seemed lost in the controversy over abortion; President Reagan seldom went to church, yet because he was identified as a "born-again" Christian and spoke the rhetoric of evangelical piety, he was viewed as the champion of the conservative religious cause. Each espoused a highly personal "version" of faith. Ferraro differed with her church's teaching on abortion and thereby incurred the wrath of many traditional Catholics, but in doing so she showed how one might arrange loyalties to church and state and combine personal and social ideals—in short, a model of how to be a good feminist, a good American, and a good Christian. President Reagan's views on personal and political freedom meshed well with conservative faith and marked him as a defender of free enterprise, traditional values, and morality—also a model for many of how to be a good American and a good Christian. America had before it two figures, very different in their views and styles, yet both could claim to be good Christians.

Item: Modern Baptists

In James Wilcox's novel *Modern Baptists* there is a provocative scene in which Bobby Pickens and his girlfriend Burma LaSteele reflect upon their religious identities. Burma's concern about Bobby's drinking turns into an existential confrontation with life:

> "Bobby, do you think you drink too much?"
> "I guess so."
> "And we're Baptists."
> "Modern Baptists can drink. It's only stuffed shirts like Dr. McFlug who don't."
> "Well, I guess I'm a modern Baptist, then."

The passage arising out of a Louisiana Southern Baptist setting conveys something of the radical thrust of today's individualism: Bobby and Burma define for themselves how a "modern" Baptist may behave. The drinking issue serves as an opportunity to revise their views on what it means to be Baptist, while at the same time continuing to make some claims upon the religious heritage. Despite strong sanctions against drinking in the southern religious context, the characters break out of this culture, assert their own individuality, and define their own religious identity. They do so with remarkable ease, suggesting that something as deeply rooted religiously and culturally as a denominational affiliation is remarkably flexible and open to recasting.

Item: Sheilaism

In *Habits of the Heart* Robert Bellah and his colleagues interview a young nurse hamed Sheila Larson, whom they describe as representative of many Americans' experience and views on religion. Speaking about her own faith and how it operates in her life, she says: "I believe in God. I'm not a religious fanatic. I can't remember the last time I went to church. My faith has carried me a long way. It's Sheilaism. Just my own little voice."[3]

Hers is a deeply personal faith involving belief in God, though not much else of a traditional sort. Highly individualized and centered in herself, the form her faith takes is distinctly personal—something she calls Sheilaism. Faith is pragmatic, something deeply experienced, a gestalt of meaning constructed out of the self. Connections between faith and going to church have been broken, and she is unlikely to find a home in any existing religious body. Authority lies within her own experience, not in an external institution. Now distant from and somewhat antagonistic toward organized religion, she looks within for whatever spiritual insights she might find.

As all three examples suggest, religion is highly voluntary in contemporary America—a matter ultimately of personal choice and conscience. Whether in matters of public and private morality, cultural and religious identity, or religious authority, there is ample evidence of a heightened individualism today. The diminished influence of the old, mainline churches and the breakup of the conformist "culture-religion" of the 1950s helped create a more diverse and fluid religious context. With the collapse of the middle, as described in the previous chapter, many new religious energies were unleashed. Coupled with these were cultural trends that have more broadly contributed to a new, more individualistic ethos—what we describe as the new voluntarism in American religious life. In this chapter we explore these cultural trends and the greater religious individualism they inspired, and especially what the trends mean for the mainline faiths.

The Heritage of Voluntarism

The roots of modern religious individualism lie deep in the heritage of religious voluntarism. Despite the nation's early Calvinist heritage, ever since the Second Great Awakening the popular faiths of Americans have been heavily Arminian. The latter's emphasis on free will, grace, and unlimited hope for conversion of all persons reinforced the value placed upon personal achievement that was dominant in the secular culture. Theology and democratic values meshed in the American experience to create a highly individualistic stance toward religion and what would come to be called the "great tradition of the American churches." This tradition emphasized religious freedom, separation of church and state, a denominational conception of the church, and, most basic of all, "voluntaryism" in matters of congregational support and involvement.[4]

Out of this heritage came the denomination as a peculiarly American socioreligious form. What developed on this continent were not churches in the European tradition, primarily confessional and territorial, nor sects, exclusive groups that set themselves against an establishment. Rather, "denominational" institutions arose, what historian Sidney E. Mead describes as a "voluntary association of like-hearted and like-minded individuals, who are united on the basis of common beliefs for the purpose of accomplishing tangible and defined objectives.[5] As it came to exist in the United States, denominationalism embodies two major social features: one, it presupposes religious pluralism and thereby accepts the legitimacy claims of other groups; two, it stands in a generally positive relationship with the society. Its churchlike features sustain a spirit of tolerance and public engagement, but it is sectlike in its appeal to the individual conscience.

Many features of popular American religion follow from this voluntary religious form. Primary emphasis is upon the free, uncoerced consent of the individual and a type of religiosity emphasizing practical, everyday faith. Voluntary faith is purposive: it is activistic, more "doing" than proper belief or creedal assent. Moral and behavioral concerns take precedence over doctrine and dogma: faith is more this-worldly than otherwordly. Religion is more a personal and inward phenomenon than something that comes to one from an objective institution: it has to do with feelings and experiences. One belongs on the basis of conviction: one chooses to join a church, one chooses the church to join. Even ecclesiastical notions are highly individualized. Historic views of the church as the body of Christ, and other views expressing a corporate character, have found little favor and have been replaced by more nominalistic conceptions of religious community. Typically Americans view religious congregations as gatherings of individuals who have chosen to be together, in institutions of their own making and over which they hold control —fostering what sometimes, in the eyes of observers from other countries, appears as "churchless Christianity."

In the larger perspective of Western history, American-style voluntary faith represents a major step in the emancipation of individual believers from the tutelage of organized religious collectivities. Arising out of the Protestant Reformation, such voluntarism is, as the early twentieth-century historian Henry K. Rowe said, "one of the revolutionary principles adopted by modern ecclesiastical organizations."[6] By eliminating the sacramental system of medieval Catholicism, and thereby emphasizing the believer's direct relation to God, the individual in Reformation theology was made autonomous and subject only to the constraints of conscience. In its early phase this notion meant the individual was responsible for his or her relation to God *within* the framework of an institutionalized church; over time the voluntary principle was extended to choosing the framework itself, to deciding as a mature individual what to believe and with whom to associate in the institutional expression of this belief. The American experience further contributed to this democraticizing process by according legitimacy to religious choice as a fundamental principle. Put simply, individuals were religiously "enfranchised" and made more responsible in the exercise of faith.

The mix of individual and communal elements has varied over time and by tradition. Catholic and Anglican traditions historically have emphasized the corporate character of faith and the integrity of the church and have assigned more value to worship and the sacramental presence in the religious community. But these are minority voices in the American experience. The dominant religious forms are those derived from congregationalist, independent, and separatist Protestant traditions. While the Puritanism of Massachusetts sustained a covenantal view that in every respect was corporate, forces both religious and cultural have over the years pulled the religious mainline in the direction of greater individual voluntarism. Religious pluralism itself has served to fracture covenental loyalties and to "relativize" the content of particular religious traditions: as denominations have divided and competed with one another, the notion of the church as a corporate body or even Americans as a "people of God" inevitably was compromised. Meanwhile, secular myths of American individualism prospered and were carried over into the life of the church: belief in one's self, laissez-faire capitalism, and democratic values generally all coincided with and reinforced a religious individualism.

The Quest for Self-Fulfillment

The new voluntarism of the 1970s and 1980s encompasses many of these older themes, yet differs significantly. With the breakup of the old cultural and religious synthesis of the more complacent Eisenhower years, the value climate within the country shifted decisively. The postwar economic boom, an upwardly mobile population, life in the suburbs, and, above all, the cold war ideology had served to create at midcentury an America in which affirmations of solidarity and normative consensus were possible. Many value commitments and behaviors, along with a generalized emphasis on religiosity, were widely shared in the fifties: conformity to social norms and other-directedness, fear of subversion and communism, commitment to family life, acceptance of military duty and war, and a favorable view toward patriotism. At the time, many families had school-age children, and most Americans, even if not themselves devout, have traditionally wanted to give their children some religious indoctrination as well as an opportunity to meet other children of the same faith. In such a climate, churchgoing was an expression of belonging and civic loyalty. Religiosity flourished as a way for individuals and families to identify themselves as Americans, and public piety was very much in evidence as an expression of the nation's core values.

In the sixties and seventies, however, a much different cultural milieu prevailed. In the early phases of this period particularly, young Americans had little fear of subversion and were greatly concerned with the evils of capitalism; they worried little about social conformity and celebrated personal freedom; they were less committed to traditional family life and were more willing to experiment with new sexual styles and family forms; more often they refused military duty and opposed an unpopular war; and they experienced widespread alienation from many institutions of the society. This was not a value climate in which religious belonging flourished, especially in the mainline religious churches. Such institutions ride the crest of popularity when things are going well, but not so in times of strain and turmoil. To many in the antiestablishment climate of the 1970s, these churches and synagogues seemed deeply implicated in a culture that itself had gone awry; they were more a target for what was wrong than a solution for the many social ills. Hence the mood of "rejecting" organized religion reached unusually high levels in these years.

Disenchantment with the American way of life both fed upon and gave momentum to a deep-seated quest for personal fulfillment. Many factors help explain why this quest was pursued so intensely during these years. Freed to a greater extent than ever before by post–World War II levels of affluence and material security, enhanced leisure, and a proliferating media of television and stereophonic sound, many Americans sought within their lives greater wholeness and meaning, a new measure of creativity and vitality, and the realization of their "potential" personhood. The breakdown of older religious norms of self-denial, the rise of more permissive child-rearing practices, and a thriving and expansive consumer culture all reinforced notions of self-gratification and enjoyment as ends in themselves. The old Puritan culture gave way to the hedonistic imperatives of a consumer society: "enjoy life," "treat yourself," "you deserve a break today." The young, the upwardly mobile, the college educated were especially touched, but they were hardly alone. A multifaceted search—material, therapeutic, and spiritual —energized many individuals and groups in the hopes for, and expectations of, a more abundant life. Indeed, the metaphor of a quest so thoroughly permeated American culture by the end of the seventies that it was, as Peter Clecak says, a major thrust among groups as diverse as "born-again Christians and atheistic feminists, gay-rights activists and red-neck males, mainline Protestants and hard-line conservatives."[7]

Pollster Daniel Yankelovich estimates that as much as 80 percent of the American population were caught up one way or another in the quest—in marriage and family, in career, in leisure.[8] Of these, he identifies about 17 percent as fairly intense seekers (he calls them "strong formers") who spend much of their time assessing and reassessing their personal lives, their jobs, their friends, their mates from the perspective of the needs and wants of the self. They tend to be under thirty-five, unmarried, college-educated, white-collar professionals. They are the ones most preoccupied with finding spiritual, mental, and physical wholeness through diet, exercise, meditation, psychotherapy, or whatever—many of them prime candidates for such quasi-spiritual activities as primal therapy sessions and *est*. Given the intensity of their quests, many have stumbled into what Yankelovich calls the "fulfillment trap," wanting more than they can have and putting self ahead of social relationships.

The majority of Americans, however, are involved less intensely in such pursuits. More moderate in their views, they retain many traditional norms and values and rely more upon stable social ties.

They enjoy the support of their families, jobs, and social networks, yet cannot escape exposure to the greater choices increasingly available to them. Many of them have embraced the quest but they do so in a more balanced fashion, setting limits on the amount of time and energy given to these pursuits. Writes Yankelovich:

> Most of them do not agonize over their inner needs and potentials. They do not fuss daily over existential life-decisions as if these were worry beads to be fingered at fretful moments. These people, especially if they are over thirty-five years of age, have mostly settled in stable commitments to family, work, friends, community, and leisure. These commitments, rather than creative forms of self-expression, fill their life space. Their inner lives are rarely subject to upheaval. The pressures that tear at the strong formers also tug at them but do not dominate their lives. The majority retain many traditional values, including a moderate commitment to the old self-denial rules, even as they struggle to achieve some measure of greater freedom, choice, and flexibility in their lives.[9]

What we observe here is a classic case of cultural diffusion. Beginning with the student movement of the sixties, the quest for self-fulfillment and a more expressive individualism spread into much of middle-class America, especially among managers, professionals, and frustrated housewives. By the late seventies, this culture had spread into more diverse, more alienated sectors of the society, including some minority and blue-collar constituencies. As the values diffused into other sectors, they became less pronounced, but nonetheless mobilized much concern for the dignity and well-being of individuals generally. Americans of all ages and backgrounds were becoming more concerned with the self—with *their* selves.

Problems of Authority and Belonging

The impact of this quest upon religion was profound, although varied and difficult to fully sort out. A more expressive individualism of this kind amounts to a massive energizing force in the spiritual realm and the unleashing of energies channeled in many directions. The bearings upon religious voluntarism were threefold:

1. *Recovery of the experiential.* In a fundamental way, the quest for fulfillment restored religion as a matter of individual experience: many Americans were to become intensively involved in the search for salvation in the many spiritual and quasi-spiritual meanings of the term. For some the quest for personal authenticity and a sense of felt wholeness took them out of the churches and into their own spiritual orbits. The many spiritual disciplines and technologies that flourished at the time held up the promise of a more genuine and compelling inner experience than that found within the religious establishment. Salvation was identical with fulfillment, something that could only be found "within" the self—and perhaps best outside organized religion. For others, personal fulfillment was seen as a by-product of Christian salvation, something found only in the life and death of Jesus. Whatever their label—evangelical, born-again Christian, neo-Pentecostal, charismatic—they were one in their stress upon wholeness and experience in faith. There was an external authority, but it was to be confirmed in personal experience. Varied and diluted were the many versions of salvation, yet they all held out hope of discovering, or rediscovering, a fuller sense of life's inner riches and possibilities.

2. *Emancipation of the self.* Salvation as a theme was closely related to a second theme—finding release from injustice and alienation. For individuals to discover their true selves, they must be freed of any obstacles standing in the way. Ascriptive barriers were downplayed, individuality and subjectivity were celebrated. Thus claims upon a better, more fulfilling life were extended to include significant numbers within virtually every social grouping—a widespread egalitarian movement sometimes described as the "democratization of personhood."[10] The categories of race, ethnicity, gender, sexual preference, age, region, physical condition, religious background, occupation, and social class were all challenged and discredited as legal and de facto barriers to the pursuit of the self. Throughout the sixties and seventies many people sought redress for historical injustices by identifying themselves as members of disadvantaged groups. Once excluded and devalued, such groups

sought a greater measure of control over their lives and acceptance of their own cultural patterns, which resulted in an upward diffusion of styles—black, southern, hillbilly, female, gay—and the end of WASP cultural domination in the minds and imaginations of most Americans. At the same time, fixed social roles and statuses lost much of their authority as many individuals sought authentic identities outside or at least a playful distance from them. For many in the privileged classes especially, this trend would mean living with greater psychic separation from established institutions and giving less importance to ascriptive loyalties and social identities.

3. *The individual against institutions.* The twin aspects of fulfillment—salvation and social justice—gave rise to greater autonomy of the individual and reinforced the view that religious institutions should serve individuals, not vice versa. Americans have long felt that institutions should bend to their needs, and in the sixties and seventies this view was very pronounced. Institutional dissent found new legitimacy on the grounds that the participants themselves could best decide if "their" church was serving them as they wished. Individuals felt inspired to claim more subjective space, to examine their beliefs and outlooks from the standpoint of their psychic needs. Consequently for many Americans, norms of belonging and ties with organized religion weakened. Religion became essentially an individual matter, something to be "worked out" on one's own terms. Whether a person becomes involved, and in what way, rests to a considerable extent on the subjective test of individual experience: is it satisfying or does it do something for the person? Since the sixties, many of the earliest Christian heresies have flourished—antinomianism, gnosticism, and especially Pelagianism— in a context emphasizing the instrumental functions or rewards of faith. By focusing on the rewards obtained, the traditionally "latent" consequences of religious involvement are brought to the fore as "manifest" positive functions. Thus emphasis upon instrumental uses and subjective validation of belief amount to one of the truly significant and subtle religious themes of the modern period.

These themes are all very much alive and discernible in the operative faiths of Americans today. Nowhere are they more apparent than in the decline of religious authority and in weakened attachments to organized religion. The two trends of course go together.

Traditional channels of authority and respect for the same—from papal "infallibility" and biblical "inerrancy" to the spiritual role of the local minister, priest, or rabbi—have been eroding for some time, but vocal and outright questioning of these structures increased dramatically in the 1960s. The bumpersticker Question Authority, which became so popular among the young, at the time symbolized the attitude of many individuals toward institutional authorities of all kinds, religious and otherwise. With such questioning came psychic withdrawal and distancing from groups, especially those that people were born into or reared in, and a turning to more intentional types of communities or more personal, highly subjective spiritual quests.

The religious quests of the countercultural years led to many new spiritual forms, some authoritarian and others more expressive, but all offering moral and religious meaning, helping youth, as Steven Tipton says, to be "saved from the sixties."[11] With some groups, such as Zen Buddhists, mystical quests often led persons into communities and shared spiritual experiences; probably for most caught up in the search for self, however, their quests have been far more personal and not linked in any lasting way with a practicing and believing community. The pursuit of self-fulfillment propelled them toward more individualistic journeys. The transformation of external authority into an internal locus of control was facilitated by the availability of consumer-oriented spiritual technologies that were "packaged" and "marketed" to those seeking them. A vast smorgasbord of spiritual therapies not only gave people options from which to choose, but did so in a way that underscored that individuals could themselves choose what they wanted.

Many of these same currents have flowed more broadly through the religious establishment. "Privatizing" trends result in individual quests and spiritual yearnings in the mainline religious sectors, pulling people in many ways. Some people have found themselves pulled away from conventional religiosity by their deeply personal quests or by a search for more support and sharing than are usually found in churches and synagogues. The quest for wholeness leads them into new spiritual enclaves, inside and outside the established institutions. Others have found in the new climate of freedom reasons to disaffiliate altogether and to adopt a more secular life-style. By far, of course, the majority of Americans maintain some ties with the mainline churches and synagogues. While "invisible religion" in the sense of faith not tied to organizations and institutions is more of an option now than in the past, still most Americans hold to some ties, even if nominal, to "visible" congregations. Privatism thrives on freedom from pressures of conformity and orthodoxy, and thus allows for a range of possible accommodations. In the religious climate of the 1960s and 1970s, conformity gave way to change and choice, opening the way for individuals to style their beliefs and behaviors—including institutional belonging—in keeping with their preferences.

Within all brands of Protestantism, a close affinity exists between faith and individualism. This religious heritage has long affirmed the believer's own responsibility to make decisions in matters of faith. Liberal Protestantism encourages members to think for themselves and to make moral choices. Members are expected to reflect on the meanings of faith and to draw out its implications for their own lives. Given the diversity of groups and traditions, there is within the moderate and liberal Protestant churches a wide range of differences in doctrinal beliefs, moral views, and social and political attitudes; theological and cultural pluralism not only reigns but is indeed widely celebrated. Loyalty to the institution often suffers when members opt for a more individualized, choose-as-you-please faith. Within the liberal Protestant constituency, in fact, there is a large, and perhaps growing, constituency best described as "believers but not belongers"[12]—that is, persons who say they hold to religious beliefs but do not actively take part in a local congregation. Religious belonging for many is no longer viewed as a presumed outgrowth of belief; it has become a matter of taste. That so many persons fit into this category of believing without belonging is itself an indication of the subtle, and institutionally eroding, effects of contemporary privatized faith. Between 95 percent and 98 percent of Americans affirm a belief in God, yet when asked about the importance of religious participation, many persons in these churches seem to have little difficulty adhering to "churchless" faith.

To a considerable extent the autonomy of the believer has become normative in the modern world in all the major faiths—Protestant, Catholic, and Jewish. Even within conservative Protestantism and Orthodox Judaism, where loyalties to tradition are stronger, there is much emphasis on individual salvation and free will in matters of faith. Over the years Protestant evangelicalism has thrived on individuals who make their own decisions: first one is "saved," then one voluntarily joins the church. Fundamentalist and orthodox religious worldviews are highly individualistic in the sense that they embrace laissez-faire economics and emphasize personal faith. The right of individuals to believe as they choose in a free and responsible manner is a cardinal tenet for religious conservatives, across faith traditions.

Popular versions of evangelical and fundamentalist faiths currently reflect an accommodating stance. Once rigid and withdrawn, the newer brands of conservative Protestantism that attract so much attention today are more engaging and culture affirming. They appeal to experiential faith and seek to "legitimate" emotions and feelings as an acceptable, middle America religious style. Expressions of deep religious experience—once mostly relegated to the unsophisticated "fringes" made up of minorities and working-class whites—are now widely prevalent among many middle-class, and especially lower-middle-class, Americans. Much attention in the mass media is given to the evangelical resurgence as a national religious movement and to prominent individuals who testify to being "born again" or Spirit filled. A far cry from the "fightin' fundies" and Holy Rollers of the revivalistic past, today's evangelicalism adopts a posture more consistent with modern rationality and good taste. It is more instrumental, with a stress upon psychological "needs" and the benefits of faith—joy, wholeness, happiness, health, and wealth. Salvation and spirituality are described as easy "steps," "laws," "principles," and "guidelines." The offensive aspects of the religious worldview (e.g., sin, hell, judgment) are often de-emphasized, while its positive and nondogmatic side is held up as normative. As James Davidson Hunter observes, conservative orthodoxy has abandoned much of its old-style asceticism and intolerance in favor of "a copacetic Protestantism—civil, soft and somewhat technical."[13] The change of ethos comes through in the popular programs of the electronic church such as the "700 Club" and the "PTL Club," which particularize and render "private" religious experience and choice. Authority for this new brand of televangelism rests less upon the traditional regard for position, education, and training and more upon the appeal and pragmatic "effectiveness" of media celebrities.

Even within the religious tradition with the greatest heritage of ecclesiastical authority—Roman Catholicism—trends toward greater individualism have been swift and at times traumatic. The case of Catholicism is fascinating because of the rapid pace of change as well as the widespread shifts and unrest brought on within this institution and community. In the early to mid-1960s, Vatican II opened the floodgates for currents of change that had been dammed for decades. The council ushered in a new climate of openness and freedom, and inspired laity and priests alike to assume a greater autonomy in matters of faith and ethics. The changes had great symbolic significance. Customs unchanged for a millennium and a half—such as the Latin mass, priests not facing the laity when celebrating the mass, and abstinence from meat on Fridays—were abandoned almost overnight and new liturgies and more democratized procedures of decision making were introduced. For rank-and-file American Catholics the changes were met with broad approval; the legitimacy accorded to greater freedom of conscience and personal responsibility in religious matters was welcomed.

Shortly after the Vatican Council closed, in 1968, Pope Paul VI issued *Humanae Vitae*, the encyclical reaffirming traditional views against birth control. This came as a surprise to many within the church, who had expected more liberalizing trends in the realm of sexual ethics. Because the encyclical followed so closely upon Vatican II with a message that seemed contrary to the spirit of the liberalizing trends, many Catholics were left confused and ambivalent toward the authority of the church. Andrew Greeley has argued that the encyclical led to a loss of respect for church authority and a turning away from the church; the "decline" trends of the period could be accounted for, he and his colleagues write, "almost entirely by a change in sexual attitudes and in attitudes toward the papacy among American Catholics."[14] A crisis in authority was provoked by the sudden attempt of the Catholic hierarchy to place limits on personal choice at a time when the larger trends in this direction were gaining momentum. Even if Greeley overestimates the importance of the encyclical and its timing, it clearly contributed to declines in church attendance and the falloff in practice and belief underway in the late 1960s.

For whatever reasons, there have been phenomenal shifts in the attitudes and outlook of American Catholics. Members of this community are making far greater choices of belief and belonging; in

TABLE 2-1

AMERICAN CATHOLICS ADHERING TO CATHOLIC BELIEFS
AND PRACTICES, 1974 AND 1979 (PERCENTAGE OF RESPONDENTS)

Practice, Belief, or Norm	Age 30 and Over 1974	Under 30 1974	1979
Attend mass weekly	50	37	37
Pray once a day	60	52	32
Christ gave leadership of church to Peter and his successors (certainly true)			
All Catholics	42	34	16
Weekly communicants only	60	45	27
The pope is infallible when he speaks as head of the church (certainly true)			
All Catholics	32	22	9
Premarital sex is morally wrong (strongly agree)			
All Catholics	35	35	17
Weekly communicants only	48	69	34
Divorce, if followed by remarriage, is wrong (strongly agree)			
All Catholics	25	17	11
Weekly communicants only	46	29	18
Artificial contraception is wrong (strongly agree)			
All Catholics	13	7	4
Weekly communicants only	24	24	13

Sources: Andrew M. Greeley, *The Religious Imagination* (Los Angeles: William H. Sadlier, 1981), pp. 204–205; Andrew M. Greeley, William C. McCready, and Kathleen McCourt, *Catholic Schools in a Declining Church* (Kansas City: Sheed and Ward, 1976), pp. 35–36; Andrew M. Greeley, "Church Authority: Beyond the Problem," *National Catholic Reporter*, September 26, 1980, 7–8. Data compiled by Patrick H. McNamara and reported in "American Catholicism in the Mid-Eighties: Pluralism and Conflict in a Changing Church," *Annals of the American Academy of Political and Social Science* 480 (July 1985), 66.

birth control, abortion, and sexual styles, more and more young Catholics regard these matters as private and thus beyond the realm of church authority. The trends for young Catholics (under age thirty) are astounding: from 1974 to 1979, a period of only five years, the changes in attitudes and practices were as great, or greater, for this cohort than were the earlier differences in 1974 between older and younger members (see table 2-1). Even among weekly communicants there have been sharp changes. A freedom-of-conscience-oriented sector of young Catholics continues to expand, little moved by exhortations couched as obligations "under the pain of sin." The Vatican's recent calls for a balanced "individualism and collectivism" seem to thwart very little the larger trends. So embedded in young Catholics today are the values of personal autonomy in forming one's conscience that formally stated doctrinal and moral imperatives appear to have little or no impact upon many of them.[15] Still, many who have drifted from mass and strict religious practice clearly think of themselves as Catholic. At present there are growing numbers of "communal Catholics" in America—well-educated, younger persons not so much involved in the institutional church, yet self-consciously, and at times even militantly, Catholic in outlook.[16]

A culture of religious individualism generally permeates American folk theology and attitudes toward religious authority. The overwhelming majority of the population—inside and outside the churches—holds to strongly individualistic views on religion (see fig. 2-1). In a Gallup poll in 1978, a staggering 81 percent of the respondents agreed with the statement "An individual should arrive at his or her own religious beliefs independent of any churches or synagogues." Seventy-eight percent (and 70 percent of churchgoers) said that one can be a "good" Christian or Jew without attending church or synagogue. In matters of belief and morality, the individual is his or her own final arbiter. Less directly pertinent to institutional religion, 84 percent of Americans looked upon individuals as able to control what happens in their own lives. Dominant patterns of the secular culture shape religious norms. For Americans, religious authority lies in the believer—not in the church, not in the Bible, despite occasional claims of infallibility and inerrancy on the part of some.

Privatized faith in the extreme knows little of communal support and fellowship; it is not a shared faith and thus is unlikely to inspire strong group loyalties and commitments. To the contrary, such individualism thrives on freedom from group constraint. In this respect one could say that the enemy of church life in this country is not so much "secularity" as it is "do-it-yourself religiosity." The latter fosters a highly personalized mode of faith which undercuts the integrality of the church and synagogue. It encourages religion à la carte—"picking and choosing" those parts of a religious tradition

FIGURE 2-1.

INDICATORS OF INDIVIDUALISM.

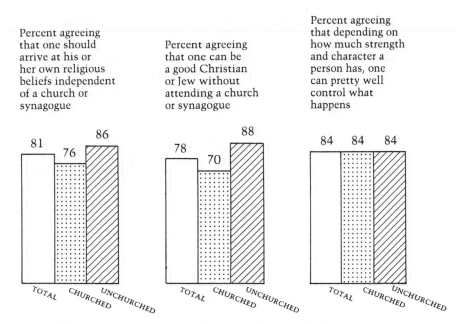

Percent agreeing that one should arrive at his or her own religious beliefs independent of a church or synagogue

Percent agreeing that one can be a good Christian or Jew without attending a church or synagogue

Percent agreeing that depending on how much strength and character a person has, one can pretty well control what happens

Source: *The Unchurched American* (Princeton: Princeton Religion Research Center and the Gallup Organization, 1978).

congenial to the individual. In a nation where orthodox notions of religious community were always weak, such individualization of belief and practice can only lead to further diminution of socioreligious group ties.

Carriers of the New Voluntarism

These changing norms of religious voluntarism were largely spearheaded by the large "baby-boom" generation of the postwar period. Seventy-five million people were born in this country between 1945 and 1965, many of whom are now in their late twenties and thirties, and a few in their forties. By virtue of their large number, this cohort now swells the young adult population, just as it did the school-age population twenty-five years ago. In 1960, 21.6 percent of the population was between the ages of eighteen and thirty-four; by 1982 the figure had increased to 30.1 percent.[17] So large a generational cohort is impressive not only in numbers but in its implications for social institutions.

For the religious establishment, the impact of the baby-boom generation was twofold: (1) it altered the age structure of the society and therefore of family-life-cycle patterns; and (2) it gave rise to a distinctive generational experience and culture. These two aspects have interacted to make this generational cohort the major "carrier" of the new voluntarism.

Age Structure and Family Life Cycle

In a very basic sense, religious patterns vary directly with the age structure of the population. When large increases occur in the school-age population, increases follow in religious membership and participation; should the number in this age group decline, so will levels of church and synagogue activity. The reason is simple: institutional religious participation is closely related to the life cycle. In his characterization of Protestant church life, sociologist Widick Schroeder describes the life-cycle patterns as follows:

> The "typical" American Protestant begins his involvement in an American church in Sunday School. . . . Voluntary teachers give generously of their time and talent, and parents prod their offspring into relatively frequent attendance, particularly in the grammer school years.
>
> The typical American Protestant reduces his church participation markedly in late adolescence and early adulthood. During this period of his life, a person is leaving his family of origin and is making the transition to the adult world. . . .
>
> After people form families of their own, they are likely to increase their involvement in church life. As did their parents before them, people in their late twenties or early thirties are likely to desire a religious instruction for their children. Consequently, they are apt to reaffiliate as their children reach Sunday School age, for they feel some increased responsibility to participate in the institution to which they are sending their children for religious instruction. Finally, as their children mature and leave this family of origin, some parents are inclined to reduce their involvement or to disaffiliate themselves.[18]

The period since 1950 offers a good example of how demography can be destiny for the churches. Throughout the fifties, and well into the sixties, the churches benefited from the young baby-boomers. Schools, churches, and kindergartens all expanded, especially in the middle-class suburbs where many Americans settled during the postwar years. Those age-groups from which church members are drawn—children and their parents—grew considerably; those sectors least likely to join or attend—older youth and young adults without school-age children—grew much less. In effect, numbers were on the side of the religious establishment. By the late fifties, religious attendance had reached an all-time high, church school programs flourished, and the construction of new churches and synagogues became a major priority for all the mainline Protestant, Catholic, and Jewish faiths. Religious membership rolls grew to accommodate an expanding religiously active population.

Late in the decade, however, the birth rate peaked, marking the beginning of a downward trend in fertility that would last for some years to come. The under-twenty age-group continued to grow during the sixties, but by less than a third of its fifties rate; by the first half of the seventies it was declining in absolute numbers. Furthermore, by the seventies the baby-boom children were reaching maturity in great numbers—the age levels at which active religious participation is less likely. This group constituted a cohort that was staggering in its numbers but foreboding in its implications for religious participation; the group constituted the largest number of youth ever in the history of the American people. Just as the churches and synagogues had earlier enjoyed the presence of these children, now they had to face their rebellion and departure.

Churches and synagogues everywhere felt the declining numbers of children and youth who normally grow up to become members. The declines were especially felt in the suburban strongholds of mainline Protestantism. Birth rates dropped more rapidly for the white upper-middle-class constituencies making up these suburban Protestant congregations. Nursery and church school enrollments dropped markedly and abruptly. Fewer children also meant fewer adults showing up at church services. Middle-class parents tend to be concerned about the socialization of their children and often feel some pressure to affiliate on their behalf. Thus as the number of young children in these families declined, many parents had less reason to remain actively involved in congregations. Denominational studies show that the declines came first in Sunday school attendance, and then within two or three years in worship attendance, and then later in church membership.[19] This succession of falloffs in religious involvement was particularly noticeable for liberal Protestant churches. These churches, more so than conservative Protestant ones, rely upon "natural growth," or the children of their own members, to replenish the memberships of their congregations. When the children fail to become members, congregations suffer. Thus demographics had a considerable impact upon the liberal and moderate branches of mainline Protestantism—those traditions most responsible for the "culture-faith" that dominated the scene at midcentury.

Cultural Experience

Numbers were important, but so was the cultural experience of the baby-boomers. They would emerge as "carriers" of a distinct set of cultural orientations which would set them apart. Exposed to experiences unlike those of any previous generation and deeply influenced by a middle-class ethos that had become insecure and unstable, many of the children of the churchgoing sector would rebel against the utilitarian culture as well as the conventional moralisms of the churches. Their break with the traditional values and life-styles combined with their numbers to make them the "lead generation" of American society. Today members of this generation are setting styles not only in religion but in such disparate cultural realms as fashion and gourmet foods, jogging and dieting, condominium ownership and sale of BMWs.

This generation had a much different social experience growing up than did their parents'. Its search for identity, for meaning and belonging, is very much unlike those of previous cohorts. It was the first true "television generation." Its members would watch nuclear test explosions, civil rights demonstrations, the assassinations of a president and other popular leaders, the sexual revolution, the Vietnam War—all in the "security" of their own living rooms. This was the generation of the Mickey Mouse Club, the hula hoop, Elvis, the Beatles, the Peace Corps, SDS, the Chicago Seven, *Playboy* magazine, and, to be sure, Campus Crusade for Christ and Young Americans for Freedom. Some are remembered as having been "hippies" and "yippies" in the late sixties and early seventies; now in their late twenties and thirties, they bear the imprint of their generation's earlier experience. A few are still alienated from the mainstream, but far more of them are now a part of it—most notably, the "yuppies" (young, urban, upwardly mobile professionals). A diverse makeup of many groupings and life-style constituencies, the young Americans who comprise this generational cohort today defy simple characterization or stereotypic labels.

Their definitions of social reality were influenced by discrepancies in American life, between the ideal and the actual, the way things ought to be and how they are. These discrepancies were so acutely perceived in the generation's formative years that few age-cohorts in recent memory have felt so intensely the pains and passions of the times. Caught up in a search for fulfillment and commitments transcending middle-class utilitarian values, many were deeply touched by the great causes and tragic events of their era. Many would find themselves drawn into the movements for social justice, for racial and gender equality. If the pursuit of self-fulfillment in the modern period has, as we described, twin components —a search both for salvation *and* social justice—then certainly baby-boomers are the generation for which this search is most alive. More so than many other generations, they came to realize that unless all people are free to pursue the limits of their potential, no one is really free to do so.

Robert Wuthnow's Bay Area research demonstrates there was a "generational unit" impact upon the churches in the sixties and seventies.[20] Some youth who were dropping out of the churches felt alienated and "turned off." But probably more important than alienation, and certainly far more widespread, was simply a growing indifference among youth to organized religion. Liberal Protestant churches particularly, but also other mainline religious institutions, felt these currents of rejection, however intense or mild. Because the constituency of many of these churches is largely middle class, the shift in value commitments affected these institutions far more severely than it did the conservative churches. The commitment to personal freedom and choice, individual autonomy, and personal quest, as well as tolerance of diversity and openness, tended to erode loyalty to the religious establishment.[21] Underlying this decline was a more basic shift in the locus of moral and religious authority, away from external sources to more internal, personal considerations: rigid and absolute norms gave way to "situational ethics"; personal choice was elevated to a new standing in moral equations, in keeping with an importance attached to individuality. Not just religious attitudes and values but notions of duty to nation, family values and sexuality, and the inherent good or evil in the democratic capitalist state came up for review. Ideas about authority and moral decision making generally were caught up in new and changing constellations of cultural values.

The climate has changed considerably since the sixties and seventies, but the themes of personal freedom and individual fulfillment remain very much alive because they were carried into the mainstream culture by the baby-boomers. Because of the size of this cohort and its distinctive outlook, change is magnified in the society as the cohort moves through each stage of life, redefining that experience and setting new styles and expectations. With the aging of the baby-boomers has come a new combination of values—a "mixture of traditional values with a liberal twist."[22] Many young Americans want stronger family and religious ties and now show greater respect for authority; some are returning to church, although it seems unlikely they will come back in large numbers. Still they remain much more tolerant of diversity than were previous generations and far more committed to finding psychological fulfillment in whatever they do. Insofar as how people relate to institutions—religious and otherwise—they continue to hold to the view that the individual is sovereign in such matters. The latest polls show that despite a return to more conformist values in some realms, on issues involving individual choice, such as personal life-style, gender roles, career, and family, young adults are still as highly committed to liberal views as ever.[23] If anything, commitment to personal freedom has increased as these values have diffused into many previously traditional sectors. And while the excesses of the "me generation" are being left behind, what Daniel Yankelovich describes as an *ethic of commitment* seems to be emerging, redefining older notions of giving and receiving in the social compact and what is deemed sacred in life.

In the new cultural climate, life-style and ideological alternatives are taken for granted: the choice to marry, have a family, combine career and family, affiliate with a religious institution. The trend is not so much for or against traditional family and religious values, but rather to be able to choose. As Yankelovich observes, today's young adults are "sorting out" the issues more than is usual for this age-group and choosing those on which to be conservative or liberal. Probably more than for any other generation, principles of choice and pluralism are accepted as a part of the scheme of things. This alone makes the baby-boomers crucial carriers of new values and outlook in contemporary American society.

The Breakdown of Ascriptive Loyalties

The force of these cultural changes on the religious establishment has been strong and more or less apparent. Some of the changes are well known to religionists and commentators alike: the old synthesis of religion and culture existing in America at mid-century has crumbled, the conformities that once prevailed have given way to greater individual choice, the moral and religious climates have greatly changed, and the matters of religious faith generally are more privatized today. Such widespread changes in the religious and cultural mood do not occur, however, without profound and often subtle shifts in the social basis of religion. These shifting group and communal parameters are generally less well known, yet are fundamental to the changing character of the American religious mainline.

Historically the major shaping influences on religious communities have been the social divisions of the society. Throughout the nineteenth century—the great era of the rise of denominational pluralism—factors such as class, race, national origin, and regionalism largely defined the boundaries of the nation's religious groupings.[24] Americans were a diverse people whose faiths reflected the realities of social and economic life. Indeed, churches divided along these lines remain so today. Just citing a few current denominations testifies to the past that is still with us: *Southern* Baptists, the *African* Methodist Episcopal Church, *Missouri Synod* Lutherans; and until recently the two largest Presbyterian bodies were split along regional lines. So powerful have been the social and economic divisions in this society that the basic structure of American denominationalism as it evolved over a century ago persists. Once established, meaning and belonging structures can have a lasting influence; communities and traditions change slowly, especially those based on ascriptive factors such as race and region.

Religion's vulnerability to social influence, and the subsequent rise of American religious pluralism, relates directly to the heritage of voluntarism. Under conditions of religious freedom and religious choice, a person's faith is shaped by social values and identity. Perhaps inevitable in a democratic order, such "quasi-*Gemeinschaft*" loyalties pose a mixed blessing. Ascription sets limits on the full expression of the voluntary principle. Choice is restricted because ascription channels religious energies along preexisting social and cultural lines and thereby subordinates religious preference per se to the larger compound of group values, interests, and ideology. Despite much rhetoric otherwise, ascriptive factors throughout American history have operated as a constraint on religious choice. For many Americans born as Baptists or Methodists or whatever, there was never a question of being anything else; family and group ties overshadowed religious preference. Faith was closely linked to custom and one's social inheritance—a given much the same as one's class standing or ethnic identity. While in principle one could shrug aside such loyalties and traditions, force of habit and upbringing are powerful influences in their own right.

There is, however, another side to ascription. One can argue that in this country much of religion's vitality is attributable to its deep social roots. Religious communities provide meaning and belonging precisely because of their ascriptive base. Andrew Greeley argues, and generally we agree, that the strength of religion in the United States rests in large part on its ability to play an ethnic, or "quasi-ethnic," function.[25] Close ties between the social and religious elements have given denominational structures particularly strong communal resources for developing religious loyalties. Their quasi-ethnic qualities inspire deeply felt commitments and identifications; they assure a context wherein beliefs and worldviews can be shared. Denominational infrastructures have undergirded personal and public faith and sustained loyalties to God and to country. Social class, ethnicity, race, and region are all critically important in this respect; they are the historic social bases, or "plausibility structures," of America's faith communities, without which it would be hard to imagine what shape the popular expressions of religion might take.

What happens when these infrastructures begin to break down? What if the social and religious elements no longer hang together? These are important questions in view of the trends toward greater religious individualism and pursuit of self-fulfillment in recent decades. In modern America, of course, many forces are operating to break apart the social fabric and to erode the bases of traditional religious loyalties. Massive structural changes since World War II— such as rising levels of education, opportunities for upward mobility, greater regional migration and geographic movement, and a high rate of divorce and family instability—have all weakened social attachments. These broader social changes have, in many respects, created the conditions for the more radically individualistic concerns and the narcissistic culture of the baby-boomers in the sixties and seventies. Certainly it is unlikely that this culture would now be so pervasive had these large-scale social changes not occurred.

Rising levels of education, especially in this period, opened up unprecedented opportunities for mobility, both socioeconomic and geographic, and for new experiences and contacts. Members of the baby-boom generation were exposed to more education, as measured both by years spent in school and by knowledge of global cultures and events, than any generation yet; the media, foreign travel, and contact with persons from other countries allowed them to have an expanded awareness of peoples and cultures. Enrollments in higher education generally rose from under 2.7 million in 1950 to almost 12.4 million in 1982, with a correspondingly dramatic increase occuring in the proportion of the population receiving a college education or other continuing education. Many of the mainline churches had only a small proportion of educated members in the 1950s, but by the 1980s a third or more of their members had been to college; the proportion with less than a high school education was smaller than one-fourth.[26] For organized religion the consequences have been important. It has had to try to accommodate a more informed and less parochial constituency; adjust to new cultural orientations and values brought on by expanding scientific and technological constituencies; bridge growing gaps between the better educated and the lesser educated on a wide range of social, political, and moral issues; and confront continuing, and at times tense, divisions between those arguing for symbolic interpretation of the Scriptures and those insisting upon a more literal approach. Perhaps no aspect of change in the social basis of American religion has produced greater strains in the past couple decades than the shifts in education and class.

Increased geographic mobility is also a factor responsible for the weakening of traditional social ties. Estimates are that annually roughly one-fourth of American families move, or at least did so in the years following World War II. So staggering are the numbers of people moving that Vance Packard some years ago entitled a book on the subject *A Nation of Strangers*.[27] Such movement takes a heavy toll on social relationships. It results in weakened ties—to family and kin, to neighborhood and community—and often a sense of homelessness, or a metaphysical loss of home. Mainline churches and synagogues especially are affected because their constituencies are among the most mobile of the society. High levels of geographic mobility erode social infrastructures undergirding corporate faith and outlook and have given rise to a new axis of cultural and religious differences between "locals," who are encapsulated in their local communities, and "cosmopolitans," whose patterns of belonging and worldviews tend to be broader.[28] The latter are in many respects the embodiment of modern individualism and a product of the educational and generational changes of the past quarter century.

All these forces of modernity entail a universalizing and differentiating process that moves toward *dissolving* ascriptively based group identities. Multiple identities get sorted into their component parts, each singled out for separate treatment. Fragmentation goes hand in hand with a person's experiences in modern life. Consider the fusions of nationality, ethnicity, and region with religion in the following collectivities: Irish Catholic, Swedish Lutheran, Russian Jew, Southern Baptist. It seems appropriate to ask, as does J. Milton Yinger: "What happens when these connections are broken? . . . What happens to the religious aspect of these multiple identities when, as a result of 'Americanization' and of geographical and social mobility, it is no longer bound to the others?"[29]

What happens, as Cuddihy observes, is that people begin using the rhetoric of "happen": "I happen to be a Presbyterian," "I happen to be a Mormon."[30] "Happen to be" means we are what we are by choice or by chance—by choice if the identity is advantageous, by chance if not. What surfaces under these conditions is the peculiarly American practice of claiming a "religious preference." Faith comes to be expressed as an opinion or point of view, something that can be easily modified or even discarded if one so chooses. Put simply, religion becomes even more privatized, more anchored in the personal and subjective sphere, and less bound by custom or social bonds.

By loosening the hold of ascriptive loyalties, the individual is freed for more autonomous decision making. The religious dimension is released from the social components, thereby enhancing personal religious responsibility and broadening the range of potential alternatives. The realms of choice are expanded, which amounts to a progressive upgrading of an individual's role in matters of faith. Logically this development is a further working out of the historic voluntary principle underlying denominationalism, in which, as Talcott Parsons says, "the individual is bound only by responsible personal commitment, not by any factor of ascription."[31] Meaning becomes differentiated from belonging, with the individual called upon to exercise greater options and to make commitments on the basis of personal choice.

Modern America thus creates for believers a situation quite different from that found in more traditional settings. Less and less bound to an inherited faith, an individual is in a position of "shopping around" in a consumer market of religious alternatives and can "pick and choose" among aspects of belief and tradition. The situation confronts believers with, as Peter Berger observes, a "heretical imperative"—the necessity of choosing a religious version and selecting out those aspects of a faith that are illuminating in one's own life and rejecting those that are not very helpful.[32] What matters is less the shared experiences and affirmations of a community of like-minded believers and more a person's own spiritual journey and quest in search of an acceptable and fulfilling belief system. The subjective aspects of faith have expanded as ascriptive and command attachments have declined.

Consequences for Religious Belonging

How has this new voluntarism affected mainline religious belonging? What are the implications of this breakdown of ascriptive loyalties for socioreligious group life? We single out several of the consequences for brief comment:

1. *The social bases of American religion are undergoing major changes.* The old lines of class, race, ethnicity, and region which gave rise to the historic patterns of denominational pluralism are not now as clearly drawn in religion as they were, say, fifty years ago. Ascriptive loyalties generally play less of a role in shaping religious communities. Modern individualism and the social transformations of the twentieth century have affected virtually every religious community. Especially in the years since World War II, the social mapping of the religious landscape has changed drastically: rising educational levels and geographic mobility have greatly weakened ascriptive social bonds; demographic shifts have altered the concentrations of religious memberships; social and cultural assimilation has leveled many of the long-standing group differences linked to custom and heritage. Old social and religious identities have eroded, and new ones have emerged along quite differing lines.

2. *The family plays less of a role today in the transmitting of religious values and identities.* Throughout much of the American past, the family was a crucial institution in transmitting religious values from one generation to the next. Even as late as the early sixties, Talcott Parsons could say about the family:

> it is to be taken for granted that the overwhelming majority will accept the religious affiliations of their parents. . . . [Even] if some should shift to another denomination it is not to be taken too tragically since the new affiliation will in most cases be included in the deeper moral community.[33]

For Parsons the family played an important role in sustaining the normative order. He believed that as long as each generation continued to "inherit" the faiths of their parents, church membership would be the means by which Americans would identify with their society and participate in the "deeper moral community." The established faiths would thereby function as the custodians of America's central values. Family, church, and values were all integrally linked in the socialization process and were evidence of how religion—either directly or indirectly—permeated mainstream American culture.

Today this triad of family-church-values no longer hangs together as well. More and more Americans have no church ties and thus no longer hold to the religious affiliations of their parents. The proportion of young Americans born as Protestants and later defecting from the churches has, in fact, increased substantially—from only 6 percent among those born in the early years of this century to 34 percent born in the years since the end of World War II.[34] For Catholics and Jews as well, the numbers have risen. Families play less of a role than they once did in transmitting religious beliefs and values; there is less of a coherent tradition to inherit. Links in the religious socialization process have become more tenuous.

3. *With the breakdown of ascriptive loyalties and the reduced role of the family in religious socialization, individually based differences in beliefs and values now operate more freely in religion.* Moral and life-style choices have come to play a more important role in religious affairs as norms of individual responsibility have become clearer. Under less pressure to adhere to old group loyalties, persons are free to make decisions on the basis of genuine *religious* preference. With conformity less of an influence, religious inclination itself becomes more of a factor.

All of this suggests a more fluid situation of religious choice, one of greater sifting and sorting on the basis of personal and ideological inclinations. Americans have always found it easy to "switch" faiths, and there appears to be greater diversity in patterns of switching now than in the past. Greeley's model of religious America as a "mosaic with permeable boundaries" is fitting: one can move in and out of a religious community; boundaries are relatively flexible and fluid.[35] Permeable boundaries are suggested in Peter H. Rossi's comment on contemporary American Catholicism: "I left the church when I was 12. At 42, I woke up and discovered that I was a Catholic again. I didn't change, but they modified the boundaries without warning me."[36]

The ease with which persons switch from one faith to another contributes to greater moral and value consensus. Individuals sharing a common outlook or behavioral style increasingly cluster around those institutions, officially or unofficially, identified with constellations of moral values and styles of which they approve. Depending on the scale which this clustering occurs, religious groups could conceivably take on clearer social and religious identities as they become more homogeneous in ideological style; greater individualism and voluntarism may thus breathe ideological vigor into many traditional groups, making them truly more reflective of personal religious preferences.

4. *American religious pluralism is being reshaped along new communal and ideological lines.* Given that boundaries are flexible and fluid, religious communities are always to some extent in flux. For reasons we have described, religious forces and movements generally have repositioned themselves in the past decade: old differences between denominations are blurred, alignments along liberal versus conservative lines have intensified; religious versus secular ideologies have crystallized; Jews and black religionists have lined up in new and somewhat unexpected ways. In a more pluralistic, more secular America, moral and ideological cleavages have taken on greater symbolic significance. So-called mainline Protestants are distinguished from evangelical and fundamentalist Protestants, less so now perhaps for their historic differences in beliefs than for their moral and cultural attitudes; Catholics have moved socially and normatively toward the center of society, making them now as vulnerable to popular moods and sentiments as any other mainline group.

With the breakdown of the old cultural synthesis, the nation now finds itself engaged in a debate over basic values and moral beliefs. People are now more aware, than perhaps at any time since midcentury, of religious diversity—the many differing traditions, opposing moral ideologies, competing visions of America and its way of life. There are heightened concerns over life-style and ideological issues and the role of religion in public life. The question of religious America is very much alive, brought to the fore by groups that now openly contend with one another to become culture-shaping influences. Tension and confrontation in a highly secular context force issues and controversies into the public arena.

5. *Differences in modes of meaning and belonging within the religious communities are becoming more pronounced.* Greater voluntarism means a greater variety of religious expression within the churches. Less inclined toward unquestioned obedience to religious authorities, individuals draw upon their own spiritual lives in defining faith and its meaning for them. There is a growing emphasis upon direct experience with God, with self, or with nature—themes that are all highly individualistic and introspective in char-

acter; biography and spiritual journey are more important than creedal statements or ecclesiastical group bonds.

Within the churches, religious styles vary considerably. They are becoming more individualized and privatized, even within a particular tradition: for example, one can be a "devout" Catholic, an "active" Catholic, a "practicing" Catholic, a "communal" Catholic, a "disaffiliated" Catholic. What this amounts to is "Selective Catholicism,"[37] or a greater freedom in choice of religious style. Not just Catholics but mainline Protestants and Jews all acknowledge a wide range of acceptable modes of belonging. At the extremes are the traditional belongers versus the more privatized do-your-own-kind-of-religion believers, "active" members and participants versus the "nominally" committed. Distinguishing among the many types of believers and belongers becomes necessary simply as a means for grasping the range of diversity now found within the churches.

A distinction of growing importance is that made between the "churched" and the "unchurched" populations. In the past, when a religious culture broadly permeated the society, this distinction was not so important; churchgoers and nonchurchgoers often adhered to a common morality, similar life-styles, and maybe even a similar public faith. A common civic faith united Americans in ways that transcended many of their subcultural differences. But with a weakening custodial role for religion in American life and less cultural conformity, the two sectors of the population have become more divergent. It has become more and more important, indeed necessary, to view church-style religiosity as one among many possible life-style and belief configurations and to look upon the changing relations between the religious and secular cultures as an important aspect of contemporary America.

To be sure, there are many influences reshaping the contemporary religious landscape, and the ones we have identified comprise hardly an exhaustive list. Many trends are underway, both within and outside of the churches, that bear upon the future of religious institutions religious pluralism. This book inquires into these changing conditions. But before we can explore the changes themselves, we must identify the major groups and traditions that make up the nation's religious mainline. Once we have defined the religious clusters and the theological families to which they belong, we shall be ready to explore the changes in greater detail.

Chapter Three

The Fragmented Mainline

When I mention religion, I mean the Christian religion; and not only the Christian religion, but the Protestant religion; and not only the Protestant religion, but the Church of England.
—PARSON THWACKUM, IN FIELDING'S *TOM JONES*

Judging from the news media, what is mainline in American religion today is distinctly conservative in cast. On television and radio one sees and hears much about the "New Christian Right" and the "electronic church"; *Time, Newsweek,* and other magazines regularly run features on evangelicals, born-again Christians, and fundamentalists. Jerry Falwell, Pat Robertson, and Jimmy Swaggert get front-page coverage as conservative religious spokesmen, while other figures with differing points of view get much less media attention. Occasionally a Catholic or Jewish voice is heard on some issue, and then often in response to a born-again Christian! Even the gurus and cult heros of the fringe who used to be media celebrities now make the news less often. And certainly few liberal Protestant voices are now heard. Edwin Scott Gaustad rightly asks: "Where are the Beechers, Abbots, Coffins, and Fosdicks of yesteryear, or the Niebuhrs and Tillichs of yesterday?"[1]

Religious establishments change from time to time and are hardly stable in times of widespread social change. New groups and movements have often arisen, displacing others and preempting their positions of power and influence. American religious history amounts to a series of successive religious shifts, with one group after another having to make room for others. Pluralism amounts to a game of shifting alliances, the rise and fall of dominant influences. As groups and conditions change, so do cultural styles and the religious ethos generally. Ours is, as Elwyn Smith says, a "voluntary establishment,"[2] a religious order that mirrors the shifting collective mood of the people and whose strength arises out of the free, uncoerced loyalties of the believers themselves. Lacking legal status, religious establishments are sustained culturally, in the mores, values, and attitudes. Always somewhat precarious and susceptible to the ebbs and flows of popular mores and values, the mainline of American religion almost inevitably takes on new shape in times of great social and cultural change.

Certainly this is what happened in the 1960s and 1970s. The established "culture-religion" that had sustained the normative faiths of most Americans lost much of its persuasive power. Consensus gave way to dissensus and a more fragmented religious order. Now in the 1980s, groups and forces contend with one another for power and influence, in an arena that has no strong religious center. The religious scene as a whole is fluid and vulnerable as one group after another engaged in revivalist politics seeks to sway the public by its own values and outlook. No longer can we identify a single dominant religious influence; instead we have a situation in which many religious and ideological forces are seeking to exert influence. In the absence of a stronger and more stable religious middle, many questions now arise: What groups and forces seek to become the culture-shaping influences of the eighties? How do they differ in behavioral styles? What are their particular claims to mainline status? How do they stand up against the pervasive influences of modern religious individualism? In this chapter we turn to the mapping of this more fragmented middle.

Features of the Religious Mainline

What is meant by the term *religious mainline*? If *mainline* means anything it means a place in the center, but even that is not easy to define in today's fluid religious context. "The 'mainline' or 'mainstream' of a phenomenon," writes Richard John Neuhaus, "would seem to be that reality which requires little explanation."[3] It is the obvious, the normative, the taken-for-granted. It is the standard of comparison against which the marginal, the fringe, the curious are all defined. But the term as used in this way came into being at a particular historical moment in America—when new religions and old-style faiths were all flourishing and gaining in popularity and the central feature of the religious establishment was its relative decline in numbers, in power and influence, and in its ability to provide identity and to inspire loyalty. Ironically, many of the old historic traditions came to be called "mainline" just at the time when their place under the sun was being challenged. It took the greater pluralism of the 1960s and 1970s to shake Americans into an awareness that something had happened to the old normative order.

It is difficult to define, positively, the features that make a group mainline. A group's *size* is important. Groups grow or decline over time, affecting their potential for influence. Yet numbers are hardly sufficient in and of themselves. History supplies many examples of how numbers can be deceiving. As early as 1850, for example, the Roman Catholic population in this country had grown to the point that they were the largest single religious denomination, but decades would pass before they would find a place in the mainline. Catholics had numbers but not much *power*. The Protestant establishment had power—social, economic, political, and cultural power. Of these, cultural power, or authority to set the norms, is of great influence in shaping notions of propriety, legitimacy, taste, and respect. It is also often quite subtle, appearing as Dorothy C. Bass says, "in places like Henry Luce's *Time/Life* empire, in leading educational institutions governed by quotas and certain ethnic habits, in the dominance of some groups in public office, as well as in many other subtle ways."[4] Power can sustain what numbers cannot and, at least for a while, thwart the force of their growing presence.

Neither numbers nor power tell us much about the religious and spiritual qualities essential to a strong and sustaining faith. Two intangible qualities are *vitality* and *claim upon the American Way*. Vitality has to do with inner resources and the strength to empower spiritually individuals and groups. A lasting synthesis of faith and culture rests upon some measure of vitality. To be in the mainline, or even to strive toward it, is to draw off deep religious resources and to comfort as well as to challenge persons in their everyday lives. It might be said that such religion has less to do with "saving faith," which refers to the way a person is finally reconciled to God, than with "ordering faith," which helps constitute civil, social, and political life from a theological point of view. Yet such faith has come to

be problematic for many. Modern pluralism works against ordering faith in the public realms. Radical religious individualism as we
know it today, with its preoccupation with concerns of the self and
neglect of the broader social dimensions, also works against ordering faith.

Some claim upon the American Way is also involved, since in this
country religion is so closely linked to core values and ideals. The
American religious mainline is very American: it resonates toward
national self-confidence, and it joins in the celebration of the hopes,
dreams, and purposes of the people. Civil religious symbols and
mythologies permeate the consciousness of Americans and are a
source of meaning and solidarity. The mainline institutions especially are a channel of continuity for Americans, linking them to the
past and to an ever-promising future. Lowell D. Streiker and Gerald
S. Strober comment on the way themes of personal and national
identity are played out in religion: "There is an *American* response
to ultimate reality which is the source of the vision of what-ought-
to-be embracing the life of each American, his society, and the
world in which he lives."[5] It is this wellspring of religious and
moral values that lies at the heart of American self-understanding
and sense of national vocation. To be mainline is to relate to this
core aspect of American experience, to evoke its symbols and meanings in the collective experience of the people.

Finally, the notion of *tension* is useful. This concept has been applied primarily in the study of sectarian movements where levels of
tension between a religious group and its environment are common.
We would expect that groups at the periphery of society would experience some normative tension. We would expect the mainline of religion to be free of such tension, given its close ties with the dominant culture and its integrative religious ideology. But in a time of
disestablishment, when many groupings are competing with one another for a secure footing in the middle, tension is unavoidable. Tension is generated by intergroup conflict: the struggle over symbols
and beliefs, over values and moral issues, over visions of America.
Tension also occurs broadly between religion and culture. Ours is a
relatively secular society in which highly traditional, otherworldly
faiths often conflict with the assumptions and values prevailing in
the political, economic, and other cultural institutions. New tensions have arisen as evangelicals and fundamentalists have come

into greater confrontation with the secular culture. These tensions arise increasingly at the center of the culture.

All these factors—numbers, power, vitality, relation to the American way, tension—bear upon the changing shape of the American religious mainline. Each amounts to a "resource" of some importance in the power plays of groups seeking to take on the mantle of the mainline. To understand these power plays and to grasp more fully what is now happening in religion, we must sort out this changing configuration of influences.

The Socioreligious Group

In *A Nation of Behavers*,[6] Martin E. Marty proposes that a useful way of mapping religion is on the basis of group behavioral patterns. Americans, he says, use religion as a means of establishing identity, linking behavior and belief in a meaningful whole. More than simply a nation of believers, America is also a nation of behavers. What distinguishes one religious group from another is social behavior—what people do, the customs they observe, their culture—and not just their words or beliefs.

Group life is a fundamental feature of religion in this country. Far more than simply formal associations, churches and synagogues are groups in which persons interact with one another, often intermarry, and share a particular set of values and ways of looking at the world. Religion's complexity in society—as institution and as community— has been the focus of much attention by previous scholars. Will Herberg defined religion as "the divine-human encounter," but also "part of the social and cultural situation."[7] Gerhard Lenski looked upon religion as the commitment of individuals to a socioreligious group—as active members of a formal church structure and as part of a communal network of individuals, families, friends, and neighbors interacting with others in the same faith.[8] Andrew Greeley speaks of religion as both a meaning-giving cultural system and a belonging-providing group.[9] This emphasis on religion as a group experience is nicely captured in Michael Novak's description of the Catholic experience in this country: "To be a Catholic is not so much to belong to an organization as to belong to a people. It is, willy-nilly, even without having chosen it, to have a differentiated point of view and sensibility, to have participated in a certain historical way of life, to have become a different sort of human being."[10]

Levels of group belonging vary. Some religious groups have fairly cohesive bonds because of their distinctive heritage or norms restricting interaction to members of the group—for example, the Amish. These groups tend to be on the social periphery rather than at the cultural center. Groups in the mainline generally have weaker attachments. To be in or near the center is to be subject to strong pressures that work against the group and against ascriptive bonds and in favor of greater individual autonomy and freedom. Cultural trends since the 1960s, as we have seen, have further eroded group bonds and foster what can only be described as more tenuous relations between the individual and the traditional support structures of religion.

Yet despite strong individualist leanings, the socioreligious attachments of Americans reach deep. The United States is, as Greeley says, a "denominational society" that encourages quasi-ethnic loyalties and grass-roots identities. Given the ties to groups and subcultures, Parson Thwackum's sentiments often lie just below the surface: "When I mention religion, I mean the Christian religion; and not only the Christian religion, but the Protestant religion; and not only the Protestant religion, but the Church of England." Such sentiments are easily aroused in a pluralist context, and especially so in times such as the present when religious alternatives have become more sharply defined.

The latest polls continue to show that nine out of ten Americans express a specific religious preference—some brand of Protestant, Catholic, Jewish, or other faith. When asked about their more specific preferences, fully 90 percent of Protestants have little difficulty naming the church of their choice. Compared with people from other modern industrial countries, Americans are far more likely to identify with, and to involve themselves in, their churches and synagogues. Affiliation is often more a badge of belonging than a mark of serious faith or conviction, yet affiliation even of a nominal sort is deemed important for personal and social reasons. Even for the "unchurched" and the not-so-religious, the denominational framework as it exists in this country is seldom far submerged in a person's consciousness. The same holds for those caught up in deeply personalized faiths. Beneath the gloss of popular subjective labels (born again, evangelical, charismatic), Americans still claim a deep grassroots religious identity: "I'm a Baptist and a born-again Southern Baptist at that," or "a post (pre) Vatican II Catholic," or "a Jew and a member of the Lubavitcher movement," or maybe even "a Lake Wobegon Lutheran."

A Typology of Mainline Faiths

What are the significant behavioral boundaries of groups in religion today? Once the historic denominational structures were more clearly identifiable, both religiously and behaviorally. Given the strong shaping influence of the Protestant ethic heritage and infusion of ascetic values into the culture, moral and behavioral aspects in religion took shape around denominational traditions. Visible differences marked one brand of faith from another, especially in the nineteenth century, as Marty describes:

> Methodists had revivals and class meetings; they did not drink
> alcoholic beverages and they wanted to reform the world. Bap-
> tists insisted on immersing adults. Baptists and Disciples
> embodied the simple life and aspired to reproduce the moral
> codes of earliest Christianity. Episcopalians favored sedate
> liturgies . . . being one species of Protestantism distanced you
> from another species and provided habit, manner, custom, rule,
> and ritual.[11]

But much less so today. Now the sharpest differences are found along broader lines. Liberals differ from conservatives, mainline Protestants from evangelicals and fundamentalists, religionists from secularists. Moral and life-style themes are readily apparent; the divisions have more to do with culture and outlook than with organizational form, polity, or ecclesiological heritage narrowly conceived. The more significant boundaries are those distinguishing one ideological cluster or tradition from another—in general religious ideology, behavioral style, and relation to mainstream American values.

Some groups are fairly easy to place in a broadly conceived religiocommunal framework: Catholics and Jews, for example. The most difficult groupings arise concerning Protestants. Many schemes have been used for classifying Protestants into religious families, typically on the basis of polity, doctrine, or historical origin.[12] We have chosen instead to emphasize religious and cultural traditions as they have developed in the United States, in keeping with our understanding of denominations as religious subcultures. Approaching the groups in this way means taking seriously theology, history, social class, group experience, race, and other factors, although the rationale for the groupings cannot be reduced to any of these individual factors.

Theological heritage is of foremost importance in distinguishing among Protestants. Differences both religious and cultural follow along theological lines. For example, Charles Y. Glock and Rodney Stark demonstrated some years ago the importance of theological differences among Protestants by showing that they vary considerably in core beliefs and institutional commitments along a liberal-to-conservative denominational continuum.[13] It is hard to imagine a typology for Protestants that does not take theological heritage into account. Since the latter part of the nineteenth century, Protestantism has been divided, according to its confrontation with modern culture, into two major theological camps: liberals versus conservatives, or modernists versus fundamentalists. The division runs deep, culturally and ideologically, and across a wide spectrum of religious concerns. It has given rise to what is described by Marty as "Public Protestantism," which was heavily influenced by post-Enlightenment theological and social thought and is concerned with life in this world and the well-being of society. In contrast, "Private Protestantism" emphasizes personal belief, strict standards of morality, and rewards and punishments in the world to come.[14]

The encounter with modernity produced a lasting split within Protestantism. The liberal wing sought to accommodate modernity by redefining religious truth in ways that minimized conflict with science and biblical higher criticism and by developing Social Gospel ministries in response to new needs arising from urbanization and industrialization. In contrast, the conservative wing insisted upon the inerrancy of the Scriptures, the primacy of religion over science, and concern with individual salvation. This split within Protestantism drew much attention in the early decades of this century, climaxing in the highly publicized Scopes trial in 1925. In its aftermath, liberals established a firm hold on the mainline churches, and conservatives largely withdrew from public life and cultivated a more passive form of faith. Liberal Protestantism absorbed much of the New Deal agenda and shared the optimism that social problems could be solved and society improved, so much so that by the late 1950s the liberal religious faith and modern liberal culture were virtually indistinguishable. Meanwhile, conservatives organized new denominations and Bible schools, and developed ministries aimed at individuals and groups hungering for traditional faith. The Scopes trial silenced the conservatives for a while, but it hardly passed a final verdict on their future, as is evident by their resurgence in the 1970s and 1980s.

While the liberal-conservative debate lives on in many religious groups, denominations tend to fall within one or another of the major camps. Groups we define as belonging to the liberal and moderate Protestant families are, broadly speaking, those that comprise the old Protestant mainline—those called public Protestants, or ecumenical churches. We distinguish between liberal Protestants and moderate Protestants partly on grounds of theology, but also on the basis of history, size, and internal diversity within the traditions. Denominations in both of these families hold membership in the National Council of Churches. Members of the conservative Protestant family, on the other hand, are heirs of the private Protestant tradition in theology and moral concerns. They include Southern Baptists, Pentecostal and holiness church members, and members of millenarian groups. Some of the denominations are members of the National Association of Evangelicals or the Pentecostal Fellowship of North America; others assiduously avoid ecumenical and interfaith involvement. None holds membership in the National Council of Churches. The divisions between liberal and moderate Protestants on the one hand and conservative Protestants on the other continue to be sharply drawn, embracing historic differences in theology and cultural attitudes.

Another factor distinguishing Protestants, which cannot be overlooked in this country, is race. Racially based religious subcultures are a reality in America. Despite efforts to integrate some congregations and some success in doing so, Protestant churches remain essentially segregated. As we shall see in the following chapter, the proportion of black members in historic white denominations is still small. The great majority of black Americans continue to identify with the distinctive black Protestant traditions arising out of the black community. Hence we distinguish a black Protestant family from the other predominately white Protestant religious families.

An Overview

Using our typology we arrive at six major religious families: Catholics, Jews, liberal Protestants, moderate Protestants, black Protestants, and conservative Protestants. In addition, we have a classification for those with no religious preference (the "nones" or the nonaffiliated) and an "other" category consisting of several diverse bodies worthy of our attention but not easily placed elsewhere. These families constitute what we believe is a useful boundary mapping of contemporary religious pluralism in America and of the major contenders in the fragmented mainline at present.

Figure 3-1 shows the breakdown for the major traditions. We utilize national survey data for a representative distribution of religious preferences (see appendix for data description and grouping procedures). Catholics and moderate Protestants are the two largest groups, each numbering about one-fourth of the population. The conservative Protestant family is the next largest constituency (15.8 percent,) followed by black Protestants (9.1 percent) and liberal Protestants (8.7 percent). These five large Christian constituencies make up the overwhelming majority of the American population— roughly 83 percent. Jews represent an additional 2.3 percent, and those with no religious affiliation 6.9 percent. These seven comprise the major families, our *dramatis personae* in the pages that follow. Of course there are scores of other religious groups, some not fitting into one of these major families because they are not easily classified along liberal or conservative lines, others that are small and non-Western in origin. We describe four of the "other" religions (Mormons, Unitarian-Universalists, Christian Scientists, and Jehovah's Witnesses), but they are minor in our story. Our attention is given to the larger religious constituencies that have some claim

FIGURE 3-1.

THE FAMILIES OF AMERICAN RELIGION.

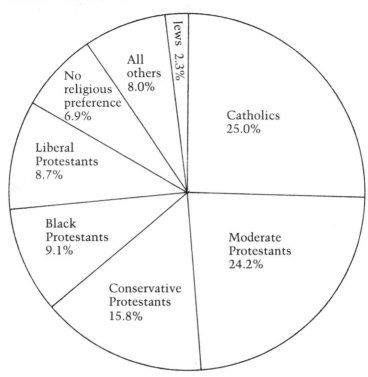

upon the mainstream culture; hence this breakdown gives us a representative and reliable profile of these major traditions as they now exist in the United States.

Patterns of religious commitment are summarized in table 3-1. Shown are data for specific denominations, for families of denominations, and for the American population as a whole. The church attendance item is based on the question "How often do you attend religious services?" Thirty-four percent of the sample attend less than once or twice a year; 21 percent are occasional attenders; and 46 percent attend nearly every week or more often. Denominational commitment was measured with the question "Would you call yourself a strong [Presbyterian]?" Overall, 43 percent of the sample consider themselves "strong" members. Membership in church-related groups is among a number of group affiliations asked of respondents in the surveys. The 38 percent who say they are members of church-

TABLE 3-1

RELIGIOUS PARTICIPATION OF RELIGIOUS GROUPS

Religious Group	Church Attendance			High Denominational Commitment	Member Church Group	Belief in Life after Death
	Low	Moderate	Regular			
National	**34**	**21**	**46**	**43**	**38**	**77**
Liberal Protestants	**37**	**24**	**39**	**33**	**43**	**82**
Episcopalians	39	28	33	32	37	79
United Church of Christ	32	24	44	39	58	80
Presbyterians	37	22	40	32	42	84
Moderate Protestants	**35**	**23**	**41**	**36**	**41**	**83**
Methodists	38	24	38	32	40	83
Lutherans	29	26	45	41	43	81
Christians (Disciples of Christ)	30	19	51	50	49	89
Northern Baptists	44	19	37	34	34	86
Reformed	25	12	64	59	48	77
Black Protestants	**20**	**25**	**56**	**52**	**51**	**72**
Methodists	17	26	57	58	57	77
Northern Baptists	27	27	46	46	43	69
Southern Baptists	15	23	62	55	55	73

TABLE 3-1 (continued)
RELIGIOUS PARTICIPATION OF RELIGIOUS GROUPS

Religious Group	Church Attendance			High Denominational Commitment	Member Church Group	Belief in Life after Death
	Low	Moderate	Regular			
Conservative Protestants	**24**	**19**	**58**	**53**	**48**	**89**
Southern Baptists	26	22	52	48	44	90
Churches of Christ	19	19	62	57	51	91
Evangelicals/Fundamentalists	18	5	77	63	64	94
Nazarenes	24	12	64	63	53	91
Pentecostals/Holiness	19	16	65	58	50	89
Assemblies of God	16	11	73	70	56	91
Churches of God	31	12	57	59	49	85
Adventists	24	13	63	59	51	78
Catholics	**25**	**20**	**55**	**42**	**30**	**75**
Jews	**48**	**39**	**13**	**42**	**38**	**27**
Others						
Mormons	27	9	64	59	61	93
Jehovah's Witnesses	13	10	77	58	49	48
Christian Scientists	31	25	44	40	35	69
Unitarian-Universalists	64	14	22	35	31	43
No religious preference	**91**	**6**	**3**	—	**4**	**47**

related groups is considerably higher than the percentage belonging to other groups (such as political organizations, professional associations, etc.). Belief in life after death is the only specific belief item available over time in the survey. The question asks simply, "Do you believe there is life after death?" Seventy-seven percent of the sample said yes.

The Religious Families

Liberal Protestants

Three groups comprise the heart of the historic Protestant mainline—the Episcopalians, the Presbyterians, and what is now called the United Church of Christ. The colonial "big three," they came to have a dominant influence early in the nation's history and became accustomed to power and influence. They occupied such a preeminent position during the nation's early years that in 1783 Yale president Ezra Stiles pictured an American future divided almost equally among Congregationalists, Presbyterians, and Episcopalians.

The nation and these churches would undergo major changes in the years following Stiles's prediction. Congregationalism struggled with the loss of its legal establishment in New England and found it difficult to adapt to life on the frontier and among immigrant groups of the nineteenth century. With an insistence on an educated clergy and a penchant for doctrinal controversy, the Presbyterians faced their own difficulties in the nineteenth century. The Episcopal Church's liturgical style and form of ecclesiastical organization seemed unattractive to many Americans. And the nineteenth-century evangelicals would come upon the scene and organize new religious bodies that would in time overtake the three, in numbers and influence.

As churches the Episcopalians, Presbyterians, and Congregationalists would come to occupy a distinct niche within the American religious economy. Despite differences in polity and background, they shared the historic Christian core faith as it was re-formed in the sixteenth century, a faith that attended more to nurture than to conversion. They came out of the modernist-fundamentalist controversies with modernists in control, inspiring bold new ventures in education, missions, charities, Social Gospel ministries. They shared a strong Anglo-American identity and a culturally established status which gave them power and influence beyond their numbers. Both their theology and their social standing encouraged an ecumenical vision and public concern, a strong social consciousness, and a mediating posture toward matters of broad societal concern. Civil rights, world peace, women's rights, the environment, and control of nuclear arms are all issues of recent concern.

Today these churches are sometimes described as "old-line" —largely because of their once historic significance and currently declining influence. Declines in institutional membership and support and a diminished influence since the 1960s point to a significant loss of vitality, more so for this sector of American religion than for any other. The self-confidence and aggressiveness with which they once engaged the culture is now missing. Optimism about the country and democratic faith, and belief that American progress and prosperity are linked with the work of God in history—once marks of liberal theology—have all faded. Commitment to social action has remained important, yet not without exacting a spiritual price; concerns for personal faith and the cure of souls are judged by many to be neglected in the pursuit of other causes. Having made more accommodations to modernity than any other major religious tradition, liberal Protestantism shows many signs of tired blood: levels of orthodox belief are low, doubt and uncertainty in matters of faith common, knowledge of the Scriptures exceedingly low. A loss of morale and mission shows up in both its public demeanor and its corporate life.

Congregational life has especially suffered, considering that the corrosive acids of modern individualism have taken a greater toll on the liberal churches than on any others. Twenty years ago Stark and Glock pointed to the weakness of socioreligious group bonds in these churches.[15] They concluded that the liberal churches were "religious audiences" rather than communities—a description even more true now than when they wrote. Levels of church attendance for liberal Protestants are well below average: 39 percent attend regularly, 24 percent attend occasionally, and 37 percent attend less often than once or twice a year. Episcopalians attend less than Presbyterians or United Church of Christ members. Liberal Protestants have weaker denominational loyalties and are less likely to be members of church-related groups. Drawing off upper-middle-class constituencies, their clienteles are the most exposed to the currents of modern individualism and the pursuits of self-fulfillment. Boundaries between the religious community and the larger culture are often vague, and commitment to the church as a gathered community of believers in which faith is shaped and nurtured is noticeably lacking.

Liberal Protestantism's cultural influence is greater than its lack of religious vitality suggests. Known for its close ties historically with the northern and eastern establishment, it still is a power and presence of some significance though less so than in the first part of the twentieth century. Persons within this tradition are disproportionately represented among the nation's civic and corporate elite. Kit and Frederica Konolige's description of Episcopalians is fitting: "the wealthiest, most eastern, best educated, and most highly placed professionally of any Christian denomination in the United States."[16] Politically the power of liberal Protestants continues to be fairly strong despite the gradual erosion of WASP influence throughout this century: all three religious groups have far more members in the U.S. Senate and House of Representatives than would be expected based on their aggregate sizes.[17] Relatively speaking, the old-line liberal Protestant community accounts for slightly less than 10 percent of the American population. Membership rolls at present show the Episcopal Church numbering about 2.8 million, the recently reunited Presbyterian Church (U.S.A.) slightly more than 3 million, and the United Church of Christ 1.7 million.

Moderate Protestants

The category "moderate Protestants" is an arbitrary grouping of five denominations, all of which are a product of nineteenth-century America: Methodists, Disciples, Northern Baptists, Lutherans, and the Reformed churches. More than just nineteenth-century origins, they have other similarities as well: all have fairly sizable constituencies, occupy a similar social location, and tend to be closely attuned to middle American values and outlook.

Three of the groups—the Methodists, Disciples, Northern Baptists—bear the imprint of their frontier origins. All grew rapidly and formed strong cultural and religious identities in the expansive years of the nineteenth century. Informality, simple faith and piety, an optimistic and confident outlook, and a deep egalitarian spirit all found expression in these truly "American" churches. Methodists especially, with their Arminian theology and practical approach to matters of faith and ecclesiology, were to become "the mainline of the mainline." President Theodore Roosevelt is reported to have said he "would rather address a Methodist audience than any other audience" because, as he put it, they "represent the great middle class and in consequence are the most representative church in America."[18] Over the years the Methodists have continued to represent much of American life, as reflected in a 1947 editorial in *Life* magazine: "In many ways it is our most characteristic church. It is short on theology, long on good works, brilliantly organized, primarily middle-class, frequently bigoted, incurably optimistic, zealously missionary, and touchingly confident of the essential goodness of the man next door."[19]

Disciples and Northern Baptists too exhibit many features of typicality and give expression to deeply ingrained American traits. The Christian Church (Disciples of Christ) is known for its staunch dedication to the principles of voluntarism and congregational autonomy. Highly pragmatic in their approach to the religious life, Disciples embody some of the most fundamental religious values—particularly their simple, noncreedal, and rational approach to Scripture. Northern Baptists are a diverse collectivity of believers in the Baptist tradition, the vast majority being members of the American Baptist Churches. While never achieving the same dominance of cultural and religious life as did their southern counterparts in their region, nonetheless the Northern Baptists would find a place in the mainstream culture as the "recognized democrats of the Protestant world." They are known for their strong emphasis upon individual conscience and religious freedom, and their congregations are among the most racially inclusive of any in the United States.

The other two members of the moderate Protestant family owe their origins to a different nineteenth-century phenomenon—the great European immigration. The Lutheran and Reformed churches were represented in colonial America, but their greatest expansion occurred from the mid-1800s through the First World War, with the massive influx of Germans, Scandinavians, and Dutch. The twentieth century has seen considerable assimilation into American life and successive consolidations of Lutheranism, the latest being the merger of three of the largest bodies (Lutheran Church in America, American Lutheran Church, and Association of Evangelical Lutheran Churches) into a single church. The union makes Lutherans now the nation's fourth largest Protestant church. The Lutheran Church—Missouri Synod, which has maintained a strict conservative doctrinal stance and has been less sympathetic toward ecumenical participation, remains independent of the newly formed church. The Reformed churches also experienced their greatest expansion in the nineteenth century. The two principal bodies that comprise this group, the Reformed Church in America and the Christian Reformed Church, share a Dutch Calvinist heritage and commitment to classical Reformed theology. They have become Americanized over time, with the larger of the two, the Reformed Church in America, generally regarded as the more assimilated into the culture at large.

Compared to old-line liberal Protestants, moderate Protestants have not had as much access to power or occupied as privileged a status in the national ethos. Their claims to being mainline have rested instead on their close ties with the people and their fundamental, grass-roots values—the ideals and standards implicit in the common American creed. Moderate Protestants are more conservative in their doctrinal beliefs and social attitudes than liberal Protestants and tend to reflect more majority American opinions and views.[20] While tending toward the middle, these constituencies, by virtue of their size, necessarily include a wide range of outlooks and opinions. Diversity in religious belief and practice and solid middle-class social location makes the group somewhat more vulnerable to the ebb and flow of popular opinion in mainstream America.

Levels of religious belonging are roughly similar to those for Americans generally. Forty-one percent of moderate Protestants are regular church attenders, 23 percent are occasional attenders, and 35 percent are "nominal" members. Lutherans, Reformed members, and Disciples show a high denominational commitment; Methodists are less strongly committed. These churches tend not to suffer as much from radical forms of religious individualism as does more liberal Protestantism, yet they suffer more than some other religious traditions do. Moderate Protestants are very much in the middle between a rampant individualism on the one hand and a more collectivist response on the other. As in many other respects, the religious group attachments of members of this family single them out as moderates—as truly mainliners.

Size is a factor in their identification as mainline. The moderate Protestant family in our typology accounts for about one-fourth of the religious population in the United States. It is the largest of the Protestant constituencies and the most representative religiously and culturally. Today the United Methodist Church is the second largest Protestant denomination, with close to 9.5 million members; the Disciples have 1.2 million; the American Baptists 1.6 million; the new Lutheran body 5.4 million; and the Reformed churches in excess of a half million.

Black Protestants

Primarily Methodist and Baptist in background, black Protestants have a distinctive religious history and group identity.[21] Historically, revivalistic Protestantism was the chief means by which blacks in the United States—having largely lost their African culture—would come to define and interpret their experience in this country. Early on, the black church emerged as an important institution, second only to the family, as a symbol and embodiment of racial solidarity and the quest for freedom and justice. Owing to a unique heritage of slavery and discrimination, Christian beliefs and symbols have taken on particular meanings for African-Americans and are closely bound up with how they view themselves and how they relate to white America.

Religion's functions in the black community have been diverse: a badly needed refuge from a hostile world, yet also a source of inspiration for social involvement. At times separatist interests have loomed large; in other times more inclusive themes have held sway. As the training ground for many black leaders—Nat Turner, Denmark Vessey, Martin Luther King, Jr., and more recently, Jesse Jackson—the black church has nurtured a vision of a just America in which blacks and whites alike could share in its bounty. The majority of participants in the black churches have promoted integration, and they have interpreted justice, liberation, love, suffering, and hope in light of the goal of creating a society in which blacks and whites could live together. Entry into the mainstream for blacks rests upon appeals to the conscience of white America and to overcoming the discrepancies between national ideals and continuing discriminatory practices. King was masterful in mobilizing religious values ("I have a Dream") as a means of breaking through to white America. Jesse Jackson's 1984 presidential candidacy represents the latest, and perhaps the most politically astute, effort yet at articulating an inclusive vision and program for the nation.

With religious symbols and community so important to blacks, members of these churches have relatively strong socioreligious group ties. Black Protestants attend worship services more than any other group except white conservative Protestants: 56 percent are regular attenders and 25 percent are occasional attenders. Black Southern Baptists are more frequent church attenders than Northern Baptists. Generally blacks have a high level of denominational commitment, much higher in fact than most other groups. With respect to membership in a church group—perhaps the best measure of communal bonds—they exceed all the other families. They are the only family for which more than one-half claim involvement in a church group. Strong bonds to church and community have served to buffer somewhat the trends toward greater religious individualism dominant in the society.[22]

Conservative Protestants

A large and diverse constituency, white Protestant conservatives share a traditional religious and cultural outlook. The tradition was shaped by several major religious reactionary strands of the late nineteenth and early twentieth centuries, most notably, the holiness revival, the Pentecostal movement, and fundamentalism. Though distinct as revivalistic movements, they shared evangelical doctrines emphasizing the necessity of a conversion experience, the authority of the Bible, and the importance of a moral life, freed especially from such barroom vices as drinking, dancing, and card playing. These latter have receded in emphasis, but religious conservatives continue to stress the importance of a strong personal moral life.

The largest distinctively evangelical denomination in the United

States today is the Southern Baptist Convention. The authority and inspiration of the Bible stands as the cornerstone of Baptist belief, and for Southern Baptists such views are decidedly literalistic. Compared with their Northern Baptist sisters and brothers, they are more conservative in both theology and life-style. They are beset at present by internal controversies—between conservatives and moderates—yet continue to hold together. All varieties of contemporary evangelicalism are present, though the vast majority are representatives of the evangelical right and center. For a "majority" faith shaping popular attitudes and values throughout its region of strength, Southern Baptists evoke a remarkably strong, almost "sectarianlike" type of commitment. Of the Southern Baptist Convention Martin Marty has said that it "remains disciplined, assertive, generally doctrinally conservative, often rather rigid, and consistently capable of retaining the loyalty of old members while aggressively programming means to recruit new ones."[23]

Other bodies included in the conservative Protestant family are the Churches of Christ, the Church of the Nazarene, the Assemblies of God, the Seventh-Day Adventists, and countless independent fundamentalist, Pentecostal, and holiness groups. Arising out of the fundamentalist-modernist disputes earlier in the century, many of these groups stand squarely within the Arminian tradition and are representatives today, generally speaking, of the evangelical right and center. Many are members of the National Association of Evangelicals, a major symbol of the evangelical presence as well as a bastion of social and political conservatism during the 1960s and 1970s. All hold to fairly rigid personal moral views and have sought to maintain distinctive religious styles, some being more successful than others. For example, members of the Assemblies of God still hold to a strict code of personal behavior, including taboos against social dancing and alcoholic beverages. Along with its Sabbatarianism and belief in an imminent second coming of Christ, the Seventh-Day Adventist church holds to distinctive views on health, medicine, and diet.

The posture of conservative Protestantism continues to be shaped by its confrontation with modernity. Although many of their earlier objections to Catholicism, Darwinism, and higher criticism of the Bible have toned down, they still resist the encroachments of modernism and secularism. They do so by holding to literalistic orthodox Christian doctrines, a view of the Bible as inerrant, and a metaphysic that assumes reality is inhabited by both physical and spiritual beings. God and the Devil wage spiritual warfare against one another in a world in which the outcome for humanity in time and space hangs in the balance. Many of the old doctrines of the evangelical worldview have lost some of their salience (e.g., notions of hell and judgment), yet continuity with many of the traditional beliefs remains intact. A survey conducted in the late 1970s for *Christianity Today* shows that two-thirds of evangelicals believe that the "Devil is a personal being who directs evil forces and influences people to do wrong"; 82 percent said they accepted the view that "God created Adam and Eve, which was the start of human life."[24]

For a long time "outsiders" to the mainline, religious conservatives now hope for a stronger hold on the culture. They have successfully called up the old symbols of American civil religion and forged a new alliance between belief in God and belief in America. If religious liberals are pessimistic and alienated from democratic faith, conservatives are optimistic and are ready to proclaim anew that what is good for the country is good for the gospel and vice versa—a message Americans have often enjoyed hearing, and one that resonated extremely well in the seventies and eighties. After the crises of Vietnam and Watergate, a new sense of national purpose and pride warmed the hearts of those who really wanted to "believe" in America. And people in this country do in fact want to believe in America, for at the core of patriotic loyalty is an affirmation about themselves. As Jerry Falwell says; "America has been great because her people have been good."

In its religious worldview and its Americanism, conservative Prottestantism is frought with paradoxes. "It is Christianity derived from an ancient book, yet shaped also by the technological age," writes George M. Marsden.[25] Often it is otherworldly and seemingly concerned only with the salvation of individuals, yet it links itself with patriotism and the moral welfare of the nation. In many respects it is antimodernist, yet in other ways strikingly modern. Intolerant and narrow-minded at times, yet it strives to be civil and widely influential. And perhaps the greatest paradox of all: it is antiestablishment in much of its rhetoric, both religiously and culturally, yet increasingly sees itself as moving into the mainline.

Whatever its worldview and stance, religious conservatism thrives upon strong socioreligious group ties. The churches in this tradition have been described as primary groups with a great deal of face-to-face association and as some of the most cohesive nonethnic communities in America. Survey data sustain these observations: church attendance rates are among the highest for any groups, with 58 percent of members attending religious services nearly every week or more often; levels of denominational loyalty are also at the top, especially among the Assemblies of God, the Nazarenes, and the splinter evangelical and fundamentalist bodies. Trends toward religious individualism have found far less acceptance within this sector of American religion than within almost any other. Certainly among large and quite diverse religious constituencies, associational and communal bonds for these churches rank remarkably high.

The conservative Protestant family of denominations, as defined in our typology, accounts for about 16 percent of the overall American population. Southern Baptists are by far the largest group, with 14 million members. Membership for other major conservative bodies numbers almost 2 million for Assemblies of God, 1.6 million for Churches of Christ, six hundred thousand for Seventh-Day Adventists, and a half million for the Nazarenes. Of course the number of evangelicals and traditional believers in America is much larger, including some who are members of moderate and liberal Protestant churches.

Roman Catholics

Today roughly one-fourth of the American population is Roman Catholic. As members of a universal religious community, American Catholics share in a historic tradition marked by a strong sacramental presence and emphasis upon mediation and communion as religious values. In the American context Catholicism has become "denominationalized" as one among many faiths in a pluralist system. In the process of accommodating religious pluralism, the church has given up many of its distinctive features in matters of doctrine and practice; since Vatican II especially, the pace of change has been momentous and accommodation to American religious norms far-reaching. Andrew Greeley writes:

. . . almost overnight, it was all right to eat meat on Friday, mass was said in English, with the priest facing the people, the laity could receive communion wafers into their own hands and minister it unto themselves or take bread and wine from the chalice, as the clergy had always done; women became lectors at mass and even ministers of holy communion; priests resigned because they wanted to marry; nuns doffed their all-encompassing habits and marched on picket lines; Protestants lost their status as heretics and schematics and became separated brothers and sisters, and Pope Paul VI issued a birth-control encyclical that was promptly rejected by outspoken Catholic scholars and then by almost nine-tenths of the laity.[26]

Opposition was loud and articulate, but more significant was the widespread acceptance of the changes: an astonishing 87 percent of the laity approved the changes in the mass by the early 1970s, while 66 percent approved all conciliar changes.[27] In a fairly short period of time, Catholicism became much more pluralistic, more voluntary, more American. Associated Press religion editor George Cornell says:

A new, broader kind of Roman Catholicism is emerging in the United States as portrayed in survey findings. It's more educated, more diverse in religious interpretations, its people at ease in differing with official positions, yet loyal to the church, confident, and devout. . . . That picture is in marked contrast to the past image of a homogeneous bloc of uniform religious views and practice, with dissenters considered leaving the fold. But now they're staying explicitly in it, comfortable in doing so, dedicated to the faith, even though often disagreeing with authorities about its implications.[28]

In the aftermath of Vatican II, Catholicism moved quickly into the mainstream of American religious life. Though never without influence in American life, it had long been more concerned with the welfare of its own members, many of them immigrants, than with shaping the national society. But the 1960s saw increased cooperation with Protestants and Jews, both in civil rights work and later in the protest against the Vietnam War. The Catholic church moved toward the center just as mainline Protestantism was losing its place as a dominant voice. By the 1980s the American bishops emerged as a kind of collective conscience for the nation. They were "activists" seeking to address great issues facing the nation and world at a time when the mood of the country had grown conservative. Addressing themselves not just to Catholics but to all Americans, the bishops jumped squarely into the central policy arenas of nuclear armament and the economy. A once-suspect Catholic leadership had become a major, if not *the* major, religious voice articulating a public vision for America.

Though Catholic church attendance has declined, it is still relatively high. Catholics attend worship services more regularly than liberal or moderate Protestants and about the same as black Protestants and conservative Protestants. Forty-two percent of Catholics consider themselves "strong" Catholics, roughly the same number as are strong in other religious traditions in the country. But more Catholics are likely to consider themselves "strong" members than do either liberal or moderate Protestants. They are somewhat less likely to be members of church-related groups (30 percent are members) than are any of the Protestants, though once again they are more generally typical of Americans. Socioreligious group ties are moderately strong, particularly within some ethnic sectors. Like all mainline religious groups, however, contemporary forms of religious individualism are much in evidence as Catholics become more pluralist in style and redefine their relations with both Rome and America.

Jews

The Jewish community in America is small—only 2 or 3 percent of the population. A religious minority held together by ethnic and cultural ties, the Jews have developed three major religious responses to the American experience: the Reform, the Conservative, and the Orthodox. These represent varying accommodations to modernity and compromises with the demands of the Americanization process for a group that has made significant progress in carving out a place for itself socially, economically, and culturally.

Long known for their identification with liberal causes and commitment to an open, achieving society, Jews seem to have shifted their concern in recent years from integration to maintaining some form of Jewish identity. Many are uneasy that they may have become too assimilated, too successful and accepted. "The position of Jews has changed so dramatically, and with such bewildering speed," writes Charles E. Silberman, "that American Jews are confused about who they are and anxious about how they fit into the society."[29] Not just developments from within Jewish life, but the changing American religious scene gives pause as well. Conservative Protestants seem to offer support to Israeli and American Jewish concerns, but right-wing-fundamentalist calls for a Christian America raise serious doubts. As a minority with more power and prominence than its numbers suggest, Jews now find themselves caught up in a posture of reexamining and forging anew their political and religious alliances.

Relative to other groups, Jews have low rates of attendance at religious services. Thirteen percent attend regularly, 39 percent attend occasionally, and 48 percent attend services less often than once or twice a year. Yet denominational commitment (42 percent consider themselves "strong" Jews) and membership in synagogue-related groups (38 percent active) are close to national norms. Associational ties in the form of synagogue and temple involvement are weak, but communal ethnic bonds are strong. While some aspects of Jewishness have eroded, other aspects are emerging as American Jews seek to express their Jewishness without inhibiting their full participation in American life. For no religious community in America has the tension between the individual's integration into the national life and commitment to his or her group been more acute or aroused greater concerns.

Other Faiths

Four smaller, but visible, groups are the Mormons, Jehovah's Witnesses, Christian Scientists, and Unitarian-Universalists. Each deserves some mention simply because they are generally well known to Americans, and each in its own way is something of a minority variant of the historic Christian faith. By virtue of their greater distance from the mainstream culture, all are known for their distinctive religious styles.

The Church of Jesus Christ of Latter-Day Saints (the Mormons) is known for the deep loyalty of its members, its stress upon family life, and its discipline and restraint in using intoxicants. Its missionary zeal and penetration into growing sectors of American life are unmatched. Rates of church attendance are high, with almost two-thirds reporting they attend regularly. Fifty-nine percent of the Mormons identify themselves as strongly committed; 61 percent are members of church-related groups. By their teachings and life-styles they offer interpretations of life that differ dramatically from those of other Americans. Today their membership is close to 3 million.

Jehovah's Witnesses are aggressively millenarian, biblical literalists, and hold that theirs is the only true faith. They are known for their refusal to salute the U.S. flag, to serve in the armed forces, and to celebrate holidays such as Christmas and Easter, and for their opposition to blood transfusions. Their attitudes toward civil authority and their persistent door-to-door recruiting set them apart from other faiths. Numbering over six hundred thousand members, they hold fervently to an interpretation of world events that the Kingdom of God will be ushered in when Christ conquers Satan in the Battle of Armageddon. On measures of socioreligious group commitment, they rank high.

Christian Scientists are known for their reading rooms and long-standing concern with healing. Sin, sickness, pain, and death are all viewed as illusions in this life to be dealt with through proper faith and utilization of spiritual power; all that is real is God, and what is not an aspect of God does not exist. The church has no ordained clergy and does not release membership statistics, although it is known that the number of churches as of 1980 was just under three thousand. Members are slightly lower in church attendance rates and group membership than Americans generally. Denominational commitment is about average, and belief in life after death is low.

Unitarian-Universalists draw upon two histories. Unitarians trace their roots as a movement out of disputes with New England Congregationalism over Trinitarian doctrine. Universalists come with a background of broad liberalism in theology and universal concern for people. Committed to a "free and disciplined search for truth," members of this community cherish universal teachings, the supreme worth of every person, and promote a vision of a world united around ideals of brotherhood, justice, and peace. Levels of institutional commitment are low, and only a minority believe in a life after death. Membership is small, roughly 140,000 today.

The Nonaffiliates

Once a marginal assortment of largely alienated and isolated Americans not well socialized into the dominant values, nonaffiliates today are much more a part of the mainstream.[30] When many middle-class youth dropped out of the churches in the 1960s, the complexion of the constituency changed. These young people became nonaffiliates more by choice than by circumstance—"cultural nones" rather than "structural nones."[31] Throughout the seventies they were strong supporters of the new cultural values emphasizing self-fulfillment and the realization of individual goals and aspirations. Organized religion seemed at odds with these pursuits, and hence many caught up in the new values turned their backs on the religious establishment.

Persons reporting they have no religious affiliation are a diverse constituency, religiously as well as culturally. Many hold beliefs in the supernatural and the mystical and often show much interest in religious and quasi-religious phenomena. Few are actually militant secularists or committed atheists in their opposition to religion. They simply have little interest in organized religion and lack membership in a conventional church or synagogue. Not surprisingly, they have the lowest levels of church attendance and activity in religious groups.

Behavioral Styles and Group Attachments

As this overview of the major groupings shows, at present there is considerable variation in the relations of religion and culture in the American mainstream. Symbols, values, meaning systems, and belonging styles all vary from one religious sector to another. In the process of accommodating modernity and the cultural upheavals of the post-1960s period, the mainline religious clusters have come to be "ordered" along an individualist-to-conformist gradient—some groupings having weak institutional bonds, others having much stronger bonds. Generally behavioral styles vary with strength of socioreligious group bonds; those groupings having high levels of cohesiveness typically are more distinctive in their behavior and identity.

These differing patterns of religious conformity are of great importance for maintaining a strong religious subculture. For groups in which membership requirements, norms of participation, and behavioral expectations are generally strong, an individual's involvement within the religious community is reinforced; alternatively, for groups where communal ties are weak and conformity of belief and outlook are unenforced, there is much less support for the individual believer. That is to say, religious groupings today vary greatly in the strength of their "plausibility structures" and in the extent to which they sustain cognitive closure and normative standards.[32] Those traditions most effective in sheltering believers from the corrosive acids of modern individualism are those that nurture communal bonds and loyalty to the group. Partly this is a matter of associational and communal ties (quasi-ethnic attachments), but theological heritage and general stance toward modernity also are factors. Countersecular movements since the sixties have sharpened religious and cultural boundaries, which in turn has inspired and strengthened social bonds, especially within the more conservative sectors.

A summary comparison based on the character of group bonds is found in table 3-2. Looking at the five major religious traditions plus nonaffiliates (no religious preference), eliminating the "other" category because of its diverse composition, we arrive at the'following rank order.

Conservative Protestants rank at the very top. They have the highest scores on institutional commitment plus rank first on traditional belief in life after death. A strong belief in traditional values and morality is reinforced by strong loyalties to religious group and doctrine. Among white Protestants, communal ties and belonging are strongest for this group, thus making it more resistant to the individualizing and privatizing trends of modern society.

Black Protestants rank next highest in institutional and group commitment. They express a strong loyalty to the religious group, though not so strong a belief in life after death. "Ethnic" factors

TABLE 3-2

RANK ORDER OF RELIGIOUS FAMILIES ON RELIGIOUS INDICATORS

Family	Institutional Commitment				Belief in Life after Death
	Church Attendance	Denominational Commitment	Member of Church-Related Group	Average Commitment Rank	
Liberal Protestants	5	6	3	4.7	3
Moderate Protestants	4	5	4	4.3	2
Black Protestants	2	2	1	1.7	5
Conservative Protestants	1	1	2	1.3	1
Catholics	3	3.5	6	4.2	4
Jews	6	3.5	5	4.8	7
No religious preference	7	7	7	7.0	6

clearly contribute to the commitment, with religious and group elements mutually reinforcing a distinct identity and sense of belonging. Communal ties generally are strong as a result of minority experience.

Catholics fall third in the ranking, both on institutional attachments and belief in life after death. They rank at midlevel on all the indicators except for membership in church-related groups. Like other mainstream faiths, Catholics enjoy a great deal of freedom in matters of belief and behavior, yet because of their ethnic heritages and greater ecclesiastical authority, ties to groups and traditions remain fairly strong.

Moderate Protestants rank fourth—about where we would expect for "middle Americans." They rank somewhat higher on church-related group activities than on church attendance or denominational commitment. More than any other family, moderate Protestants are characterized by "average" levels of religious commitment. Less bound by group loyalties than either conservative Protestants or black Protestants, they are somewhat more individualistic in religious and life-style choices.

Liberal Protestants rank fifth in level of institutional commitment. They rank somewhat higher on church-related activities, but church attendance and denominational commitment are low. In belief in life after death they rank somewhat higher. Ties to institutional religion are obviously weak. Less socially encapsulated and bound by ascriptive ties, members of these churches are more vulnerable to the privatizing trends of modern society.

Jews have the lowest level of institutional commitment. Though fairly weak in commitment to synagogue attendance, they rank higher on both religious group activity and strength of group ties. In belief in life after death they rank at the very bottom—even below nonaffiliates. Ties to tradition and minority experience are far more important than common belief for this group, making it more an ethnic than a religious collectivity in many respects.

Unfortunately, few data are available on religious belief and attitudes broken down by groups as we have defined them. It is reasonable to expect, however, that such patterns are consistent with the ranking observed earlier. Previous surveys have documented for Protestants a liberal-to-conservative spectrum of belief generally paralleling the rank order of groups, based upon institutional com-

TABLE 3-3
PERCENTAGE WHO SAY RELIGION IS VERY IMPORTANT IN THEIR OWN LIVES

Denomination	Percent
Episcopalians	37
Presbyterians	55
Methodists	56
Lutherans	55
Southern Baptists	72
Catholics	56
Jews	25

Source: *Religion in America 1984*, Gallup Report No 222.

mitment. Stark and Glock's study of American piety in the midsixties, for example, documented widespread differences between liberals and conservatives, and between Protestants and Catholics, in orthodox belief, devotionalism, religious experience, and religious knowledge. Literalistic versus mythological interpretations of such matters as the Virgin Birth, the existence of the Devil, and miracles vary greatly across the religious traditions—in much the same way that levels of institutional commitment vary. Measures of belief and the cognitive salience of religion correlate with commitment to religious institutions and groups, providing a strong basis for expecting a fairly coherent and integrated system of belief and practice for each of the major traditions.

We have data, broken down by several of the larger denominations, on the "importance of religion." The Gallup organization regularly asks the question "How important would you say religion is in your life?" Though not a tenet of belief, the question provides insight into the expressed salience of religion to individuals and thus may be considered a measure of personal, or "privatized," religious significance. Responses from 1983 surveys broken down for the denominations are shown in table 3-3.

The groups vary in the importance they attach to religion, consistent with our rank order. Fifty-six percent of Americans generally say religion is "very important" in their lives—with Methodists and Catholics right on the national mark. That Methodists, our quintessential American Protestant group, and Catholics, most recently assimilated into the mainstream, embody national religious sentiment as they do seems fitting. Among Protestants, Methodists, Lutherans, and Presbyterians hover at the national norm. Episcopalians, the weakest of our three liberal Protestant denominations in terms of institutional commitment, are considerably less likely (37 percent) to report that religion is personally very important. Southern Baptists, the only conservative Protestant group for which data are available, rank at the very top (72 percent). Predictably, Jews rank below all the other groups in reported saliency of personal religion.

Conclusion

This mapping of the religious scene demonstrates that there are major religious and ideological clusters in contemporary America. These clusters provide varying cognitive and behavioral orientations for millions of Americans, alternative symbolic frames by which people interpret their lives. Further, the mapping shows that it is useful to examine the groupings on the basis of their relation to the core, mainstream culture—in terms of size, power, tension, vitality, and claims upon the American Way. In a time when there is no dominant religious force, we must look at all the competing groups and the ways they seek to influence the public realms. The relations of religion and culture are dynamic and varied; to understand how they are changing, some attention to ideological groupings and behavioral styles is essential.

Today these clusters have surpassed the denominations themselves as the fundamental divisions in American religious life. The typology is especially helpful for highlighting the various levels of religious individualism or lack of strong social cohesiveness. The trends toward greater individualism and privatism are of crucial importance to organized religion, yet as we have seen, the patterns vary considerably from one tradition to another. Levels of cohesiveness, importance of religion, and moral and religious styles all vary along predictable group lines.

So important are these groupings that we must explore their changing social and geographic locations in contemporary America. The fact that the public square has become "naked," to hark back to Neuhaus's description, suggests the likelihood of profound transformations in the social basis of religion in this country. Greater individualism has led to a weakening of many of the old ascriptive attachments and a repositioning of religious groups and forces in the social structure. We look next at the social context of American religion and its changes in the modern period. Perhaps no other aspect of change is of greater importance for grasping what is happening to the religious mainline.

Chapter Four

The Social Sources of Denominationalism Revisited

For if religion supplies the energy, the goal, and the motive of sectarian movements, social factors no less decidedly supply the occasion, and determine the form the religious dynamic will take.
—H. RICHARD NIEBUHR

More than fifty years have passed since the publication in 1929 of H. Richard Niebuhr's classic *The Social Sources of Denominationalism*. His was a benchmark work in several respects: it set forth the denomination as a distinctive American religion form; it showed how sects evolve in the direction of churchlike structures; and most important, it established the primacy of social, rather than religious, factors as the basis of the nation's religious pluralism. As a theologian and ethicist, he lamented what he called the "ethical failure of a divided church," yet recognized as few others have the truly "secular character" of American religious life. Commentators ever since have pointed to religion's vulnerability to social and cultural influences and to the fact that in this country especially religion and society are inextricably bound together. In a democratic order with a strong heritage of individualism and voluntarism, nonreligious factors play a decisive part in shaping the religious landscape.

Niebuhr emphasized the importance of the major structural divisions of the society—namely class, race, national origins, and regionalism—as sources of religious subcultures. He looked back upon an America in its formative period when a young, dynamic nation and its institutions were taking shape. The influences upon religion were the same as those upon the nation. Throughout the nineteenth century the forces shaping religion and culture were those arising out of an emergent class structure, a diverse ethnic population, and growing cleavages along racial and regional lines. These were all powerful forces moulding the country and its way of life; they would become the ascriptive bases around which religious life would be organized and would have a lasting impact upon group identity and the way in which Americans experienced their lives.

From the vantage point of the 1980s, many changes have occurred in the social basis of American religion. Many of the old parochial boundaries separating the religious subcultures have broken down: social and cultural changes have "leveled" some of the long-standing historic differences separating churches and denominations; widespread social upheavals and cultural shifts have weakened ties to organized religion and led to increasing numbers of secular "non-affiliates," who have little or no connection with the churches. Modernity has brought about greater individualism and privatism in religious life—trends undermining many of the old ascriptive bases of denominational structures and encouraging greater choice and more personal forms of belief. Not surprisingly, boundaries between faiths as well as those between faith and culture have been, and continue to be, redrawn—and thus call for a new mapping if we are to grasp the changing social location of the mainline faiths.

So we are led to ask: To what extent have the old social sources declined in importance? What are the social profiles of the various groups at present? What are the basic structural differences in religion today? Following Niebuhr's lead, we explore in this chapter the sources that he identified and their more recent developments: social class, ethnicity, region, and race.

Social Class

The relation between social class and religion in this country has always been fluid and dynamic. Though religious groups are often formed in direct response to economic concerns, seldom do they remain for long committed to their original ideologies or unchanged in their constituencies. In an open and mobile society, there is considerable opportunity for upward social movement and thus a changing class basis for religion. The "churches of the disinherited," as Niebuhr observed, often become the "churches of the middle class." Sectarian groups tend to be unstable and over time typically are transformed into churches—or more exactly, as Niebuhr pointed out, into denominations. External as well as internal dynamics propel religious groups, at least most of them, in the direction of becoming established institutions. Historically in the United States, a group's sectlike or churchlike religious characteristics have varied largely with its social class standing.

The Methodists are a prime example. Beginning with a popular following on the frontier and later finding a following among the urban working classes, over time the Methodists have evolved into a solidly middle-class Protestant denomination. In so doing the group left behind many of its earlier sectarian traits of revolt and opposition to become a more accommodating, mainline religious body. In styles of religious belief and observance, members changed as their social characteristics and relation to society changed. This pattern of religious change was to be repeated, time and again, in American religious history. As John Wilson says, "Methodists, Baptists, Disciples, and even Holiness sects, all once associated with the unwashed and illiterate, have entered the ranks of religious respectability. A Disciple became President of the United States in 1963 and a Southern Baptist followed in 1977."[1]

Several features of the American experience help explain the shifting social and economic bases for religion. Historically, close association of democratic and religious values have exposed the work ethic to the most deprived groups and thereby legitimated a commitment to individual striving, hard work, and worldly success. An achievement-oriented society made it possible for upwardly mobile individuals to "switch" denominations, especially if their social attainments were generally greater than those of the groups in which they were born and reared. As we shall see in a later chapter, upward switching is a common pattern at all levels of the religious status hierarchy.

In a dynamic society, religious groups themselves often experience collective upward mobility. With economic growth and opportunities for migration, in the late nineteenth and twentieth centuries many groups of working-class origins advanced fairly rapidly.

Often in as few as three generations, the composition of a religious movement has changed considerably. The upward mobility of older Protestant churches was facilitated by the large numbers of immigrants of low standing, largely of Catholic and Jewish background. By entering the lowest levels of the class structure at the time of arrival, their presence served to raise the status of more established groups. In much the same way, the movement of blacks, Puerto Ricans, Mexican-Americans, and, more recently, Asian immigrants to the cities has bolstered the status levels of many white sectarians who otherwise would occupy the lowest rungs on the status ladder.

Thus religious constituencies in this country can be ordered fairly easily along a status hierarchy. The hierarchy rests largely upon time of entry into the system and subsequent pace of assimilation. The colonial "big three"—the Episcopalians, the Congregationalists, the Presbyterians—have maintained high-status positions from the time of the nation's founding to the present. Their social standing is largely a product of history. Other groups have experienced far greater changes in status and economic position, but generally their standing at any given time reflects when they entered the system. Methodism, for example, as it evolved into a middle-class faith, opened the way for many new sectarian movements among the displaced classes—the Nazarenes, the Adventists, and numerous Pentecostal and holiness groups. These groups rank well behind the Methodists in socioeconomic standing, reflecting the lag of a century or more in their origins. Thus while the religious system is highly fluid in the sense that new churches are formed, the sect-to-denomination pattern of upward-shifting status is fairly constant. Groups fall into rank pretty much on the basis of their standing in this on-going cycle of religious movements, first breaking away and then evolving toward a more mainline position. The Jews are a major exception; despite their relatively recent arrival in sizable numbers, nonetheless they rank among the highest of the groups.

In the period since World War II, the socioeconomic basis of American religion has undergone dramatic changes. The postwar economy, the growth of the middle class, and suburban expansion all contributed to new patterns of class and religion. Table 4-1 shows this change by comparing the status order of groups in the mid-1940s and with the more current period.[2] Lack of comparable

TABLE 4-1

STATUS HIERARCHY OF THE DENOMINATIONS AND MAJOR SHIFTS, 1945–1946 TO PRESENT

1945–46	*Current*
Top rank	
Christian Scientists	Unitarian-Universalists
Episcopalians	Jews
Congregationalists	Episcopalians
Presbyterians	Presbyterians
Jews	United Church of Christ
Middle rank	
Reformed	Mormons
Methodists	No religious preference
Lutherans	Christian Scientists
Disciples	Methodists
	Catholics
	Lutherans
	Misc. Evangelicals/Fundamentalists
	Christians (Disciples of Christ)
	White Northern Baptists
	Churches of Christ
	Reformed
Bottom rank	
Protestant Sectarians	White Southern Baptists
Catholics	Adventists
Baptists	Nazarenes
Mormons	Assemblies of God
No religious preference	Jehovah's Witnesses
	Black Northern Baptists
	Black Methodists
	Misc. Pentecostals/Holiness
	Churches of God
	Black Southern Baptists

data for some of the groups limits the comparison, but still we can grasp the major aspects of class changes for the religious mainline during this time.

Those groups comprising the historic religious elite experienced relatively little change in status rankings during this time. With the exception of Christian Scientists, all the top-ranking bodies from the mid-1940s continue in their high-status positions. Unitarian-Universalists, Jews, Episcopalians, Presbyterians, and the United Church of Christ comprise the elite—essentially a WASP and Jewish mix of upper-status groups. On all the status indicators—education, family income, occupational prestige, and perceived social class—they continue to hold their own, unchallenged by any of the other groups (see table 4-2).

By far the greatest status changes have occurred at the middle and bottom ranks. Especially striking has been the upward movement of Catholics. Since World War II Catholics have enjoyed impressive social and economic gains. New generations of younger Catholics, more educated and acculturated to American life than their parents, now find their way into jobs and careers unknown to previous generations. In 1957, for example, 29 percent of Catholics held white-collar jobs; by the mid-1970s that figure had increased to 48 percent.[3] This exceeds the gains of any of the large mainline Protestant bodies during this period. Protestant-Catholic status differences generally vanished during this period, with Catholics even pulling ahead of Protestants in some respects. Today Catholics generally resemble moderate Protestants in their socioeconomic profile; each group contains about equal proportions of persons who are better educated, employed in the higher-paying occupations, and say they consider themselves members of the higher-ranking classes.[4] Together the two groups make up a significant portion of the nation's mainstream, and as much as any large group can be, they are at the cultural and religious center.

Upward movement is a pattern for many conservative groups as well. Mormons, for example, show a phenomenal shift: they have moved from the lowest-ranking religious group in the mid-1940s to the top of the middle rank. On all the status indicators their standing places them along with, if not ahead of, many of the mainline Protestants and Catholics. Evangelical and fundamentalist Protestants have likewise made substantial status gains. Whereas in 1960 only 7 percent of members in evangelical and fundamentalist denominations had attended some college, by the mid-1970s that figure was 23 percent—a striking rate of increase for so short a period of time.[5] These gains stand out against more liberal mainline Protestants, whose educational base hardly changed at all during this period. The current profile shows that the evangelical/fundamentalist group ranks right along with Lutherans, Disciples, and Northern Baptists and has the highest status levels of any in the conservative Protestant family. Increasingly represented in the lower-middle echelons of American life, growing numbers of religious conservatives have gained entrance into the mainstream and

TABLE 4-2
SOCIOECONOMIC STATUS OF RELIGIOUS GROUPS

Religious Group	Education				Family Income			Perceived Social Class		
	Less Than High School	High School Graduate	College Graduate	Mean Years	Under $10,000	$10,000– $20,000	Over $20,000	Mean Occu- pational Prestige	Lower/ Working	Middle/ Upper
National	33	52	14	11.8	36	34	30	38.7	53	47
Liberal Protestants	19	54	27	13.2	26	31	43	44.2	34	66
Episcopalians	15	51	34	13.8	25	31	44	45.6	28	72
United Church of Christ	18	61	21	12.8	26	31	43	42.7	37	63
Presbyterians	21	54	25	13.0	27	31	42	43.9	37	63
Moderate Protestants	31	57	13	11.9	34	36	30	39.5	50	50
Methodists	26	59	12	12.2	34	34	32	41.2	45	55
Lutherans	29	59	12	11.9	32	38	31	39.5	52	48
Christians (Disciples of Christ)	40	49	11	11.5	39	36	28	37.5	53	47
Northern Baptists	39	53	8	11.4	36	36	28	36.6	58	42
Reformed	44	43	13	11.3	40	40	21	38.2	57	43
Black Protestants	53	41	7	10.3	60	26	15	30.9	69	31

TABLE 4-2 (continued)
SOCIOECONOMIC STATUS OF RELIGIOUS GROUPS

Religious Group	Education				Family Income			Perceived Occupational	Perceived Social Class	
	Less Than High School	High School Graduate	College Graduate	Mean Years	Under $10,000	$10,000–$20,000	Over $20,000	Mean Occupational Prestige	Lower/Working	Middle/Upper
Methodists	44	45	11	10.8	57	27	15	33.1	64	36
Northern Baptists	47	46	7	10.9	54	29	17	32.5	70	30
Southern Baptists	60	35	5	9.7	65	22	12	28.8	69	31
Conservative Protestants	**46**	**47**	**8**	**10.8**	**43**	**35**	**22**	**36.3**	**63**	**37**
Southern Baptists	45	46	6	10.9	41	37	23	37.3	60	40
Churches of Christ	41	51	9	11.1	38	35	27	37.6	62	38
Evangelicals/Fundamentalists	32	53	15	11.7	37	35	27	38.2	65	45
Nazarenes	42	51	7	11.1	44	37	19	36.2	67	33
Pentecostals/Holiness	53	45	2	10.0	53	31	16	31.8	70	30
Assemblies of God	50	49	2	10.4	36	40	24	35.8	66	34
Churches of God	62	34	4	9.7	53	31	17	33.2	73	27
Adventists	41	47	12	11.4	52	31	17	36.8	64	36
Catholics	**31**	**57**	**12**	**11.9**	**31**	**35**	**34**	**38.9**	**52**	**48**
Jews	**15**	**48**	**38**	**13.9**	**22**	**27**	**50**	**46.7**	**20**	**80**
Others										
Mormons	23	59	18	13.3	23	39	38	38.8	52	48
Jehovah's Witnesses	41	58	1	10.6	44	32	23	32.8	72	28
Christian Scientists	15	59	25	12.9	40	30	30	42.0	38	62
Unitarian-Universalists	6	22	72	15.7	16	32	52	52.5	14	86
No religious preference	**25**	**50**	**25**	**12.9**	**34**	**34**	**32**	**40.8**	**52**	**48**

are now enjoying a much improved social and economic standing than in the past. Once they were the "churches of the disinherited," located on the fringes of middle-class society, but hardly anymore. Vance Packard could speak of "The Long Road from Pentecostal to Episcopal" in his 1959 best-seller, *The Status Seekers*, in what was an apt description at the time.[6] But the fact is that Pentecostals have moved uptown and into the suburbs and have become more socially respectable, thus shortening the distance between these two status affiliations within Protestantism.

One sign of the new status is the shift in cultural views and identities—many religious conservatives now prefer to call themselves "charismatics" and "neo-Pentecostals" instead of "Holy Rollers," and some prefer "biblical inerrantists" rather than "fundamentalists." More securely positioned in middle America and deeply concerned about the threat of secular humanism, many conservatives have discovered one another in a common cause. Sects that were once bitter foes—for example, Mormons and many Christian evangelical and fundamentalist groups—now find themselves brought together in their opposition to many moral and secular trends. Once passive and withdrawn from the culture and warring among themselves, now they are more unified around a common enemy and have taken on the mantle as defender of the country and its way of life. Old stereotypes, from the days of H. L. Mencken, about fundamentalists and evangelicals as marginal and culturally deprived are outdated and no longer fit in a time of substantial upward mobility and enhanced status. The new standing is apparent on talk shows such as the "700 Club" and on glossy bumperstickers on cars parked in suburban shopping centers across America proclaiming such messages as Maybe Your God is Dead, But I Talked with Mine This Morning.

Not only Catholics and conservative Protestants but the nonaffiliates as well have made spectacular status gains during this period. The remarkable upward movement of this more secular constituency is evident in their shift from the very bottom of the bottom rank in the mid-1940s to an upper-middle position by the 1980s. Those with no religious affiliation exceed the national average today on every status indicator. They rank almost with liberal Protestants in education, above moderate Protestants on most status measures, and closely parallel Catholics in overall socioeconomic profile.

Once an alienated and marginal group, they are now well educated, highly professional, and among the most mobile of all sectors of the population—and thus increasingly at the center of the culture. Many fit the description "yuppie" in status characteristics and life-styles.

Over the past couple decades the relationship between middle-class status and church membership appears to have weakened. At midcentury the linkage between religion and class was fairly strong: the college educated participated more in the churches than did the lesser educated, and the middle classes generally were more active in congregations. Both church membership and religious participation were sensitive to middle-class status. These patterns began to change in the sixties and seventies. The polls showed a gradual decline in religious attendance across the classes, but especially among the college educated. Downward trends have continued to the point that now there are slight differences in participation across educational levels. Middle- and working-class styles of religiosity generally seem to have moved in the direction of greater convergence.

Moreover, the rise of a more socially respectable and increasingly visible secular constituency has contributed to a reordering of the class basis for religion. Among the upper-middle classes especially, there emerged a more distinct ideological split between religionists and secularists. The post-1960s religious dropouts were a precipitating factor, but more general developments as well helped create this division. With the expansion of science and education, the media, and the "knowledge" industry generally in the post–World War II years, a new stratum (often described as "new class") emerged, deriving its livelihood from the creation and dissemination of ideas and information, as distinct from the old bourgeoisie, or entrepreneurial class. The two classes sharply differ in values and interests and are engaged in what is sometimes described as a *Kulturkampf*—a battle of class cultures.[7] On both sides of the conflict are clusters of values and views ranging from national policy to matters of personal life-style. While the interrelations among values and attitudes are not always consistent, generally the capitalist and laissez-faire values of the older business class are pitted against the more "statist," or governmental interventionist, orientations of the new class.

The distinction between these two classes helps in understanding the dividing lines between and within the religious communities. The New Religious Right strongly identifies with the older business class, and by virtue of its momentum has helped to broaden the base of bourgeois values and interests in the sector known since the 1960s as middle America. A rising socioeconomic status, combined with a growing sense of a moral and religious crisis, has led many conservative Protestants to see themselves as the new custodians of American democratic faith and the old bourgeois morality. Traditionally many Roman Catholics, Lutherans, and moderate evangelicals within Protestantism have also been of the old class—strongly bourgeois in their outlook and behavior. A feature of the old class culture, as Richard John Neuhaus observes, is that it is not uncomfortable with religion and religiously grounded values playing a prominent role in public affairs.[8] Many of a more secular humanist persuasion within the upper-middle classes disagree. This very issue in fact has become a source of debate and contention in many circles—that is, whether, and if so in what way, a particular faith or tradition should exercise a custodianship over the culture.

The conflicts generated by these ideological differences are greatest in the mainline, moderate-to-liberal Protestant traditions. With a conservative Protestant upsurge, on the one hand, and a growing secular humanist constituency, on the other, many of the churches in the moderate-to-liberal Protestant traditions are now caught up in a struggle of worldviews and moral values. With the optimism of democratic faith having waned in the years since World War II, these churches have become cast as critics of American institutions and the country's domestic and foreign policies. Even if not avowedly critical, their postures toward God, country, and the American Way of Life seem not to match those of others in loyalty and passion. Large proportions of their members are corporate managers and professionals—upwards of one-third in the old-line liberal Protestant churches and perhaps as many as one-fourth of those in some of the moderate Protestant denominations.[9] These traditions are now more exposed than others to critical currents of opinion and the secular challenges of modernity. Both their size and the relation of their members to the more modernized sectors of the society dispose them toward value conflict and ideological clashes. More diverse in their constituencies and more open to pluralism, frequently they find themselves in a strange and precarious situation—at odds with other religious faiths and seemingly allied with more tolerant secular forces.

Ethnicity

A second source of historic significance in shaping American religion is ethnicity, or national origin. Alongside the churches of the disinherited and the middle class, Niebuhr spoke of the "national churches" and the "churches of the immigrants." These were the religious communities of the European immigrants, old-style structures that in due time were transformed through the process of assimilation into American-style denominations. The immigrant cultural heritage would of course play a central theme in the formation of the nation and all its institutions. Hardly any aspect of the country's way of life, and certainly not its religious life, would escape the imprint of this heritage. With the great numbers of immigrants crossing the Atlantic and the many national backgrounds they brought with them, the foundations were laid for religious pluralism as we know it today in the United States.

Immigration thrust these faiths into a new and different cultural context. Groups were confronted with a choice: either conform to the prevailing American religious norms or try to hold on to distinctive heritages. The first involved accommodation, which meant giving up dogmatic formulations of faith and relying more upon individual religious concerns and feelings. Exposure to the democratic political process would inevitably undermine historic ecclesiastical structures—the churches would have to become less authoritarian, and ties between the churches and their native lands would be broken. Conformity to American norms meant transformation of these communities into voluntary faiths.

But the Americanization process was neither uniform for all groups nor without counterpressures. New religious movements often arose out of resistance to accommodationist trends. For example, the Missouri Synod of Lutheranism was formed not simply because of doctrinal controversy but also to resist the broader changes underway in Lutheranism in its new environment. Even when schism did not result, the voluntary and competitive religious order often provided the immigrant churches with a need for greater self-consciousness and opportunity to fly their own group colors. For many this need for a distinct sense of identity generated a strong appreciation for ethnic and national heritage. Life in the New World propelled them toward becoming "quasi-*Gemeinschaft*" groups, with stress upon cultural bonds and communal belonging.

The pace of cultural and religious assimilation is evident in the declining use of foreign language in the churches. Before the great immigration era came to an end in the early 1920s, foreign language use was widespread. The 1916 Census of Religious Bodies reported that fully a fourth of all church and synagogue members were in congregations in which foreign language was used in worship services. For some Jewish, Lutheran, and Reformed groups, a majority of the congregations conducted services in a foreign language; 35 percent of Roman Catholic congregations conducted services in a language other than English.[10] Foreign languages bolstered a sense of ethnic identification and served a vital integrative function within many immigrant communities. Today foreign language use has all but disappeared (except among recent Hispanic and Asian-American immigrants): only 5.4 percent of white Catholics are foreign born, and just 2 percent of white Protestants.[11]

Despite the decline of foreign language use, ethnic ties and consciousness of national origins have hardly disappeared. Among American Catholics, for example, the largest and most diverse religious population in terms of national origins, many remain remarkably close to the immigrant experience. Andrew Greeley estimates that 15 percent of the Catholic population is first generation, 25 percent is second generation, 40 percent is third generation, and 20 percent is fourth generation—which means that two-fifths are either immigrants or the children of immigrants.[12] It is virtually impossible to sort out the ethnic versus the religious components of Catholic life: the beliefs and practices of a people tell a story of meaning and belonging that has taken shape in collective experience. Because of their widely differing experiences, Catholic ethnic groups vary in religious styles: German Catholics are the most likely to go to church, the most likely to believe in life after death, and the least likely to enter into a religiously mixed marriage; Irish and Slavic Catholics demonstrate less religious loyalty than Germans; and Italian and Hispanic Catholics demonstrate the least loyalty.[13]

White Protestants, in contrast, are further removed from the immigrant experience. The English, Scottish, Scotch-Irish, and Welsh were the first to be absorbed socially into the Anglo-Saxon Protestant core. Later large segments of the non-British Protestant groups —Swedes, Norwegians, Danes, Germans, and Dutch—merged with one another and with the Anglo-Americans. Despite the assimilation of many Protestant national origin groups into a more inclusive religious and cultural community, ethnic ties and traditions are still alive for many with non-British backgrounds. We simply cannot speak of American Protestantism in quite the same way we do of American Catholicism or American Judaism. There is no single identifiable socioreligious community for white Protestants; for reasons of both size and diversity, the ties and experiences uniting them are weaker than for Catholics or Jews. With so many groups, traditions, and theologies, generalizing about them can be hazardous: "As colonist and immigrant, Englishman and Swede, Episcopalian and Baptist, cosmopolite and hillbilly, executive and laborer, liberal and conservative, northerner and southerner," writes Charles H. Anderson, "the 'white Protestant' is so various that the label appears meaningless."[14]

Today the religious groups vary greatly in their ethnic makeup and consciousness of national origins. Table 4-3 reports on these patterns for the religious subcultures. Respondents in the General Social Surveys were asked, "From what countries or part of the world did your ancestors come?" If a single country was named, as was the case for 54 percent of the sample, it was recorded as the individual's heritage. If more than one country was named, the individual was asked, "Which one of these countries do you feel closer to?" An additional 24 percent were able to choose a single country. Another 11 percent were unable to choose a single country, and 11 percent could not identify their ancestry. In our discussion we have included only those persons who were able to name a single country or choose a country to which they felt closest. For ethnic background we follow the lead of the National Opinion Research Center, using twelve national origin categories appropriate to the American population.

Liberal Protestants trace their foreign ancestries to two major countries closely tied in culture and history—Britain and Germany. In keeping with their WASP character, 39 percent of the Episcopa-

TABLE 4-3

ETHNIC HERITAGE OF RELIGIOUS GROUPS

	British	German	Scandi-navian	Irish	Italian	French	Slavic	Hisp-anic	African	U.S. Only	Other Group	Can't Choose One Group	None
National	**15**	**18**	**5**	**10**	**5**	**3**	**7**	**4**	**7**	**3**	**4**	**10**	**11**
Liberal Protestants	**33**	**22**	**5**	**8**	**1**	**3**	**3**	*****	**3**	**1**	**3**	**15**	**4**
Episcopalians	39	14	3	9	1	4	3	1	6	2	3	13	3
United Church of Christ	24	36	6	6	2	4	2	*	*	2	2	16	2
Presbyterians	32	22	5	9	1	2	3	*	2	1	2	15	5
Moderate Protestants	**20**	**31**	**11**	**9**	**1**	**2**	**3**	**1**	*****	**1**	**3**	**11**	**8**
Methodists	29	23	5	11	1	3	2	1	*	1	2	13	11
Lutherans	9	43	26	3	1	2	3	1	1	*	1	8	3
Christians (Disciples of Christ)	22	21	3	11	*	3	2	1	2	1	2	17	14
Northern Baptists	35	22	5	14	1	2	3	1	*	2	5	11	11
Reformed	7	74	3	*	1	*	*	*	1	*	4	9	1
Black Protestants	*****	*****	*****	*****	*****	*****	*****	**1**	**52**	**13**	**6**	**3**	**25**
Methodists	*	*	*	*	*	*	*	*	53	8	6	4	27
Northern Baptists	*	*	*	*	*	*	*	1	52	16	5	4	22
Southern Baptists	*	*	*	*	*	*	*	*	53	11	6	3	27

TABLE 4-3 (continued)
ETHNIC HERITAGE OF RELIGIOUS GROUPS

	British	German	Scandi- navian	Irish	Italian	French	Slavic	Hisp- anic	African	U.S. Only	Other Group	Can't Choose One Group	None
Conservative Protestants	18	14	2	12	1	2	*	2	4	3	7	8	28
Southern Baptists	21	14	1	14	1	2	*	*	*	2	6	8	33
Church of Christ	17	14	2	17	*	1	1	1	4	2	9	11	21
Evangelicals/ Fundamentalists	20	32	9	6	*	1	3	3	3	2	3	13	7
Nazarenes	17	17	5	12	1	3	*	3	3	5	6	9	21
Pentecostals/Holiness	10	11	2	6	2	*	1	6	16	6	9	7	25
Assemblies of God	15	14	2	21	1	2	*	3	3	4	6	9	20
Church of God	14	11	1	12	1	3	2	*	10	7	6	5	29
Adventists	17	18	5	9	*	3	*	10	9	1	7	9	12
Catholics	6	15	2	14	15	5	15	10	2	1	4	9	2
Jews	2	10	*	1	2	1	57	1	*	*	2	24	*
Others													
Mormons	33	16	7	8	1	2	1	3	1	*	4	16	7
Jehovah's Witnesses	8	14	*	5	3	1	4	6	18	7	9	11	13
Christian Scientists	27	23	2	15	*	*	6	*	*	6	6	13	2
Unitarian-Universalists	42	6	*	3	3	8	11	*	*	*	*	25	3
No religious preference	15	17	4	9	4	3	9	3	5	2	6	14	9

* Less than 0.5 percent.

lians, 32 percent of the Presbyterians, and 24 percent of the United Church of Christ members list England, Wales, Scotland, or English-speaking Canada as the country from which their ancestors came. The percentage would probably be even higher for United Church of Christ members, who come out of the heavily British-background Congregational Christian churches; half of the United Church of Christ sample are of German origin, reflecting the importance of the Congregational Christian union with the predominately German Evangelical and Reformed church. Episcopalians of non-British ancestry come from diverse backgrounds, German and Irish being the most dominant. Many Presbyterians are German and Irish, again pointing to a broad Anglo-Saxon Protestant heritage. No group comes close to matching liberal Protestants in being more closely linked to the nation's historic Anglo-American core culture.

The moderate Protestant family consists of five distinct traditions that were shaped by quite diverse nineteenth-century ethnic streams: the Methodists, Disciples of Christ, and Northern Baptists were shaped by the settling of the frontier, and the Lutheran and Reformed churches by successive waves of ethnic immigrants. The ethnic backgrounds of the "frontier" denominations are similar—primarily English, German, and Irish. Persons of British ancestry account for 29 percent of the Methodists, 22 percent of the Disciples of Christ, and 35 percent of the Northern Baptists. A considerable number within each group give their background as German: 23 percent of the Methodists, 21 percent of the Disciples, and 22 percent of the Northern Baptists. The Irish are the third most frequently represented, with 14 percent of the Northern Baptists and 11 percent each for the Disciples and Methodists. Those belonging to these churches differ from their more liberal Protestant kin less in national background than in their more indigenous, frontier American experience.

In comparison, the Lutheran and Reformed denominations retain stronger ethnic traditions. Forty-three percent of Lutherans report their background as German and another 26 percent as Scandinavian. Seventy-four percent of the Reformed members are classified in the German cluster of national origins. Breaking the data down further to specific nationalities, 47 percent of the Lutherans trace their roots to Germany, 1 percent to the Netherlands, 12 percent to Norway, 7 percent to Finland, 6 percent to Sweden, and 4 percent to

Denmark. Of the Reformed members, 44 percent are of Dutch and 37 percent are German. Ethnic ties and customs continue to be important in giving these communities a sense of identity.

Most members of the three black Protestant groups give their ancestral background as African. Fifty-three percent of the black Methodists, 53 percent of the Southern Baptists, and 52 percent of the Northern Baptists identify themselves as African in origin. Remaining members of each group trace their origins primarily as "U.S. only" or some other group, or they do not identify an ancestry. Perhaps best described as Afro-American, a common black ancestry and minority experience binds members of these faith communities.

Conservative Protestants comprise a variety of backgrounds and heritages, closely approximating white America's ethnic and national origins profile. British ancestry is most often reported by Southern Baptists, Church of Christ, Church of God, and Assemblies of God. German origins are represented in most groups, most notably among evangelical and fundamentalist bodies. The Irish account for sizable constituencies among the Assemblies of God, the Church of Christ, Southern Baptists, and the Church of God. Generally large numbers of the Irish are affiliated with the conservative Protestant family and the "frontier" churches. Persons of African descent also account for sizable proportions of the members in some of the predominately white conservative churches: about 16 percent of the Pentecostal and holiness churches and 10 percent of Church of God.

The American Catholic population is a mix of persons from countries with very different histories and cultures. White Catholics trace their roots to four major sources: German, Italian, Slavic, and Irish. The next largest group of Catholics are Hispanic, then British and French. A few claim descent from other diverse backgrounds. No other religious group in America combines as many large, diverse nationality subgroups as do the Catholics; for this reason there are noticeable ethnic variations in religious styles within the boundaries of the Catholic community. To a great extent, ethnicity functions within American Catholicism as the equivalent of denominationalism within Protestantism.

With the smaller religious populations, we can only sketch their ethnic backgrounds. American Jews are predominately Slavic. Fully

57 percent of the Jews in the sample are of Slavic background, and another 15 percent trace their roots to Germany. Mormons, Christian Scientists, and Unitarian-Universalists are all heavily British in origin. Jehovah's Witnesses alone are the only predominately white group with a larger proportion of followers who trace their descent to Africa than to any single European nationality.

Those with no religious preference parallel closely the national backgrounds of Americans generally. Seventeen percent of those without a religious preference are of German background, 15 percent British, 9 percent Irish, 9 percent Slavic, 4 percent Italian, and 4 percent Scandinavian. Other groups are represented roughly in proportion to their distribution in the total population. This more secular constituency cuts across "old stock" and "new stock" and shows every indication of becoming a truly American cultural and ideological creation. What this might mean for the future is not fully known, but it seems to imply a broad cultural and life-style constituency without any strong and particularistic ethnic roots.

Remarkably little is known at present about the changing ethnic makeup of the religious groups or the meanings attached to ethnicity and national origins in congregations. Immigration is now once again a factor of significance for many groups. The "new immigrants" of recent years, Latin and Asian in origin, have strong cultural and religious bonds, which will no doubt continue to shape the religious communities. Catholicism especially will be influenced by these newer immigrant streams and will continue to have distinct ethnic enclaves within it. The Spanish-speaking constituency will expand more rapidly than any other sector within American Catholicism. Thus it is reasonable to expect a gradual but significant shift in Catholic constituency and religious and spiritual life as these influences are assimilated in the years ahead.

Protestantism is undergoing changes in its ethnic makeup as well, but mainly in its conservative wing. Many conservative Protestant churches are now recruiting heavily among Spanish-speaking as well as Korean and other Asian populations: ethnic membership increased by 48 percent for the Assemblies of God and by 70 percent for the Southern Baptists over the past decade.[15] Meanwhile, growth is nonexistent or minor in most of the old-line, liberal denominations. If these patterns continue we would expect in the future to see more sharply drawn ethnic profiles between conservative and liberal Protestants.

No doubt ethnic religions will also continue to flourish among native Americans, Jews, and many urban minorities of non-Western background. Even for white Protestants, whose distance from an immigrant past is much greater and whose assimilation is largely a matter of history, their national origins cast a long shadow. The "WASPness" of most white Protestant groups is never far removed from the conscious level. And in a pluralistic society of Jews, Catholics, blacks, Hispanics, and others who define themselves as groups in relation to one another, a self-conscious WASP community is almost assured. Yet the fact that this community is crisscrossed by many divisions, most notably social class, region, and denomination, works against its being highly solidified. By and large, for America's religious subcultures the patterns are complex, and seldom if ever does a single factor, ethnicity or any other, operate alone in shaping a group's identity.

For Americans of European descent, ethnicity has declined significantly as a decisive influence on religious life. Upward mobility and growth of the middle classes after World War II led younger generations of "hyphenated Americans" to move beyond the ethnic enclaves in which they grew up. A more assimilated culture and society mean that many churches no longer have as strong an ethnic-based support structure as in the past. Congregational memberships are now less ethnically homogeneous as a result of greater intermarriage, changing class compositions, and geographic mobility. With the blending of the population, national origin ties and consciousness have waned for large proportions of white America. According to the General Social Surveys, large numbers in all the religious groups can neither choose a single country of origin nor identify their ancestry. Thirty percent or more in some mainstream Protestant denominations are without a meaningful ethnic identity. Conservative Protestants especially seem to have large proportions of their members who have lost much of their ethnic past—perhaps because so many of them are from the South, where regional identities have over time tended to replace ethnic loyalties. Even outside the South, ethnic ties seem to have lost much of their importance as a basis for group attachment and identity. This fact, along with the shift upward in socioeconomic status, may suggest a shift of some significance in the cultural and religious consciousness of the conservative wing of Protestantism, although it is far from obvious what this might mean for the future.

At the institutional level as well, there has been an erosion of older ethnic barriers within mainline Protestantism. Denominational mergers of recent times suggest that religious groups are now better able to transcend narrow ethnic or national backgrounds. To cite a major example, the Evangelical and Reformed church in 1957 united with the Congregational Christian Churches to form the United Church of Christ—the first such merger to cross both ethnic and ecclesiastical polity lines. More recently various Lutheran bodies, once divided mainly by national and ethnic heritage, have entered into merger debate and are now taking further steps toward Lutheran unity. Such examples of churches reaching out to others of a different background in the interest of unity point to a triumph of ecumenical vision and a lessening hold of ethnic attachments upon religious communities.

Region

Another great historic influence on religion was regionalism. East versus West, North versus South—these regions came to represent more than geography as they developed distinct ways of life and cultural traditions. Nor has regionalism died out in contemporary America, and a major reason why is religion itself.[16] In all the regions, religions contribute to their distinctiveness by helping mould the ethos and outlook. A religious community that has been dominant, or at least very prominent, for a long time has many things making it a formidable force: its extensive infrastructure; its visibility; its size and stability; and the mere fact of its being the ranking faith. Baptists in the South, Mormons in Utah, Lutherans in the Dakotas, and Catholics in New England and the Southwest are examples of groups and places blending together in a common identity.

From the very early days, the westward expansion generated new religious styles. The frontier, advancing across a huge continent, set into motion theological and ecclesiastical controversies along the way which lasted for a long span of time in the nation's history. Frontier life nurtured individualism, self-sufficiency, and antipathy to authoritative control; its challenges served to break the bonds of cultural tradition and fostered a new and egalitarian consciousness. So different were the experiences and challenges that inevitably tensions broke out while trying to harmonize the way of life and interests of the frontier with the eastern establishment. Rural versus urban cultural differences have overlapped with those of region, thus enhancing distinctions between the more sober and sophisticated easterners and the primitive farmers and settlers of the West.

Three major frontier churches emerged in the 1800s—the Methodists, the Baptists, and the Disciples of Christ.[17] The Baptists and the Methodists attracted large followings, largely because their religious teachings and ecclesiologies were easily adaptable to frontier conditions. An emphasis upon personal conversion, lay ministry, and practical faith and morality fit in well with the spirit of the region. Fervent preaching and evangelistic camp meetings met with great success; an itinerant ministry and the circuit system of preaching, among Methodists especially, were ingenious organizational devices for exercising religious control over a large and expanding population. The Disciples, unlike the Baptists and Methodists, were a native-born frontier religious movement. They also held revivals, appealed to the emotions, ordained clergy with little or no theological education, and organized their churches on the sectarian principle. Although they did not reach as big a following, they embodied in many respects the genuine frontier spirit of religious individualism. Over time, and particularly in the twentieth century, the religious landscape in the West has changed as new immigrants and new religions have come on the scene, yet the influences of these earlier moderate-style Protestants have had a lasting affect in giving the region a distinctive religious character.

As the frontier became more settled, the churches born of the revivals took on form as major rural institutions. These popular churches were more than religious communities: they became social centers in hamlets and villages throughout rural America. This was especially true in the West, where there were fewer large cities and much open space. With the growth of cities during the nineteenth century, the established faiths of the cities came more and more to be distinguished from the simpler ways of belief and prac-

tice in the rural areas. Known for their doctrinal simplicity and traditional morality, rural and small-town churches have long been the
stronghold of Protestantism throughout the country; they have also
been the source of much of its leadership and have influenced its institutional styles and moral and religious flavor. The frontier heritage gave rise to an ethic of self-restraint and self-reliance—moral
ideals that have continued to distinguish the West from other regions of the country. In religious practices as well, westerners remain distinctive: they attend church and are involved in organized
religion much less than the people of any other region.[18]

Aside from the churches of East and West, there were also those of
North and South. The Mason-Dixon line came to symbolize differences of tradition and sentiments over slavery, and finally the Civil
War itself. Particularly in the years after 1830, slavery was the chief
moral issue around which regional controversy and bitterness developed. But even earlier, the views and outlook of the two regions had
begun to diverge. The South with its agricultural economy moved in
a direction that deviated from the industrial and commercial North:
it lacked a large and influential middle class and a strong intellectual heritage, and its way of life reflected the region's rural and
small-town character, its greater isolation and traditionalism. By
the time of the Civil War, a myriad of moral, social, cultural, and
economic factors separated the regions from one another.

In the mid-1840s sectarian bodies such as the Baptists and Methodists split into southern and northern branches. Moral disputes
over slavery figured prominently in these divisions. For Presbyterians, Lutherans, and Episcopalians, the divisions were more political
than moral. Separation did not occur until the war, and then primarily as result of broader regional interests and loyalties. Episcopalians
divided only during the brief span of the war and never to the point
of creating separate institutional structures. Presbyterians and Lutherans created separate regional structures which would last for decades, indeed, in the case of Presbyterians, for more than a century.

Religious life as a whole in the South took on a distinctive quality
that reflected more than institutional schisms. Historical, social,
and geographical factors converged to fashion a peculiar religious
syndrome. The frontier tradition of revivalism and appeal to emotions and a simple faith persisted in the small towns and rural areas
within the region long after the course of mainline American reli-

gion had begun to change and adapt to urban life and pluralism. Religious conservatism helped immunize southerners against cultural as well as religious influences from the outside and thus contributed to the making of a separate and distinct religious subculture. Southern Protestants successfully withstood three important developments occurring more generally in American Protestantism early in this century: the concern for unity of the church, a liberalizing of theology, and the Social Gospel movement. Lack of exposure to these broader theological and moral currents helps explain the persistence of a regional faith and the southern church's failure, throughout this century, to enter into serious debate on issues of modernity and social activism.[19]

The region continues to be dominated by a Baptist-Methodist hegemony of conservative and evangelical faith—what Samuel S. Hill, Jr., describes as "popular southern Protestantism."[20] In some southern states the combined Baptist-Methodist membership runs more than 80 percent of the reported Protestant affiliation and well beyond a majority of the total religious population. By virtue of its numbers, the popular piety of these two low-church groups sets the tone throughout much of the region. A close, comfortable alliance exists between the popular churches and southern culture, which makes for a congenial blend of religious beliefs with regional attitudes and thought forms. The result is a highly subjective theology, rural and small-town values and outlook, and traditional morality. A central theme is the individualist and verticalist character of salvation, primarily something between the believer and God. Sustained by theological fundamentalism and a puritan moral ethic, the "old-time religion" of Dixie is unlike that found anywhere else in the world.

Of course there have been changes—in the South and elsewhere. Considering the megatrends of urbanization, industrialization, and population movement throughout the United States in the twentieth century, we would expect some regional blending. In an era when Kentucky Fried Chicken franchises and McDonald's outlets can be found on Interstate 80 from New York City to San Francisco, where one drumstick or hamburger tastes exactly like another, one can hardly dismiss the possibility of greater national homogeneity. Yet it is easy to exaggerate just how homogeneous American society is becoming. The truth is that in religion as in many other aspects of culture, regionalism persists to a far greater extent than is often realized. One recent study suggests, in fact, that migrants who move to a new region tend to adapt to the religious styles of that region rather than add to its diversity.[21] So long as this remains true, migration should not be accompanied by a decline in the distinctiveness of the various religious and cultural regions. Ethnic pride and local tradition join with historic patterns to assure a continuing diverse culture.

To determine the extent to which religious patterns for the regions have changed, in table 4-4 we examine data from the 1926 Census of Religious Bodies and current church membership statistics. These data allow us to compare a half-century span during which there have been enormous social, cultural, and economic changes in all the regions. But have there been corresponding shifts in the religious geography? Are Americans' religious beliefs and practices becoming more alike or are people holding on to their distinct regional religious traditions?

On the basis of this comparison, we see that liberal Protestants —Episcopalians, Presbyterians, and members of the United Church of Christ—are still overly concentrated in the Northeast, though less so than they once were (see table 4-4). Episcopalians over the past fifty years have shifted to the South and West; indeed, more than a third of Episcopalians are in the South today. The United Church of Christ has gained members in all regions outside the Northeast; the greatest gains are in the Midwest, where roughly 44 percent of its members are now located. The Presbyterians have lost members in the Northeast as well, and their greatest regional gains are now occurring in the West.

Taken as a whole, these figures underscore a good deal of popular wisdom about the erosion of the "eastern establishment" of liberal Protestantism and the shift to the Sunbelt. Many from within this religious tradition have followed corporate and managerial careers that have drawn them to other regions. National demographic and economic trends since midcentury have significantly undercut the historic regional strongholds of WASP power and influence. More than losing simply members, the East has lost a great deal of its influence as the center of Protestant thought and the institutional base for mainline religious leadership. Geographic mobility contributes to a greater religious pluralism despite the fact that, as we

TABLE 4-4

REGIONAL DISTRIBUTION OF SELECTED RELIGIOUS BODIES, 1926–1980

Body (1980 name)	East 1926	East 1980	Midwest 1926	Midwest 1980	South 1926	South 1980	West 1926	West 1980
Episcopal Church	52.5	32.3	19.0	17.0	20.6	36.1	7.9	14.6
United Church of Christ	46.8	38.2	39.4	43.7	7.1	9.5	6.7	8.6
United Presbyterian Church	41.2	31.4	38.4	38.8	9.8	11.8	10.6	18.0
Presbyterian Church in U.S.	—	—	4.1	5.5	95.8	94.5	0.1	—
United Methodist Church	17.8	14.9	34.2	28.6	43.3	50.1	4.7	6.3
Lutheran bodies	24.7	15.9	64.1	61.1	7.8	12.0	3.4	11.0
Christian Church (Disciples)	3.9	2.9	53.6	43.4	33.6	42.2	8.9	11.5
American Baptist Churches	41.5	33.0	39.6	33.2	7.2	17.1	11.6	16.7
Reformed bodies	45.0	25.0	51.8	60.7	0.3	1.6	2.9	12.7
African Methodist Episcopal (Zion)	11.4	24.5	6.3	11.6	81.0	62.4	1.2	1.4
Christian Methodist Episcopal	1.4	5.1	9.7	11.0	87.9	76.4	0.9	7.5
Southern Baptist Convention	—	0.3	8.0	8.5	91.7	86.0	0.3	5.3
Churches of Christ	0.7	1.7	18.2	14.6	78.4	72.9	2.7	10.8
Christian and Missionary Alliance	45.5	31.2	25.1	25.1	15.3	23.3	14.1	20.3
Salvation Army	32.8	21.1	36.0	36.5	14.4	27.7	16.8	14.7
Church of the Nazarene	8.0	7.4	38.3	35.8	32.3	33.3	21.3	23.5
Assemblies of God	12.0	10.6	30.9	22.3	33.5	42.0	23.6	25.0
Pentecostal Holiness	3.0	1.2	2.2	3.4	94.8	90.7	—	4.6
Mormons	0.6	2.5	2.0	5.5	5.1	10.5	92.2	81.5
Unitarian-Universalist Association	68.4	42.9	21.2	21.7	5.7	19.3	4.7	16.1
Seventh-Day Adventist Church	14.3	11.7	34.0	20.1	19.2	29.4	32.5	36.8
Roman Catholic Church	49.5	39.7	32.0	28.9	10.8	15.7	7.7	15.7

Sources: U.S. Bureau of the Census, Religious Bodies, 1926, Washington, D.C.; and Bernard Quinn, Herman Anderson, Martin Bradley, Paul Goetting, and Peggy Shriver, Churches and Church Membership in the United States, 1980 (Atlanta: Glenmary Research Center, 1982).
Notes: All figures represent percentage in the region.

noted earlier, regional religious cultures generally persist. Many migrants to the Sunbelt have indeed joined the more popular churches of the South and Southwest, yet many others have not changed their affiliations. Often they carry with them their old affiliations but adapt to the prevailing religious styles and ideologies in the places they settle.

Regional patterns appear to have been more constant for moderate Protestants over the past half century. Virtually all of these bodies continue to be concentrated in their regions of historic strength. Today half of the United Methodists are in the South—a figure proportionately higher now than it was in the 1920s. Lutherans continue to be heavily based in the Midwest despite impressive gains in the West. The Disciples have added members in the South but are still more represented in the Midwest than in any other region. Sixty percent of the members in the Reformed bodies remain in the Midwest where they have been strong throughout this century. An exception are the American Baptists, who, like liberal Protestants, are less concentrated in the East now than in the past. Today they are about equally represented in the East and Midwest. Generally, the greater stability for this sector of mainline Protestantism is accounted for by their larger numbers and regional concentrations.

Membership statistics were available for only two of the black Protestant denominations—the African Methodist Episcopal Zion and the Christian Methodist Episcopal. Both continue to be highly concentrated in the South, though less so now than in the 1920s. Both have increasing numbers of members outside the South. Throughout much of this century blacks have migrated to other regions, and particularly to the large cities of the Northeast and Midwest, which has given these churches less of a rural and small-town southern base.

Conservative Protestants, more so than others, are concentrated in the regions of their historic strength. Because many of these denominational bodies are located primarily in the southern region, they continue to be encapsulated by this regional subculture. The largest of these, the Southern Baptists, report that 86 percent of its members are from below the Mason-Dixon line. Several other groups report similar memberships: 73 percent of the members of the Churches of Christ, 42 percent of the members of the Assemblies of God, and more than 90 percent of Pentecostal Holiness members are southerners. For all these groups the proportion of members who are southern has declined only slightly since 1926. The southern roots for these traditions are deep and change only gradually. Next to the South, the Midwest continues as a conservative stronghold. The Church of the Nazarene and the Salvation Army are both still concentrated in the Midwest as they were in the past. In many respects the bulk of the membership constituencies for these bodies have not changed drastically throughout this century.

There are, however, signs of change. Many conservative Protestant bodies are currently growing more rapidly outside their regions of origin than within them. Even Southern Baptists, so closely bound with a regional culture, show the fastest rates of growth outside the South, and especially in the Northeast.[22] Seventh-Day Adventists, long strong in the Midwest and South, are now rapidly expanding into the western states. Southern-born evangelicals are moving into other territories, but their regional memberships reflect this outward movement very slowly.

For the most part, Roman Catholics continue to be found disproportionately in the regions of their traditional strength. Historically they settled in the urban centers of the industrial northeastern and Great Lakes states, where the majority are still found; about 40 percent remain in the Northeast today, compared with 1926 when about half of the Catholic population lived in the region. In the intervening years Catholic membership expanded throughout the nation, in the South and West particularly. As their numbers have grown, they have become more dispersed throughout the country. By far the largest single denomination in the United States today, Catholics are found in significant numbers in all regions and types of locales.

Two other groups with distinctly regional concentrations are the Mormons and Unitarian-Universalists. Well over 80 percent of Mormons are still found in the West, despite their rapid growth in many other parts of the country. Unitarian-Universalists are still a predominately eastern group, though less so today than in the past. In both instances the concentrations help to give the religious groups a strong and continuing regional identity.

Survey data confirm the regional profiles in church membership patterns and reveal much the same levels of religious concentration (see table 4-5). The General Social Surveys show many evangelicals and fundamentalists outside the South. Members of the more distinctly evangelical and fundamentalist splinter bodies are less southern than any of the other larger conservative Protestant groupings. In addition to having a somewhat higher socioeconomic standing, they are also more dispersed geographically. The members are predominantly midwestern, but many are found in every region, with the smallest number in the South. Particularly striking is the large proportion in the Northeast—22 percent. Many, especially Appalachian whites better known as hillbillies, migrated out of the South after World War II and settled in towns and cities, often in the Midwest and Northeast. They have carried with them their transplanted "southern-style" faiths. Regional movement of this kind, combined with Jimmy Carter's election as president in 1976 as a born-again Southern Baptist, no doubt helps explain the emergence of a broader national base for evangelicalism and fundamentalism. These faiths have long been sustained by traditions deeply rooted in the American South, and they continue so today through the cultural diaspora of southerners into the other regions of the country.[23]

As seen in table 4-5, more Americans live in the small towns and moderate-sized cities than in any other single community type. This grouping becomes clear when classifying Americans by means of a fourfold community typology: central cities of the hundred largest metropolitan areas, suburbs of these large cities, moderate-to-smaller urban areas, and rural areas. The churches follow the people wherever they live, and the great majority of those who are members of predominately white religious groups are found in small towns and cities.

Among white Protestants are widespread differences related to community type. Liberal Protestants are overrepresented in the suburbs and small towns and underrepresented in the largest cities; they have fewer members in rural areas than either the moderate or conservative clusters. The Episcopal Church, with only 10 percent of its members living in rural areas, is the most urban of the liberal denominations. Fully 56 percent of its respondents reside in metropolitan areas, and they are about equally split between central city and suburb. The Episcopalians, Presbyterians, and United Church of Christ all have more members in the suburbs of the large cities than in the rural areas. In contrast, the moderate Protestants have larger rural constituencies than suburban. Except for Lutherans, who have

TABLE 4-5
RELIGIOUS GROUPS, REGION, AND COMMUNITY TYPE

	Region				Community Type			
	Northeast	Middle West	South	West	Central Cities	Suburb	Other Urban	Other Rural
National	**22**	**29**	**34**	**16**	**25**	**22**	**37**	**17**
Liberal Protestants	**31**	**26**	**25**	**18**	**20**	**26**	**40**	**15**
Episcopalians	34	13	30	23	28	28	35	10
United Church of Christ	45	42	3	11	9	24	50	17
Presbyterians	26	29	29	17	19	25	40	17
Moderate Protestants	**14**	**45**	**23**	**18**	**15**	**19**	**42**	**25**
Methodists	10	34	42	13	14	17	42	27
Lutherans	20	56	11	13	14	22	43	22
Christians (Disciples of Christ)	4	43	27	25	17	15	42	26
Northern Baptists	14	53	—	33	16	22	39	23
Reformed	42	44	3	12	7	17	42	35
Black Protestants	**15**	**21**	**57**	**7**	**52**	**13**	**25**	**10**
Methodists	19	15	61	5	47	13	27	13
Northern Baptists	32	51	—	17	69	19	10	2
Southern Baptists	—	—	100	—	40	9	37	15

TABLE 4-5 (continued)
RELIGIOUS GROUPS, REGION, AND COMMUNITY TYPE

	Region				Community Type			
	Northeast	Middle West	South	West	Central Cities	Suburb	Other Urban	Other Rural
Conservative Protestants	**4**	**10**	**79**	**7**	**18**	**13**	**43**	**27**
Southern Baptists	—	—	100	—	14	11	45	30
Churches of Christ	3	21	67	10	21	14	48	17
Evangelicals/Fundamentalists	22	43	16	20	21	16	46	18
Nazarenes	12	28	40	21	17	15	49	19
Pentecostals/Holiness	12	21	49	18	27	16	33	24
Assemblies of God	5	15	54	27	18	10	53	20
Churches of God	3	21	67	8	16	11	36	37
Adventists	13	27	31	30	32	27	32	9
Catholics	**37**	**31**	**16**	**16**	**26**	**29**	**35**	**11**
Jews	**56**	**14**	**14**	**15**	**51**	**33**	**15**	**2**
Others								
Mormons	5	7	17	72	18	25	48	9
Jehovah's Witnesses	16	20	31	32	25	22	47	6
Christian Scientists	33	21	15	54	19	40	35	6
Unitarian-Universalists	33	25	22	19	31	44	25	0
No religious preference	**23**	**26**	**21**	**31**	**36**	**22**	**32**	**10**

about equal rural and suburban constituencies, all the rest have considerably larger proportions of rural members. Rural predominance is even more pronounced for the conservatives. Most of the large conservative bodies have sizable rural memberships plus great numbers residing in the smaller cities and small towns. This is true for the Southern Baptists, the Church of Christ, Nazarenes, Pentecostal/holiness sects, Assemblies of God, and the Church of God. Interestingly, those we have categorized more specifically as evangelical/fundamentalist do not differ from other conservative groups in geographic location. Adventists and Jehovah's Witnesses differ somewhat from the others in having a stronger hold in the large cities and suburbs.

With their rising socioeconomic status, Catholics have changed their distribution substantially. No longer are Catholics disproportionately found in the large cities. More live in the suburbs than in the central cities; they are more likely to be suburban than any other major group except for Jews. Only 11 percent are rural, which is considerably less than most white Protestants. For the most part the data underscore the image of an upwardly mobile, middle-class American Catholic population, located in about the same places as members of other mainline religious groups.

The most urban groups of all are the black Protestants, Jews, Christian Scientists, and Unitarian-Universalists. Among black Protestants the most urban are the Northern Baptists, which is explained by the migration of blacks to northern cities; however, even black Southern Baptists and the more regionally distributed black Methodists are highly urban. Since the days of immigration, Jews have lived predominately in the large cities. Over half in this sample live in the large cities, and 84 percent live in the large cities and suburbs. Likewise with Christian Scientists and Unitarian-Universalists: 59 percent and 75 percent, respectively, are found in the large cities. Unlike blacks and Jews, who tend to remain in central cities, the majority of Christian Scientists and Unitarian-Universalists live in the suburbs.

While at one time very much a rural constituency, the nonaffiliates now can be found in significant numbers just about everywhere. They are more likely to be found in the West, supporting the notion of an "Unchurched Belt" on the West Coast.[24] But they are well represented across America; even in the South, where one would expect they would not be so prevalent, they are almost as common as in other regions. They are urban and, indeed, are over-represented in the large cities. Far from being marginal, nonaffiliates today are among the most exposed of all groups to the forces of modernity and secularism in contemporary United States.

Thus there is both continuity and change in the regional and urban-rural locations of American religious groups. Religious strongholds are still found in areas of a group's historic strength: the most obvious examples are white Protestantism's continuing small-town and rural base, conservative Protestantism's strong roots in the South, and the Jews' continuing strength in the cities. The religious geography of the nation remains a good index of the cultural and demographic history of the American people. But the geographic base is shifting: liberal Protestant strongholds of the Northeast have declined; evangelical and fundamentalist Protestants are expanding throughout the nation; both Catholics and secular nonaffiliates have made spectacular moves into neighborhoods and places where only a few decades ago they were regarded as strangers; blacks are largely an urban constituency. The changes are gradual and often invisible, but nonetheless real. Region's diminishing hold on the churches is apparent in the Presbyterians' recent move toward merger. Separated into northern and southern branches ever since the Civil War, these two are now forming a large, unified Presbyterian church. This development is an important one within mainline Protestantism, if only because it testifies to the power of religious heritage over a long history of regional bitterness and division.

Race

Of all the divisions among the churches, the color line is the most rigid and enduring. Frequently in the 1960s it was said that "eleven o'clock on Sunday morning is the most segregated hour of the week"—an observation that still rings all too true in the 1980s.[25] Racial separation is more institutionally complete and more practiced than any other form of ascription in the churches; it is far more pervasive than that based upon social class or ethnicity. Heritage and prejudice combine to sustain a color line in the churches, despite the commitment of many to eradicate its presence.

The rise of the black churches testifies to the heritage of racism and, in particular, to events surrounding the Civil War and Emancipation. Prior to the Civil War—both in the South and North—it was not uncommon for white and black Christians to worship together. Though hardly enjoying fellowship on equal terms, often they were members of the same congregations. Missionary work by Methodists and Baptists among southern slaves led to converts frequently becoming members of the churches; occasionally entire congregations of blacks were organized as part of the same denomination. Mixed congregations were fairly prevalent in the North, at least in the early years, before the rigid norms of Jim Crow segregation hardened racial lines throughout the churches.

Separate black congregations became more common in the early 1800s. Frequently blacks were encouraged to worship by themselves or to meet at a time different from the white members' service. The independent congregations that resulted tended at first to remain loyal to the old denominations. In time, however, the same difficulties that had led to schisms of the local churches came to divide the mixed denominations. Thus the African Methodist Episcopal Church came to be organized as a separate denomination in Philadelphia in 1816, and the African Methodist Episcopal Church Zion in New York in 1821. Both emerged as a result of decades of friction between white and black members and from strong determination on the part of free blacks to have their own religious organization.

The great impetus to separate black denominations came with the Civil War and Emancipation. These events unleashed strong feelings of freedom among blacks as well as heightened racial consciousness among whites. Except for Episcopalians, all the major denominations with large memberships in the South would face division along racial lines. Black Baptist churches were the first to break away and create their own associations as early as 1866. Gradually these were consolidated, leading to the formation of the National Baptist Convention in 1895. The Cumberland Presbyterian Church split in 1869, as did the main body of Southern Presbyterians in 1874, resulting in the creation of "colored" churches of the same name. In 1866, blacks who had been members of the Southern Methodist church withdrew to form the Colored Methodist Episcopal Church. Many black Methodists also joined the African Methodist Episcopal and African Methodist Episcopal Zion churches, which in the years after the war grew rapidly. These two northern groups moved quickly to the newly freed constituency in the South, so quickly that by 1896 the A.M.E. Church claimed 452,725 members and the A.M.E. Zion 349,788.[26]

By the century's end the independent black churches claimed 2.7 million members in a black population of about 8.3 million. In only four decades from the time of emancipation, the "invisible institution" of antebellum days had become visible and the black church had emerged as a crucial center of social and religious activity. It was the one institution over which blacks maintained control. The price of autonomy and self-control was a separate and segregated church, one effectively cut off socially and religiously from white America.

Racially separate structures have existed for well over 150 years. In his day Niebuhr estimated that 88 percent of black church members belonged to black denominations.[27] At the time the vast majority of black church members were affiliated with one of four large denominations: the National Baptist Convention, the African Methodist Episcopal, the African Methodist Episcopal Zion, and the Colored Methodist Episcopal. His figures were taken from the Census of Religious Bodies of 1926, which showed black denominations' membership at around 45 million. A much smaller number of blacks, perhaps 650,000, belonged to predominately white denominations and were generally segregated into separate jurisdictions or congregations. Niebuhr lamented the extent of racial division in the churches and expressed great concern that instead of showing signs of healing it would become more acute. Future efforts at church union, he feared, would accentuate the color line within the churches and thus result in more, not less, racial segregation at the denominational level.

What has happened over the past fifty years? The answer depends largely on the level at which the question is posed. At the broadest institutional level, there has been little change in the extent of racial separation. Over the years schisms within the black denominations have given rise to still more racially based religious structures. For example, the National Baptist Convention, the oldest black denomination, split in 1915 in a dispute that formed two separate structures: the National Baptist Convention in the USA, Inc., and the National Baptist Convention in America. In 1961 a splinter group withdrew from the National Baptist Convention in the USA, Inc., to create the Progressive National Baptist Convention. Traditions other than Methodist and Baptist have also flourished in more recent decades. With the migration of large numbers of blacks from rural to urban areas and from the South to the North, many sects and storefront churches have arisen to meet the needs of ghetto blacks. The largest of these is the Church of God in Christ, which has approximately four hundred thousand members and an estimated forty-five hundred churches. The religious life of blacks has become more diverse in the twentieth century, resulting in even more racially separate structures and a more variegated pattern of religious groups and traditions.

The most recent membership figures for blacks in the major denominations are listed in table 4-6. Shown are the reported memberships for black denominations and estimated memberships within the predominately white denominations. The largest black denomination is still the National Baptist Convention in the USA, Inc., with more than 5 million members. Next largest is the National Baptist Convention of America, followed by the three Methodist bodies and the Progressive National Baptists. All together the six bodies account for over 12.5 million members. In comparison, blacks in predominately white denominations number somewhere between 1.5 million to 2 million. Using the liberal estimate of black membership in the major white Protestant denominations as shown in table 4-6, we arrive at a total of 1,861,159—which suggests that roughly 85 percent of all black Protestant memberships are in the black denominations. Against Niebuhr's estimate of 88 percent in 1929, we can only conclude that the past fifty years have brought little change in the overall structural basis of racially separate "black" and "white" churches.

Most of the white denominations have only a small proportion of black members. Two percent to 3 percent black membership is the typical pattern. However two denominations report large numbers of black members: the American Baptists and Seventh-Day Adventists. Among moderate to liberal churches the American Baptists are probably the most racially integrated, and for the conservatives the same holds for the Seventh-Day Adventists. Even so, in both these

TABLE 4-6

BLACK MEMBERSHIP OF SELECTED DENOMINATIONS

	Total Adherents	Estimated Black Adherents	Percent Black Adherents
Episcopal Church	2,823,399	141,170	5.0
United Church of Christ	2,096,014	66,395	3.2
United Presbyterian Church	2,974,186	86,747	2.9
Presbyterian Church in U.S.	1,038,649	11,494	1.1
United Methodist Church	11,552,111[a]	435,105	3.8
Lutheran Church in America	2,911,817	37,000	1.3
Lutheran Church—Missouri Synod	2,622,847	79,883	3.0
Christian Church (Disciples of Christ)	1,212,977	44,282	3.7
American Baptist Churches	1,922,467	520,274	27.1
Christian Reformed Church	211,894	1,208	0.6
Reformed Church in America	371,048	3,710	1.0
African Methodist Episcopal	2,050,000[b]		
African Methodist Episcopal Zion	1,134,176[b]		
Christian Methodist Episcopal	786,707[c]		
National Baptist Convention USA, Inc.	5,500,000[d]		
National Baptist Convention of America	2,668,799[e]		
Progressive National Baptist Convention, Inc.	521,692		
Southern Baptist Convention	16,281,692	97,423	0.6
Churches of Christ	1,600,177	129,670	8.1
Church of the Nazarene	885,749	13,000	1.5
Church of God (Cleveland, Tenn.)	474,315	12,000	2.5
Christian and Missionary Alliance	170,643	1,098	0.6
Seventh-Day Adventist	668,611	180,700	27.0
Roman Catholic Church	47,502,152	916,854	1.9

Sources: Data supplied by individual denominations to the Glenmary Research Center or to the authors. Totals are for adherents and utilize adjustment formulas outlined in Quinn et al., Churches and Church Membership.

[a] 1974 data

[b] Data for 1980 taken from Yearbook of American and Canadian Churches, 1982

[c] Data for 1981 taken from Yearbook of American and Canadian Churches, 1982

[d] Data for 1958 taken from Yearbook of American and Canadian Churches, 1982

[e] Data for 1956 taken from Yearbook of American and Canadian Churches, 1982

denominations most blacks belong to single-race congregations, thus making the "integration" reported by the figures somewhat illusory. There are also over nine hundred thousand black Catholics, yet this figure represents only about 2 percent of the American Catholic population. The extent of racial integration in the "white" churches, whether Protestant or Catholic, is still small, hardly enough to refute the charge that the church remains among the most segregated major institutions in the society.

At other levels there has been some progress toward achieving greater racial inclusiveness. Racially based structures within the predominately white churches have largely been eliminated. In the United Methodist Church, for example, the "Central Jurisdiction" which for many years segregated thousands of blacks from whites no longer exists. Once a symbol of separatism in Methodism, its elimination was a major step forward toward a more inclusive church. Even if it did little to bring about racially integrated congregations within the denomination, the change opened the way for greater unity and interracial contact. More visible at the bureaucratic and leadership levels than for local congregations, nonetheless such action is a testimony of commitment to Christian ideals. In the United Methodist Church, the Episcopal Church, the United Church of Christ, and others, nonwhites are now being given leadership positions that only a decade or so ago were the province almost exclusively of whites.

Within many local congregations there has also been some progress. The civil rights movement of the 1960s undoubtedly helped open the doors of the churches to persons of all races. The extent of improved interracial church participation is difficult to judge. Twenty-five years ago Liston Pope calculated that less than 2 percent of white congregations had black members.[28] Since then the figure has clearly risen although we have no comparable data for the present. Findings from the General Social Surveys in 1978 and 1980, which asked white respondents about the racial composition of their churches, reveal that a surprisingly large proportion (38 percent) say they attend worship services with blacks.[29] Living in urban areas, in the Northeast and West, and having moved away from the state in which one was reared were associated with interracial worship. Such experiences were cited more by Catholics than by Protestants, and more by liberal Protestants than by conservative

Protestants. Probably this finding represents the presence of a small number of upwardly mobile blacks attending predominately white churches rather than anything approaching genuine racial integration, but even so, it is an index of racial change for many congregations.

Whatever the advances of the past quarter century, there is no denying that progress toward genuine racial integration in the churches has been slow. And there is little reason to expect that the pace of change will pick up in the immediate future. The persisting realities of residential segregation, friendship and interaction networks, the privatism of religious life, and denominational loyalties all but assure that racial changes in religious institutions will be slow. Unless some re-ordering of the society occurs, racial separation in the churches will continue as a sign of a deep-seated disjuncture between the ideals and practices of American life. Maybe in some spiritual sense American churchgoers see themselves as belonging to a "kingdom beyond caste," but the congregations they join remain status-conscious voluntary organizations.

Conclusion

The sources of denominationalism identified by Niebuhr more than fifty years ago are still important for understanding the social bases of American religion. The nation's faith communities continue to be divided along lines of social class, ethnicity, region, and race. Expectations in the 1950s of an emerging cultural and religious unity in America proved overly optimistic. No massive institutional mergers have occurred across major denominational lines, nor has a Protestant-Catholic-Jewish mode of pluralism of the sort Herberg thought was emerging taken shape as a social reality. Diversity remains the singular fact of American religious life, despite mass cultural trends in consumption and behavioral styles and the growth of an urban, mobile, national society.

We should not, however, minimize the changes that have occurred during this time. The religious map of America is much different today from the time when Niebuhr wrote, nor has it lived up to the predictions of the theorists in the 1950s and early 1960s. At least five general aspects of the current social mapping of religion distinguish it from the past and are worth noting:

1. The ascriptive bases of the religious communities have declined, creating a more fluid and voluntary religious system. Class, ethnicity, region, race—all have lost force in shaping religious and cultural identities. Old class and ethnic patterns especially have diminished in importance while at the same time new aspects of each have emerged, for example, the "new class" and "new immigrant" patterns. Niebuhr himself anticipated a fluid and changing situation and was struck with the potential for religious mobility in a democratic, achievement-oriented social order. He foresaw old lines of cleavage being erased and new ones emerging as the society experienced changes. His well-known sect-to-denomination hypothesis rested on the assumption that upward social movement was possible, allowing working-class sectarians to evolve into middle-class denominations. This type of change was particularly prominent in earlier years characterized by economic expansion and high rates of intergenerational mobility. Collective mobility of this kind is probably of less importance today than individual mobility—both social and geographic—in shaping religious loyalties. Since the 1960s the country has undergone something of an "equality revolution," as one movement after another has challenged the limits of ascription and opened up opportunities for individuals to pursue their goals. Weakened ascriptive ties and greater ease of movement for individuals facilitate greater religious choice.

2. The social boundaries distinguishing the major mainline traditions continue to be identifiable. Within-family differences between denominations have blurred while between-family differences are visible. Trends toward assimilation have not been as encompassing and homogenizing as was once thought; instead they have occurred along definite structural and ideological lines. What has emerged is not a "triple melting-pot" or a "common-core Protestantism," but a more complex mosaic of religious cultures. Protestantism is fundamentally divided along lines of race and liberal-conservative ideology. Race is the greatest obstacle to religious unity and will continue to be a source of structural separation. Ideology has reemerged as a strong and revitalizing force, polarizing the Protestant

house into divisive factions. Still another source of diversity is the emergence of a more secular constituency. This collectivity is characterized by a high social standing, urban residence, and exposure generally to the processes of modernity and signifies a changing and more diverse pattern of pluralism in contemporary America. Generally we can identify distinct social and geographic characteristics for the major traditions, such as liberal Protestants, moderate Protestants, black Protestants, conservative Protestants, Catholics, Jews, and secular nonaffiliates.

3. A WASP elite retains its position in the status order, but its dominance over the culture has declined significantly since the 1960s. Mainline Protestants (especially the moderates) and Catholics now occupy increasingly similar social, economic, and power niches; boundaries of class and geographic residence greatly overlap. Both can be considered mainline—socially, culturally, and religiously. Catholics have moved toward the center at a rapid pace and in a relatively short period of time, making them in some respects the greatest beneficiaries of the more fluid and voluntary religious order of the post-1960s.

4. The white Protestant establishment suffers from a serious and deeply rooted ideological division. The split arises between, on the one hand, a resurgent religious conservatism as espoused by traditionalists who have recently found their way into middle America and, on the other hand, a growing secularity and openness on the part of many better-educated, more cosmopolitan, upper-middle classes. Social class figures prominently in this division but in a new way. Of greater importance than the old cleavage between working class and middle class is the current split within the middle class between the traditional entrepreneurial and the "new class" sectors. This split is an axis of ideological dispute and controversy over values and life-styles. Primarily a class-based phenomenon, it is also sustained by regional and rural-urban differences in American church life. Conservative Protestants tend more to be small-town and rural dwellers and disproportionately southern; liberal Protestants are found more in large cities and suburbs and in the Northeast.

5. There is a weakened link between middle-class status and church membership. Churchgoing norms have eroded in the more affluent middle class, as reflected in the emergence of a more self-

consciously secular, or at least religiously indifferent, constituency consisting mainly of persons who have left the mainline churches. In matters of social standing, life-style, and values, this new secular, unchurched sector is as much in the cultural mainstream as any of the mainline religious constituencies; indeed, they are more so than many such groups. As a result of the attenuated ties between religion and class, the gap between religious and secular cultures is widening.

In sum, the evidence points to what we are calling the new voluntarism—a more fluid and flexible religious situation. Individualism and privatism are becoming more pronounced in matters of belief and life-style; consequently, the "social sources" of religious belonging no longer have as much hold upon individual religious styles as in the past. Faith is shaped less by social background factors and more by the personal choices and values of the believers themselves. Given these new trends in American religion, we must examine further the changing profiles by exploring the religious demographics. If the social basis of religion is changing, there is good reason to expect changes in the demographics as well.

Chapter Five

The Demography
of Religious Change

Are the churches dying?

—DEAN M. KELLEY

For so blunt a question to be asked in the early seventies about the future of the churches was a sure sign that times were changing. The fact that the question was posed by an executive of the National Council of Churches, long the coordinating headquarters of the Protestant mainline, underscored the point even more. Kelley's book *Why the Conservative Churches Are Growing* became a conversation piece, capturing the mood of the times much as had Will Herberg's *Protestant—Catholic—Jew* in an earlier period. Many cults, sects, and religious movements appear on the scene and then disappear; indeed, we have come to expect that many of them will be short-lived. But what about the more established, mainline churches and synagogues? Were they too following a course of institutional decline? Was their future really that uncertain?

Kelley's data gave little basis for optimism. With a massive array of membership figures and related statistics, he documented sharp growth for conservative and sectarian bodies but precipitous decline for many of the older, historic religious traditions. The mood of the country had changed since the more expansive and optimistic growth period of the 1950s, when virtually all religious institutions as well as "religion in general" seemed to flourish. Growth was now more selective, and the demographics offered proof of the changing religious fortunes. The mainline churches were not about to die, but they were in trouble.

From the vantage point of the mid-1980s we can ponder why

Kelley's book attracted so much attention. Much of it had to do with the "shock" of facing up to a changing religious milieu and hearing about it from the establishment itself, yet in some respects the facts presented were not all that new. It was not the first time we learned that the conservative churches were experiencing a great surge in growth. The sectarian wing of Protestantism has been expanding throughout most of this century. Ever since the modernist-fundamentalist struggles of the 1920s and 1930s, this wing has grown. Even in the more conformist 1950s there had been signs of mounting conservative momentum. Henry P. Van Dusen, in what is surely one of the few *Life* magazine articles ever regularly cited in scholarly footnotes, called attention to a rapidly emerging "Third Force" in Christendom (alongside traditional Protestantism and Catholicism), composed of Adventists, Pentecostals, Nazarenes, Jehovah's Witnesses, and many small holiness sects.[1] Nor had religious conservatives suddenly overtaken liberals in rates of membership growth. The annual yearbooks had shown for decades that many of the newer, conservative bodies were growing far more rapidly than the older, more established groups. The division within Protestantism into liberal and conservative camps had been widening for some time and was apparent to anyone who took the time to tally the membership figures of the churches.[2]

What was eye-catching, however, and quite alarming for some were the *minus* signs in the growth rates. Minus signs pointed to absolute declines in the membership statistics, and year after year for an extended period of time—which was a new phenomenon in American religious history. To be sure, there had been drop-offs in membership at one time or another in the past. One such period was the "religious depression" of the late 1920s and early 1930s, but it neither lasted as long nor had so significant an impact on the membership base of the churches as did the declines beginning in the 1960s. By the time Kelley wrote his book in 1972, the memberships of some liberal Protestant churches had dropped by hundreds of thousands; by the end of the decade they were lower still. The fact that other religious traditions showed parallel losses helped underscore the significance of the changes. Catholic growth slowed, and many Reform synagogues experienced declines. The minus signs stood out all the more when compared with the conservative churches, which continued to grow in both decades, often at exceed-

FIGURE 5-1.

GROWTH PATTERNS FOR SELECTED DENOMINATIONS.

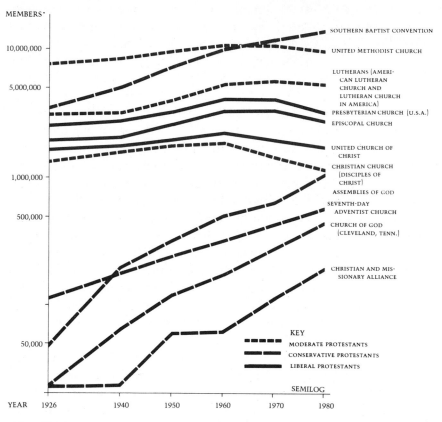

*Adjusted for mergers.

ingly high rates of 50 percent or more. Even the huge Southern Baptist Convention, the largest of the conservative bodies, continued to grow at rates well over 15 percent per decade. A glance at the membership statistics made clear that the denominations were on differing trajectories, some growing and others not (see fig. 5-1).

Now it appears the mainline decline may have bottomed out. Some of the churches that suffered losses are reporting modest gains, and others, while not growing, at least appear more stable.[3] Yet there is no evidence that a genuine turnaround has begun. The liberal Protestant community is mired in a depression, one that is far more serious and deeper than it has suffered at any time in this century. Large numbers of Catholics and Jews have also defected. All of this points to a changing religious establishment and changing relations of religion and culture in the modern period. Twenty years of membership decline and loss of the young have left a fundamentally altered religious mainline. Even if the declines have leveled off, these institutions will bear the imprint of these demographic shifts for many years. Imbalances of this magnitude work themselves out slowly, and not without lasting scars.

One thing the differential patterns of growth and decline has done is to raise concern about the changing social and demographic profile of religious America. Kelley's charts and graphs jolted us into recognizing that religious communities have quite differing demographies and that the ways in which they grow, or fail to grow, bear directly on their institutional destinies. Recent developments have made us newly aware that congregations are very much "earthen vessels"—no less so than other social institutions, they are shaped by a myriad of influences in their environments. Sometimes they grow, and sometimes they suffer losses, depending on both their internal and external conditions; not to understand them in this way is to overlook their fundamental human character. Increasingly, religionists and social analysts alike are turning to religious demographics for church planning and helping religious groups understand their growth potential. Indeed, compiling and interpreting these facts is one of the new growth industries in religious research today. George Gallup, Jr.'s Princeton Religion Research Center, for example, is one of many thriving research enterprises now collecting and analyzing data on religion. A growing storehouse of reliable and representative data on varied aspects of religion makes it possible to describe, better than ever before, the trends now reshaping the religious mainline in the United States.

Two Basic Demographics: Age and Family Patterns

Of all the information now available, two basic demographics are the age structures and family patterns for the religious groups. By examining these we are able to determine, in the first instance, the "location" of a particular group in the larger

American population and, in the second, the fundamental relations between religion and family. Far from being constants, or common features of the mainline groups, these two can vary in ways that are important for understanding how religion fits into the social structure. In both instances the demographics point to significant shifts since midcentury and changing institutional patterns for religion in America.

Aging Constituencies

Normally religious involvement varies by age, which means that churches and synagogues have a disproportionate number of older people within them. This observation has long been made by commentators, indeed for as long as we have had reliable data on congregations. In the 1930s the Lynds, for example, commented on "the same preponderance of gray-haired persons" that they observed in Middletown's churches.[4] Returning to Middletown in the late seventies, Theodore Caplow and his research associates found much the same patterns; they concluded that "regular attendance and intermittent attendance increase for each increment of age."[5]

Age differentials in religion have become even more pronounced since midcentury. The reason for this is simple: the American population is growing older. Low birth and death rates have pushed the average age upward. This finding might not be of much significance if all groups were affected uniformly, but such is hardly the case. Some religious groups, depending on their location relative to the mainstream culture, are far more influenced by general population trends than are others.

Mainline Protestants especially have aged. For some Protestant denominations there have been noticeable increases in the average age levels.[6] The proportion of members fifty years of age or older within these churches has grown considerably in just the last twenty-five years:

	1957	1983
Episcopalians	36%	46%
Methodists	40%	49%
Lutherans	36%	45%
Presbyterians	42%	49%
Baptists	33%	40%

TABLE 5-1

PERCENTAGE DISTRIBUTION OF RELIGIOUS FAMILIES BY AGE

Family	18–34	35–54	55+
Liberal Protestants	27	34	39
Moderate Protestants	31	32	38
Black Protestants	37	31	32
Conservative Protestants	35	34	31
Catholics	40	34	27
Jews	31	31	38
No religious preference	59	26	15

While this trend is most evident in the Protestant mainline churches (both old-line and moderate), the Catholic and Jewish communities have aged as well. Similar proportions of members fifty or older increased for Catholics during this period from 31 percent to 34 percent and for Jews from 33 percent to 39 percent. Religious constituencies generally have aged while just the opposite is true for those with no religious preference: nonaffiliates are considerably younger today than they were a quarter century ago. As the social composition of this secular constituency has undergone a metamorphosis, so too has its demographics. With large numbers of youth dropping out of the churches in the 1960s, and religious nonaffiliation becoming more acceptable, the average age within this sector declined significantly.

Among the religious communities there are disparities in age structures, some being more lopsided than others. This is apparent in table 5-1, which looks at the percentage distribution of mainline religious group members by age. Affiliates of all faiths are older than nonaffiliates; Jews are older than both Protestants and Catholics; Protestants are older than Catholics. Within Protestantism there are some striking differences: white Protestants are older than black Protestants, and liberal Protestants are older than conservative Protestants.

More is involved here than simply the aging of the American population: in the seventies and eighties the greater voluntarism of young Americans took many out of the churches and synagogues and in turn "pushed" the average age levels upward. Protestants, Catholics, and Jews all felt the impact of growing numbers of disaffected and "unchurched" members, the upshot of which was to shift the location of religious mainstream in the direction of a somewhat older age base. Age would thus join the list of social correlates, along with class, ethnicity, and region, as an aspect of fundamental change for these historic traditions. Perhaps no other feature is so apparent in observing many congregations today.

The age shift would have its most profound consequences for Protestantism. Within this community a growing age gap now exacerbates existing tensions and cleavages between liberals-moderates and conservatives. By the 1980s liberal Protestants were on the average almost four years older than conservative Protestants. United Church of Christ members have, along with Christian Scientists, the oldest constituencies, with mean ages greater than fifty years of age. Forty-three percent of the United Church of Christ, 41 percent of Methodists, and 42 percent of Disciples of Christ are age fifty-five or older. This stands in marked contrast to the lower mean ages of the conservative Protestant denominations, the lowest being 41.2 for Pentecostal/holiness members. Not one of the conservative Protestant groups has as many as 40 percent of its members over fifty-five years of age; fewer than one-third of Jehovah's Witnesses, Pentecostals, and Assemblies of God members are this age or older.

Young adults under the age of thirty-five, on the other hand, account for only 26 percent of the members of the Reformed church, 21 percent of the United Church of Christ, and 28 percent of the Methodists. Proportionately these numbers are small, a fact that becomes clear when one considers that almost 40 percent of the nation's adult population belongs to the eighteen-to-thirty-four age category. Young adults are far better represented in the conservative churches: more than 50 percent of Jehovah's Witnesses belong to this younger category. Compared with moderate and liberal Protestants, the conservative churches are more successful in holding on to their young members.

The fact is that liberal, mainline Protestant denominations are aging more rapidly than the more evangelical, fundamentalist faiths. A lopsided age distribution obtains broadly within the liberal Protestant sector, resulting in death rates that are high and likely to become higher still unless the denominations are able to replenish their ranks with younger members in their child-rearing years. As it stands at present, the situation amounts to what Benton Johnson describes as a fundamental "demographic weakness" for liberal Protestantism, and one that does not augur well for its future.[7] For the other religious traditions the age shifts are not as critical, although they are discernible and creating institutional repercussions.

The youthful rebellion against the churches served also to broaden the age gap between the religious and secular cultures. Fifty-nine percent of nonaffiliates are under thirty-five years of age, which is much higher than for any of the religious clusters; only 15 percent of nonaffiliates are age fifty-five or older. The age profile for this more secular constituency has shifted dramatically in the post-1960s period. Nonaffiliates have on the average become younger as they have become more educated and more affluent, all of this happening when the mainline churches were aging. The combination of trends now creates a widening cultural rift between the religious and nonreligious sectors.

Family Patterns

Another set of demographic changes are underway in the relations between family life and religion. Both of these fundamental institutions have had to adjust to the dominant values of individualism, freedom, and equality in the modern world. Both also have had to accommodate the massive social and cultural upheavals of the post-1960s period. New life-styles, changing roles for women, increased divorce rates, and new family forms all pose serious challenges to the traditional family—especially the Norman Rockwell portrait of the normative American family consisting of the husband who is the breadwinner, the wife who is the homemaker, and young children in the home.

Today almost one-fifth of all families are maintained by single parents, about two-fifths have dual wage earners, and one-tenth of the population lives in nonfamily arrangements.[8] Varying patterns of family and household types have become more and more common, and the highly sentimentalized view of the traditional family is now very much a minority family type. Consequently, a huge "gap" exists between the idealized image of the American family and the great diversity of family patterns that now exist. And increasingly, as the range of new family and household types has expanded, so too have ways in which religious institutions accommodate these changes.

Family patterns vary across religious traditions, more so than is often realized. Norman Rockwell's normative family is most commonly found among conservative Protestants and next among moderate Protestants. Seventy-one percent of the conservatives and 68

TABLE 5-2

PERCENTAGE DISTRIBUTION OF RELIGIOUS FAMILIES BY MARITAL
STATUS

Family	Married	Widowed	Separated/ Divorced	Never Married
Liberal Protestants	66	12	10	12
Moderate Protestants	68	12	9	11
Black Protestants	46	14	21	19
Conservative Protestants	71	10	10	9
Catholics	65	9	9	18
Jews	65	12	7	16
No religious preference	48	4	14	34

percent of the moderates are married. For many Protestants of the
center and right, the more evangelical and fundamentalist ones especially, the nuclear family is considered not only normative in
American culture but God given. This pattern is viewed as in keeping with the "biblical concept of the family," which defines marriage as heterosexual and lifelong and the primary function of the
family as that of home building and parenting. Roles in the family
are traditional: the conservatives strongly prefer that women remain in the home or that, if they must work outside, it not interfere
with child-rearing responsibilities. Theological conservatives encourage churches and synagogues to exercise social control and socialization functions that support the traditional family, though not
without some difficulty in the face of secular pressures.

For Jews, Catholics, and liberal Protestants, there is a wider diversity of marital and family styles. All three have large numbers of
singles, reflecting the growing number of Americans choosing not to
marry or, more commonly, to postpone marriage until a later age,
and sizable numbers of widowed. That the numbers of the widowed
would be high for Jews and liberal Protestants is understandable
given their above-average age structures. The proportion who are
separated or divorced is not unusually high (except for Episcopalians); the proportion of Jews who are separated or divorced is actually the lowest, at 7 percent of all the major groupings. While the nuclear family is held up as a model, norms of pluralism and freedom
of choice are deeply ingrained within these traditions. There is less
emphasis upon maintaining a particular family style and more openness to diversity. Even within the Catholic community, where traditional family norms are deeply ingrained, there is awareness of di-

versity among the laity and among many parish priests and a
growing effort to deal with changing family forms. Most mainline
churches and synagogues recognize a variety of family patterns and
life-styles, and in official stands and statements religious authorities
have moved toward a greater nurturance and support. Such emphasis does not mean abandoning values crucial for the survival of the
family but rather, as William V. D'Antonio points out, helping people to "draw out the love and caring features of religious
teachings."[9]

Two of the religious constituencies differ significantly from the
mainstream family norms. Black Protestants have the lowest proportion of married persons, the highest separated or divorced and
widowed, and large numbers of singles, which is not surprising in
view of the long history of strains on the black family. The growing
number of single-parent families and serial marriages within this
community suggests that it may become even more distinctive in
its religious and family patterns. Also not surprising, the nonaffiliates have the highest number of singles and, next to blacks, the
highest number of separated and divorced—34 percent and 14 percent respectively. Considering that many of the nonaffiliates are
young, many will likely marry in time, but it is also evident that
this subculture will remain distinctive for its large number of "alternative" households. Neither of the two groups is likely to become
an exemplar of, much less a strong advocate for, the traditional
family.

Factors Affecting Religious Growth

Both the aging of the mainline religious constituencies and their changing relations with the family bear upon the
theme that has become of such paramount concern in recent years
—whether the churches are growing or declining. This is a complex
issue involving internal institutional as well as contextual factors,
and one that has attracted much attention in both scholarly and
popular circles. Here our concern is not so much to identify the various reasons why some churches grow and others do not as it is to describe specifically the demography of religious change.

The size of a group's membership over time is dependent upon
two fundamental sets of factors: its natural growth and its net gains
or losses from conversion. Most faiths are able to hold the loyalty

of a majority of the children born to members, and thus the higher
the fertility among members the greater the likelihood of numerical growth. Such growth is so obvious that it is usually taken for
granted. In contrast, conversion involves the addition or subtraction
of members by means of willful choice. Persons join or leave on
their own accord—"religious switching" as sociologists describe
such movement. A group with a sufficiently high birth rate can,
within limits, lose substantial numbers to other faiths and still grow
faster than its rivals. Provided it does not lose too many of its members, the group will grow simply because of the large numbers of
children born to its members. By the same token, a group with a low
birth rate and a high death rate can be a net gainer as a result of con-
versions and still show membership declines over time. Its losses
due to deaths exceed its gains from membership transfer.

These two sets of factors are critically important in the demographic balance and thus determine whether a congregation, or
church, grows or shrinks in its membership base (see fig. 5-2). So important are they for understanding the changing American religious
mainline that we give extended treatment to them in the pages that
follow.

Birth Rates

Within the natural growth equation the most significant variable is the birth rate, which varies across traditions and
over time as well. Factors of theological heritage as well as group
experience combine to create differential fertilities, which once in
place tend to be perpetuated. Norms of family size and birth control
all vary from one religious subculture to another. Conformity to religious norms is itself a factor. Among Catholics, for example, John
Scanzoni found that religious devoutness and traditional attitudes
toward sex were mutually supportive: "Wives who have been more
traditional have been more devout, which in turn reinforces and perhaps increases traditionalism, and so forth. Acting together, both elements have evidently resulted in larger families."[10]

Catholics' birth rates are higher than Protestants' or Jews', Protestants' are higher than Jews', and blacks' higher than whites'. Among
white Protestants there are differences that, for the most part, reflect
the wide span of class and educational levels found within this large

FIGURE 5-2.

THE DEMOGRAPHY OF RELIGIOUS FAMILY GROWTH AND DECLINE.

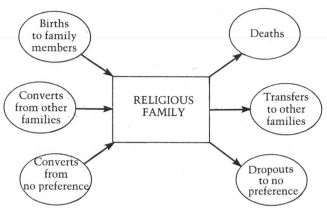

religious family. Thus Methodists typically have had more children than Episcopalians, but fewer than Nazarenes, Jehovah's Witnesses, or many other conservative Protestants. In some instances where fertility levels are high, class may not be so important; for example, the Mormons, Hutterites, and Mennonites lay great emphasis upon the regeneration of the community of believers and have created close ties between kinship and religious roles. But these are minority faiths outside the mainstream, where, generally speaking, fertility varies in direct relation to a group's socioeconomic standing. As with political party affiliation, personal and family styles, and social attitudes, fertility is a fairly sensitive index of status and class.

Those groups that have collectively moved upward in the social structure have typically experienced declining fertility. Churches originating as working-class movements a hundred years or more ago and evolving into middle-class constituencies in the early decades of this century have experienced this pattern. The number of children born to Methodists, for example, dropped as members moved from the farms and small towns to the cities and adopted more middle-class values and life-styles. With the exception of Catholics, whose church prohibits artificial birth control, only small minorities in other religious communities have recognized any religious direction on matters of contraception—maybe as few as 20 percent of the most religious Protestants and 30 percent of the most devout Jews. Consequently, nonreligious factors have had a greater influence in shaping fertility patterns. Urbanization, the changing relations of work and family, women in the work force, and better methods of birth control have all contributed to a reduced fertility.

More generally, norms of family size vary from one period to another. The postwar baby boom of the 1950s is a good example. At midcentury, birth rates were at an all-time high for the modern period, and familial and child-centered themes (for example, The Family That Prays Together, Stays Together) figured prominently in the religious milieu of the period. Middle-class families with three or more children were not uncommon in those years, and more often than not, new parents followed their children to the Sunday schools and churches. "A Little Child Shall Lead Them" was the title of Dennison Nash's popular essay on the role of children in bringing about the so-called religious revival at the time.[11] The symbolism of religion, family, and country was pervasive; for the religious establishment, the market was bullish indeed.

In the late 1950s, however, birth rates began trending downward. The postwar baby boom peaked and was followed by an extended period of declining or stabilized low fertility. The declines affected virtually all sectors of the society. Among young Catholics, for example, the declines throughout this period were especially evident. In a Gallup poll conducted in 1971, 58 percent of Catholics interviewed agreed that one could ignore *Humanae Vitae*, the pope's encyclical proscribing birth control, and still be a good Catholic.[12] Only 40 percent of the priests surveyed in 1969 agreed with the encyclical, and opposition was almost unanimous among the younger priests.[13] For a variety of reasons the gap in birth rates for Protestants and Catholics was narrowing. Even by the late fifties, overall birth rates for Protestants and Catholics under forty-five years of age were already coming together.[14] Throughout the sixties and seventies, the gap continued to diminish. Broad changes in the society and within Catholicism led in the direction of greater convergence—in fertility as in many other cultural aspects.

Today Catholic and mainline Protestant birth rates are roughly similar, but differences remain among the Protestant communities. Table 5-3 shows the number of children born per woman, both the total figures and those broken down by age. With the exception of blacks, conservative Protestants have the highest birth rates of any

TABLE 5-3

AVERAGE NUMBER OF BIRTHS PER WOMAN BY RELIGIOUS FAMILY

Family	Total	Age 45+	Under Age 45
Liberal Protestants	1.97	2.27	1.60
Moderate Protestants	2.27	2.67	1.80
Black Protestants	2.62	3.08	2.24
Conservative Protestants	2.54	3.12	2.01
Catholics	2.20	2.75	1.82
Jews	1.69	1.96	1.37
No religious preference	1.39	2.30	1.18
National	2.25	2.75	1.73

of the religious families (for older women the rates are even higher than that of blacks). Despite declining birth rates and converging patterns generally in the United States, historic differentials within Protestantism are still readily apparent. At present, differences *within* Protestantism far transcend those between Protestants and Catholics.

The patterns are indeed striking. Among women under forty-five years of age, the child-to-woman ratio is 2.01 within the conservative Protestant family as compared to 1.60 for liberal Protestants. This translates into four-tenths of a child less for every liberal Protestant adult female under forty-five. If indeed liberal Protestant women had as many babies as do conservative Protestant women, the size of the liberal sector would increase by more than 2.2 million! Not only, however, do liberal Protestant women have fewer children, but there are fewer women in these churches in the child-bearing ages. Thus numbers and fertility work against a strong and sustained liberal mainline: the natural growth potential for the liberal denominations is fairly weak, while the opposite is true for conservative bodies.

Against conservative Protestantism's strong demographic base, the other white religious communities have far less potential for growth. None of the others are positioned as well in age structure and family patterns—the essential prerequisites for a strong fertility. Except for Northern Baptists and Reformed members, birth rates for the under-forty-five females in the moderate Protestant family are relatively low, almost as low as for liberal Protestants. Catholics' birth rates are similar to those of moderate Protestants: both hover around the national average. Young Jewish women have the lowest fertility of any comparably aged, religiously affiliated Americans. The nonaffiliates have the lowest of all of the major groupings, especially for the under-forty-five category. The nonaffiliates, Unitarian-Universalists, and Christian Scientists have, in that order, the lowest birth rates among younger women. In contrast, black Protestants have exceedingly high birth rates, the very highest in fact among young women.

Religious Switching

Religious switching is another significant factor in the demographic equation of mainline religion. Inflow and outflow amount to a migratory stream of religious movement—in and out of the established faith communities. Some churches benefit from what is described as the "circulation of the saints," that is, they pick up members from other churches; other churches pick up fewer members this way and must aggressively proselytize from among those who have no religious background. As with inflow, so with outflow. Churches and synagogues lose members either to another faith community or to the more secular, nonreligious sector. Losing members to the former does not mean that these members have lost faith, but rather that they are simply opting for a different religious style; losses to the ranks of the nonaffiliated are more serious and may suggest a general secular drift as a competitor to faith.

Movement from one church to another is common in the United States, especially among Protestants. The most common pattern is an "upward movement" of switching from low-status to high-status denominational affiliations. Long observed in Protestant church life, this type of switching has contributed to the making of a diverse and socially conscious denominational order. Much impressionistic evidence, throughout the nineteenth century and much of the twentieth, points to religious movement associated with upward social mobility. Closely linked symbolically with the prevailing mobility ethos, religious switching has often been celebrated as part of the American Way of Life. Abraham Lincoln's own celebrated life course was not all that atypical religiously: from a hard-shell Baptist background, through a "good" marriage and a successful law practice, to regular Presbyterian attendance.[15] Americans can generally relate to the character type that Peter Berger describes as "the young

Baptist salesman who becomes an Episcopalian sales executive."[16] Education, hard work, success, good marriage, recognition—all are values given expression in the upward religious movement, which Jay Demerath amusingly describes as "playing musical church to a status-striving tune."[17]

The best "hard" evidence on religious switching is found in Rodney Stark and Charles Y. Glock's *American Piety*. Using 1963 survey data from California and a 1965 national survey, they observed "upward" movement among Protestants from conservative to more liberal denominations.[18] Liberal churches benefited for two reasons: first, upward social mobility tended to propel people into more liberal, higher-status churches; and, second, people found the demythologized beliefs of the liberal churches more congruent with modern life. While the pattern of liberal movement was especially pronounced in California, there was ample evidence of similar switching nationally as well. The groups with the greatest gains were the Episcopalians, Presbyterians, and to a lesser extent the Congregationalists. Conservative Protestant bodies lost in the switching process, as did Methodists and Lutherans. By far the greatest losses were experienced by non-Christian groups and those with no religious preference. Religious nonaffiliates declined by 31 percent in the national study. Overall, in the sixties the pattern demonstrated conservative Protestant switching losses, modest gains for moderate Protestants, and the greatest gains for liberal Protestants.

Stark and Glock's findings offer a portrait of upward shifts in a bullish religious market. Whether their description accurately fits the past or is an inflated pattern peculiar to the period we do not know. Unfortunately, historical data on which to judge either the amount of movement or its significance are lacking. But we believe it is reasonable to conclude that in this century such movement was a source of growth and vitality for many mainline religious institutions. Especially in times of economic growth and middle-class expansion such as the post–World War II era, high-status Protestant churches likely benefited from above-average levels of religious switching. Old-line establishment churches such as the Episcopal and Presbyterian often received membership transfers from lower-status churches; so did Congregationalism, particularly in New England and the Midwest. A dynamic, achievement-oriented society generated a secular, accommodating religious stance favoring these churches. Higher-status churches have benefited up the line; upwardly mobile Nazarenes and Baptists often became Methodists, affluent Methodists joined the Presbyterians, and many out of diverse backgrounds, if successful, found a home with the Episcopalians. Thus one religious tradition after another in the mainline has enjoyed gains from this pattern of membership flow.

The portrait given us by Stark and Glock underscores another observation: sectarian and conservative Protestant bodies recruit more successfully among the nonaffiliated than do liberal Protestants. This finding is in keeping with the more evangelical character of these traditions and hardly comes as any surprise. But it is an important observation about the basic historic structure of religious movement in the United States. An inflow of members at the "bottom" of the religious establishment has served to replenish low-status memberships and has assured a continuing large pool of upward religious switchers. Large numbers of Americans, whatever their current religious affiliation, were first introduced to, or indoctrinated into, Christianity within the more conservative and moderate branches of American Protestantism.

This portrait of religious America was no longer fitting after the tumultuous sixties. To claim a religious affiliation was "in" during the fifties and early sixties; religious belonging was consistent with the conformist pressures of the period. In an era of expansion and mobility generally, upward religious movement created a favorable milieu for the mainline churches. Conformist cultural and religious themes helped create something of an artificial prosperity and gave the impression that mainline Protestantism (and to a lesser extent an Americanized Catholicism and Judaism) was healthier than it really was. The religious institutions were on the brink of a "gathering storm"—confronting civil rights and other divisive issues of the 1960s. The counterculture, Vietnam, and the crisis of authority for the established structures would shatter the older bourgeois styles of status-driven religiosity. Both the culture and the role of religion within it were to change and so would patterns of religious switching.

Current Patterns of Switching

What about religious switching today? Is the proportion of switchers relative to nonswitchers still fairly high? How have the patterns of switching changed? The following news release issued in June of 1980 is worthy of note:

> LESS THAN HALF REMAIN IN SAME DENOMINATION
> Princeton, N.J. Fewer than half of U.S. adults (43 percent) say they have always been a member of their present religion, or denomination, as determined by a recent Gallup survey.[19]

Many surveys and studies show that at least 40 percent of American Protestants have at one time or another switched denominational affiliations.[20] Switching within this tradition remains much higher due to its size and diversity of churches. For Catholics and Jews there is less switching "in" or "out," but all indications are that it has increased in recent years. Not only has switching increased since the 1960s, but patterns of movement generally have changed. The new voluntarism, involving greater individual choice and preference, has produced more diverse types of switching and far more value-laden and symbolic movement into and out of the religious communities.

To grasp the full import of switching, we must look at both its quantitative and qualitative aspects. Even the quantitative switching, which in one sense is obvious, must be sorted out carefully. We begin with levels of stability for the religious groups. By *stability* we mean the extent to which those who grow up in a religious group stay with it throughout their lives. The more stable a group, the stronger most likely will be its institutional attachments and religious bonds and the more likely it will add the children of its members. Obviously a crucial dimension, stability points to a group's capacity to sustain and "hold on" to its members in what is a fluid and competitive religious market.

Groups vary far more than might be expected in how well they hold on to their members. Jews and Catholics do much better than Protestants: 87 percent and 85 percent, respectively, remain in their faiths. Eighty percent of Mormons and 78 percent of Jehovah's Witnesses continue to maintain their original religious ties. Among more mainline Protestants, the range is wide—from 75 percent (Lutherans) to 37 percent (evangelicals and fundamentalists). A ranking of Protestant denominations shows the following groups to be the most stable: Lutherans, 75 percent; black Northern Baptists, 73 percent; white Southern Baptists, 73 percent; Pentecostals and holiness, 70 percent; Adventists, 69 percent; and black Methodists, 69%. At the bottom of the rank order, or the least stable, are three disparate groups: Christian Scientists, 39 percent; Unitarian-Universalists, 39 percent; and evangelicals and fundamentalists, 37 percent.

Most of the large, Protestant mainline denominations fall in the middle. Episcopalians (65 percent), Methodists (63 percent), United Church of Christ (61 percent), Disciples (58 percent), and Presbyterians (60 percent) all have majorities that have remained stable, yet there are large numbers of switchers. This is not too surprising: to be in the mainline is to be in the middle, tending toward neither extreme. By virtue of their size and social location, they are the religious institutions most likely to experience tensions arising out of the larger society. The cross-pressures of switching versus non-switching are felt most acutely within these structures.

One thing is clear—membership stability is not a matter simply of liberal or conservative theology. Groups in the most stable category do not all share a strong conservative theology, nor are those least stable necessarily similar in this respect. Christian Scientists and Unitarian-Universalists are among the most liberal; many evangelicals and fundamentalists are known to switch to other churches. Stability appears to be more a reflection of communal belonging. Mormons, Lutherans, Jehovah's Witnesses, black Baptists and Methodists, and white Southern Baptists all have strong ethnic or quasi-ethnic loyalties, at least compared with more mainline groups. The role of communal attachments in creating stability becomes even more apparent in view of the fact that nonaffiliates are also among the least stable of all groupings. Only 45 percent of those reared as nonaffiliates have retained a nonreligious preference. Known to be highly individualistic and to have weak communal attachments, they are also unstable as a constituency of nonbelievers or, more correctly, nonbelongers.

Looking at the religious families, we see even better the significance of ethnic and group ties. Stability in this context refers to the percentage of persons raised in a family group who remain within that family; for example, a person raised an Episcopalian who is now a Presbyterian is classified as remaining in the liberal Protestant family. Of course this means the amount of switching is less than when grouped in more specific denominational categories, but such grouping helps show levels of stability for the larger religiocultural traditions in America today. Arranged on the basis of the percentage remaining within the family, the ordering is as follows: Jews, 87 percent; black Protestants, 87 percent; Catholics, 85 percent; conservative Protestants, 78 percent; moderate Protestants, 74 percent; liberal Protestants, 67 percent; and no religious preference, 45 percent. The relation between group identity and membership stability within the family is evident: the stronger the quasi-ethnic bonds, the more likely members will stay within their traditions. Jews, Catholics, and black Protestants are more likely to remain within their families than are conservative and moderate Protestants, who in turn are more likely to do so than liberal Protestants. That levels of stability parallel so closely *gemeinschaft*-like group attachments is itself revealing about the contextual boundaries that set limits on religious switching even in the highly individualized culture of modern America.

There is another aspect to switching: a group's capacity to *attract* new members. Net gains or losses for a particular group are a function of both its stability (or the number it retains) and its attractiveness (or the number who switch in). Thus very stable religious groups need not attract many persons in order to show a net gain, but denominations that lose many of their members must attract large numbers of new members if they are to avoid net losses through switching.

With this in mind, we can begin to see how the flow of members varies for the various religious traditions. Table 5-4 shows switching patterns for the seven mainline groupings. For each the table gives the number of sample members who were raised in the family, the number who were raised in another family or without a religious preference, and the number brought up in the tradition who have switched out either to another family or to no religious preference. To illustrate: there were 1,255 members raised in liberal Protestant denominations. To this number were added 431 persons from other families and 27 with no religious preference. Subtracted were 311 persons raised as liberal Protestants who are now affiliated with another religious family and 101 who now list no religious preference. Overall, the liberal Protestant family has a net gain of 46 members, or 3.7 percent. By looking closely at the membership flows, we can draw several conclusions about religious change today.

TABLE 5-4

FAMILY GAINS AND LOSSES DUE TO SWITCHING

Denominational Family	Total		Under Age 45		Age 45+	
	Number in Sample	Percent	Number in Sample	Percent	Number in Sample	Percent
Liberal Protestants						
Base (age 16)	1,255	100.0	635	100.0	620	100.0
From other families	431	34.3	154	24.3	277	44.7
From nonaffiliation	27	2.2	18	2.8	9	1.5
To other families	(311)	−24.8	(159)	−25.0	(152)	−24.5
To nonaffiliation	(101)	−8.0	(73)	−11.5	(28)	−4.5
Net gain/loss	46	3.7	(60)	−9.4	106	17.1
Moderate Protestants						
Base (age 16)	3,896	100.0	1,862	100.0	2,034	100.0
From other families	708	18.2	353	19.0	355	17.5
From nonaffiliation	84	2.2	41	2.2	43	2.1
To other families	(796)	−20.4	(340)	−18.3	(456)	−22.4
To nonaffiliation	(225)	−5.8	(167)	−9.0	(58)	−2.9
Net gain/loss	(229)	−5.9	(113)	−6.1	(116)	−5.7
Black Protestants						
Base (age 16)	1,499	100.0	814	100.0	685	100.0
From other families	33	2.2	20	2.5	13	1.9
From nonaffiliation	3	0.2	3	0.4	0	0
To other families	(133)	−8.9	(62)	−7.6	(71)	−10.4
To nonaffiliation	(63)	−4.2	(55)	−6.8	(8)	−1.2
Net gain/loss	(160)	−10.7	(94)	−11.5	(66)	−9.6

TABLE 5-4 (continued)
FAMILY GAINS AND LOSSES DUE TO SWITCHING

Conservative Protestants						
Base (age 16)	2,307	100.0	1,278	100.0	1,029	100.0
From other families	550	23.8	272	21.3	278	27.0
From nonaffiliation	53	2.3	32	2.5	21	2.0
To other families	(448)	−19.4	(208)	−16.3	(240)	−23.3
To nonaffiliation	(90)	−3.9	(72)	−5.6	(18)	−1.7
Net gain/loss	65	2.8	24	1.9	41	4.0
Catholics						
Base (age 16)	4,012	100.0	2,438	100.0	1,574	100.0
From other families	331	8.3	178	7.3	153	9.7
From nonaffiliation	37	0.9	18	0.7	19	1.2
To other families	(287)	−7.2	(175)	−7.2	(112)	−7.1
To nonaffiliation	(294)	−7.3	(245)	−10.0	(49)	−3.1
Net gain/loss	(213)	−5.3	(224)	−9.2	11	0.7
Jews						
Base (age 16)	357	100.0	171	100.0	168	100.0
From other families	19	5.3	12	7.0	7	4.2
From nonaffiliation	3	0.8	3	1.8	0	0
To other families	(12)	−3.4	(7)	−4.1	(5)	−3.0
To nonaffiliation	(36)	−10.1	(23)	−13.5	(13)	−7.7
Net gain/loss	(26)	−7.3	(15)	−8.8	(11)	−6.5
No religious preference						
Base (age 16)	387	100.0	247	100.0	140	100.0
From other families	809	209.0	635	257.1	174	124.3
To other families	(207)	−53.5	(115)	−46.6	(92)	−65.7
Net gain/loss	602	155.6	520	210.5	82	58.6

Liberal Gains Offset By Losses

Many mainline Protestant churches enjoy membership gains from other churches but lose equal numbers, if not more, to the ranks of the nonaffiliates. Liberal Protestants show a gain of 34.3 percent through transfers *from* other families, which is offset by a loss of 24.8 percent *to* other families, or a resulting net interfamily gain of 9.5 percent. This suggests that liberal Protestantism is attractive as a religious alternative and actually does better in interfamily switching than any other religious family. Liberal churches continue to pick up members out of the conservative churches. But with other types of membership flow they do not come out as well. Liberal churches show a gain of 2.2 percent from the nonaffiliates, which is offset by a loss of 8.0 percent to them, or a net loss of 5.8 percent. This leads to the observation, one which goes against popular wisdom, that the challenge to liberal Protestantism comes not so much from the conservative faiths as from the growing secular drift of many of their not-so-highly-committed members.

Secular Drift Across the Religious Spectrum

The big "winner" in the switching game is the growing secular constituency. Of all seven groupings, nonaffiliates are the greatest beneficiary of switching; all the groups lose more persons to this category than they receive from it. In the exchange, Jews, liberal Protestants, and Catholics have the greatest losses, while conservative Protestants come closest to holding their own. The liberal religious traditions especially have a serious institutional problem of holding on to their own.

Stark and Glock hypothesized some twenty years ago that the leftward trend of switching might not end with movement into the liberal churches, but that in time many liberals might simply drop out of the churches altogether. They surmised that should this happen, what had seemed like a favorable situation for liberal Protestantism could turn into a serious problem of membership collapse.[21] To some extent, their predictions appear to have been borne out. Liberal Protestantism's greatest losses come from those dropping out of religion altogether. But Catholics and Jews, and to a lesser extent some conservative Protestants, also lose considerable numbers to the nonaffiliate ranks. What was once a liberal Protestant "problem" is now more generally one for the mainline faiths.

The only group showing net gains among younger members is the nonaffiliates. All the religious families lose considerably higher proportions of their younger members to this group than they receive from it. In this exchange, Jews, liberal Protestants, and Catholics experience exceptionally high losses among those under forty-five years of age. All three families lose great numbers of youth and young adults to the nonaffiliates. Conservative Protestants do somewhat better; they hold on to more of their younger members, yet still lose in the exchange. In every case the rate of loss to nonaffiliation for the younger group exceeds that of persons forty-five and older. This trend differs from the 1950s and 1960s, when proportionately more were leaving the ranks of the "unchurched" to affiliate with one or another of the major national faiths. Disaffiliation, and indifference generally to organized religion, is much more of a reality today for the churches and synagogues. Maybe it was the case, as Dennison Nash said, that the religious revival of the fifties came about as a result of "A Little Child Leading Them," but we might add with just a little whimsy that in the seventies and eighties a religious depression resulted when "A Teen-Ager or Young Adult Dropped Out."

Older Switchers Within the Religious Communities

Many of the mainline Protestant and Catholic churches pick up more recruits from other religious communities than they lose, yet it is important to note who these persons are. The net switching gains for liberal Protestants are wholly accounted for by *older* switchers. Among older persons this community experiences a net gain of 17.1 percent, among younger persons a loss of 9.4 percent. Conservative Protestants and Catholics pick up older members and break even or lose the young. Both increasing numbers of switchers to nonaffiliation and a decline in the number of persons switching from other religious communities have contributed to this more pronounced age-related phenomenon. Generally, religion's "market share" of potential recruits has grown older.

Losses in the Middle

The big "losers" are the moderate Protestants. The large middle America denominations—Methodists, Lutherans, Disciples, Northern Baptists, Reformed—have disproportionately lost to other groups since the 1960s. Because of their size and close identity with the mainstream culture, they have been unable to hold their own and have become the major suppliers of recruits to other faiths. As the nation's cultural and religious center has weakened, movement is greatest at the extremes—in the conservative religious and the secular, nonaffiliated directions. Such switching reflects the more fragmented and polarized culture that so rocked the religious establishment in the sixties and seventies. The strains run deep in the large moderate Protestant bodies, those truly mainline in faith and cultural experience.

The Switchers

Who are the switchers? What are their social and life-style characteristics? How do they differ from nonswitchers? Considering how many switchers there are and their importance for American religion, we must inquire further about them. As we have seen, patterns of switching currently are much too complex for simple generalizations about the switchers. In recent years switching patterns have become more diverse, reflecting the greater variety of styles of belief and behavior. By looking at the switching profiles, we can learn a great deal about the religious disestablishment of the sixties and seventies and about the many currents of change now reshaping the religious landscape (see table 5-5).

Again, we draw several conclusions:

1. *The overriding factor of age.* The profile data confirm what we already know—age is a major predictor of switching patterns. Young persons are vastly overrepresented among those who switch to nonaffiliation. As many as 80 percent of those who have disaffiliated from some of the religious families are under forty-five years of age. Age differences stand out in Protestant interfamily switching. Those switching into the liberal Protestant family from other traditions are older. Sixty-four percent of those who switch into liberal Protestantism from another religious family are over forty-five years of age. Fifty percent of those switching from other families to both moderate and conservative Protestant families are of this age. While we do not know the age of individuals when they made a

TABLE 5-5
SELECTED CHARACTERISTICS OF SWITCHERS

Family	Percent under 45	Mean Age	Mean Education	Mean Occupational Prestige	% Regular Worship Attenders	% Strong Members
Liberal Protestants						
No change	48	47.2	13.2	43.8	34	32
From other families	36	51.2	13.3	45.6	48	37
From nonaffiliation	67	41.7	13.6	42.8	33	28
To other families	51	46.8	13.1	42.5	57	43
To nonaffiliation	72	36.8	14.1	45.4	2	—
Moderate Protestants						
No change	47	47.6	12.0	39.5	39	36
From other families	50	46.7	12.0	40.4	50	38
From nonaffiliation	49	45.4	11.5	37.3	42	33
To other families	43	49.3	12.3	41.3	57	45
To nonaffiliation	74	37.3	13.1	40.0	3	—
Black Protestants						
No change	54	44.5	10.4	31.0	55	13
From other families	*	*	*	*	*	*
From nonaffiliation	*	*	*	*	*	*
To other families	47	44.8	11.1	32.2	74	56
To nonaffiliation	87	34.0	11.5	32.2	3	—
Conservative Protestants						
No change	56	43.9	10.8	36.4	54	52
From other families	50	47.5	10.9	36.3	69	59
From nonaffiliation	60	39.9	9.9	35.6	70	54
To other families	46	47.4	11.7	40.6	49	39
To nonaffiliation	80	35.8	11.0	37.0	4	—

TABLE 5-5 (continued)
SELECTED CHARACTERISTICS OF SWITCHERS

Family	Percent under 45	Mean Age	Mean Education	Mean Occupational Prestige	% Regular Worship Attenders	% Strong Members
Catholics						
No change	59	42.5	11.9	38.8	53	43
From other families	54	44.9	12.3	38.8	52	32
From nonaffiliation	49	45.9	11.9	37.9	62	34
To other families	61	42.1	11.8	38.6	50	39
To nonaffiliation	83	34.4	13.5	41.8	4	—
Jews						
No change	46	49.2	14.0	47.3	13	43
From other families	*	*	*	*	*	*
From nonaffiliation	*	*	*	*	*	*
To other families	58	41.3	12.5	34.8	*	*
To nonaffiliation	64	39.7	15.4	53.8	0	—
No religious preference						
No change	73	35.3	12.0	38.5	2	—
From other families	79	35.9	13.1	41.1	3	—
To other families	56	43.3	11.5	37.7	51	38

* Too few cases for meaningful analysis.

change of affiliation, the data suggest two possible conclusions: switching to liberal Protestantism occurs mainly among older persons or switching to this family may have been more common in earlier periods than in the recent past. Very likely both are correct and, if so, bear implications for the future course of change within American Protestantism.

Switching currently contributes to the lopsided age composition of the liberal churches. Because these churches lose so many of their young and receive as members a disproportionate share of older persons, their constituencies continue to age. No other religious family is so adversely affected. Disaffiliation by the young has raised the average age levels in all the families, but in most instances this is somewhat offset by a favorable membership transfer. Among conservative Protestants, for example, there is almost no discrepancy between the ages of those switching in and those switching out (among religious families); the overall age level of these denominations is essentially unaffected by interfamily switching. The members moderate Protestants pick up are younger than those they lose to other denominations. Catholics pick up members who are older than the ones they lose in the exchange, but whatever demographic imbalances may result are "made up" by a favorable fertility.

2. *Upward switching.* All evidence points to less upward switching, or conservative-to-liberal transfer of religious membership, now than in the past. Net gains resulting from switching for liberal Protestants are not as marked today as they were in previous decades; there seems to have been a falloff in what had once been an important source of their growth during the 1950s and 1960s. Conservative Protestants show net gains from switching today, in contrast to their earlier losses; they are losing proportionately fewer to other faiths today because of their greater attraction and appeal in the religious marketplace. Because greater numbers of affluent, well-educated persons are becoming nonaffiliates, liberal churches are drained of many who in times past were more likely to join these churches. There appears to be little question that the old historic pattern of intragenerational switching—from conservative to liberal Protestant denominations—has declined and no longer plays as important a role in sustaining a vital membership for the liberal churches.

Some upward switching still occurs primarily among those with higher levels of education and occupational prestige. As in the past, contemporary switching helps enhance status differences among Protestants. The social characteristics and status trajectories for the several streams of switchers differ. Those leaving the liberal churches for other churches have lower educational and occupational standing than "stayers," or those remaining, or than those who switch in from other churches. In other words, interfamily switching contributes to the higher social status of liberal Protestants. But the opposite is true for conservative Protestantism. While switchers into this family have education and occupational prestige that are close to those of stayers, the status levels are lower for the joiners than for persons raised in the family who switch to other groups. Much the same holds for moderate Protestants. Unquestionably there remains an upward switching pattern within Protestantism of older, well-educated, and higher-status members.

Upward switching is not simply a Protestant phenomenon. Catholics too appear to enjoy status gains as a result of the circulation of the saints. Those switching into this faith have a higher socioeconomic standing than those who leave for another religious affiliation. New recruits to Catholicism have equal if not greater status than those who are born and reared within the faith. More distinct switching patterns here indicate broad changes in Catholicism, especially in its relation to American culture. As Catholicism has moved into the religious mainstream, its patterns of recruiting have changed to reflect the greater mobility and status of its members.

3. *Mobility and secular drift.* There is an emerging second type of religious movement associated with upward mobility: switching into the ranks of the nonaffiliated. Those who switch to no religious preference have significantly more education and higher occupational prestige than those who remain religiously affiliated. This is true across all the religious families, for Protestants, Catholics, and Jews. Many born and reared in the established faiths and who are upwardly mobile are dropping out and becoming a part of the growing nonaffiliated sector. At the same time, recruits into the churches from the nonaffiliated have less education and lower occupational prestige than those who switch the opposite way—from a faith to nonaffiliated. Switching thus contributes to the emergence of a

more sharply crystallized image of nonaffiliates as an increasingly mobile, high-achieving group.

By and large, interfamily switching serves to maintain rather than lessen status differences among the religious communities in America. Even the more diverse switching patterns of recent times and the emergence of a more distinct secular, nonaffiliated constituency appear not to have eroded historic class differences among Protestants. If anything, switching has enhanced these contrasts and contributed to the greater religious and ideological pluralism of contemporary America.

The "Quality" of Converts

In the circulation of the saints that occurs within Protestantism, mainline Protestant churches take in many affluent, well-educated, upwardly mobile members. But what about the level of *religious* commitment of those picked up? As church members are they more or less committed than converts to conservative Protestant churches? There is reason to expect that the liberal denominations fail to attract the highly committed. Rodney Stark and Charles Y. Glock two decades ago concluded that "liberal denominations fare badly in generating member commitment."[22] More recently Kirk Hadaway, in a study of the "quality" of switchers to various denominations, concluded that while more liberal groups have larger net gains as a result of switching, "conservative denominations pick up the 'better' converts."[23]

The data at hand shed some light on these interesting questions. The evidence in table 5-5 suggests that "joiners" make good attenders and strong members, often better ones than those who have remained all their lives in a particular tradition. Among "stayers," regular worship is highest for Catholics and conservative Protestants, but lower for black Protestants, moderate Protestants, and liberal Protestants. It is very low for Jews and those with no preference. In contrast, religious "joiners" have significantly higher rates of religious participation (more true in the case of religious attendance than "strong" membership). This is particularly true of persons switching to conservative Protestantism and Catholicism; persons raised with no preference who switch to these groups have the highest participation rates shown in the table (70 percent and 62 percent, respectively). Even for liberal Protestants, those switching in tend to participate about as much as those who have been with the tradition all their lives. Across the religious spectrum, then, it appears that recruits are a source of on-going institutional vitality.

Thus there is little basis for believing that religious switching itself undermines institutional commitment or leads persons to lessened religious involvement; if anything, switching from one faith to another is probably the occasion for greater clarity of choice and deliberateness. As conformity has given way to greater choice in lifestyle and religious affiliation, opportunity for a more genuine type of commitment becomes possible. In an age of religious voluntarism, switching may well be a means of enhancing personal faith as well as institutional commitment and should not be viewed as simply an expression of how secular forces erode faith.

But the "quality" of switchers does indeed vary. Liberal and moderate mainline Protestants attract persons who are less active than those they lose to other groups, whereas those who switch to the conservative Protestant family are more active than those who leave. A difference is evident among those both switching in and switching out. For example, 48 percent of the "new" liberal Protestants raised in other families are regular attenders as compared to 69 percent of those switching to conservative Protestantism and 52 percent of those switching to Catholicism. Those picked up by the liberal churches are, as Hadaway suggests, less committed. And it is also true that these churches lose their most faithful participants. Among those switching out of the liberal Protestant tradition to other faiths, 57 percent are regular attenders—a much greater percentage than that of its stayers. Forty-three percent of those leaving are "strong" members—a higher percentage than that for the stayers or for any new recruits. Typically those leaving a liberal church for another church find one in which they can become more involved. A principle of consistency seems to operate: persons whose levels of religious commitment differ from the prevailing norms within their respective traditions, whether liberal or conservative, tend to switch to a group more in keeping with their particular styles.

The quality of converts thus adds to the list of woes for liberal churches. To compensate for their low natural growth and high death rates, they must rely upon transfers from other faiths in order to maintain a steady membership. But falloff in membership transfers of this kind places the churches in a weak demographic position, and the fact that they fail to pick up the better converts further erodes their institutional strength. Both numbers and levels of member commitment work against them.

This lack of commitment helps explain a puzzling feature about switching and church growth. While liberal Protestant churches enjoy net gains from switching, these churches have suffered severe membership losses for two decades now. Why would the churches benefiting from the switching not also be growing? Of course the survey data on switching have to do with "religious preference," not church membership, which may account partly for the discrepancy. And we do not know when individuals in the surveys may have switched. The average age of switchers into these churches may have risen, which might also be a factor. The most likely explanation is that some may say they have switched but in fact are mental affiliates—that is, they do not actually join or become active participants with these churches. Mental affiliates show up in the polls but not on the churches' rolls.

For Catholics, patterns are similar to those for conservative Protestants. Both tend to pick up "better" converts than they lose. Both of these large communities show considerable power in attracting highly committed members, and they do so across a broad spectrum of social and religious backgrounds. Both recruit persons from the nonaffiliated category as well as from other religious families. Sixty-two percent of those switching from nonaffiliation to Catholicism, and 70 percent of those switching to conservative Protestantism, are regular worshipers. Levels of commitment for the recruits are in each instance considerably higher than those of long-standing members. The more liberal and moderate Protestants fare less well in reaching the unchurched and reactivating their faiths. Those switching from a nonreligious background appear to adopt a style of institutional commitment in keeping with standards of practice within the churches they join. They truly "join" and often become good members.

Three Streams of Religious Movement

Today there are three distinct streams of religious movement reshaping the religious mainline: two amount to circulation of the saints within the religious establishment, and the third involves a drift out of the religious communities. The first stream is the liberal movement, characterized generally by rising status levels for many Americans. Those shifting into liberal churches are typically older, more educated, and hold more prestigeous occupations; they tend to be relatively liberal on many moral and social issues. They are less active religiously than those they leave behind in other churches and synagogues. While such switching has declined somewhat in recent decades, it is still a discernible pattern accompanying upward mobility and entry into the mainstream. Liberal Protestants and Catholics, and to a lesser extent Reform Jews, all benefit from such switching. Older switchers account for a disproportionate amount of such movement. In the United States in the 1980s, the moral and ideological views of the switchers have become more pronounced, suggesting that those who choose to identify with these traditions may do so with greater awareness of, and possible conviction for, what they represent in the larger framework of American religious pluralism at present.

A second stream is the conservative movement, perhaps best understood primarily as a reaction to the secular trends of modern society and accommodation of the mainline faiths to the culture. Those switching to the conservative churches tend to be somewhat younger, less educated, and of lower social standing; they are often opposed to such issues as the ERA, abortion, gay rights, and the extension of civil liberties. They are more committed to traditional religious values and moral principles. Such switching is very much ideological in character and seems to have increased in recent years as a response to the moral and religious ambiguities of the times. Largely it is a white Protestant phenomenon, and the losses it creates are felt most within the large, moderate bodies.

The third movement, or growth of the secular constituency, is qualitatively different. It cuts across religious families and breaks with the cognitive and moral worlds associated with the religious traditions. Amid all the flux of the recent period, this group has become the main beneficiary. For every person raised without religion

who adopts a church, three persons forsake the churches for no institutional religious affiliation. Those who become nonaffiliates are
young, predominately male, well educated, more committed to alternative life-styles, and oriented generally to an ethic of personal
growth and self-fulfillment. Though we have no hard data on which
to judge, these persons appear to be more "new class" in outlook and
ideology. They may be religious in a deeply personal sense, but affiliation with a congregation is not deemed essential to their spiritual quests.

This greater diversity in switching patterns signifies, as noted earlier, the migratory character of faith in a modern, pluralistic society:
people move "in" and "out" of faith communities with considerable
ease. Americans have always been known for how easily they cross
boundaries of faith, and they seem to be doing so even more now
than in the past. A new religious order appears to be in the making
in which life-style choice and moral values play a bigger part in the
selection of a religious (or nonreligious) affiliation. The religious individualism of modern America encourages sifting and sorting on
the basis of shifting perceptions of institutions and definitions of
personal need. Individual preferences in matters of faith operate
more freely; believers are less bound by the strictures of group belonging, by custom and tradition. As conformity in religious life has
declined, choice has become a more important factor.

Conclusion

The demography of American religion offers many
clues to how and why the religious establishment is changing. Age
structures and family patterns are becoming more diversified in the
religious mainline. These fundamental shifts in the social and demographic structure have implications for the social location and
institutional characteristics of religion, now and for the future.

Generally demographers who study population dynamics concern
themselves with three basic variables—births, deaths, and migration. All three of these bear upon the changing religious scene. As
we have seen, differential birth rates are important, death rates are
crucial especially for those traditions with low birth rates, and religious switching, or the migration equivalent, has become more sig-

nificant in the modern period. A particular church or tradition may enjoy added numbers as a result of a favorable birth rate or net gains from switching, or both; similarly it may suffer serious institutional losses depending upon how the numbers fall. Both natural growth and additions by switching are crucial elements that figure in the formula of institutional and group survival. It is difficult to imagine that either will become any less important as considerations in the future, and one or the other may well become even more critical. Switching as a factor especially is likely to take on greater significance.

Demography has proven to be destiny for American Protestantism. Since midcentury, demographic and switching trends have literally reshaped the Protestant establishment. Declining birth rates have diminished the chances that liberal Protestants will reproduce themselves. Liberal churches continue to attract upwardly mobile switchers but at a reduced rate, and those they attract tend not to be very active. The liberal churches at present suffer from a severe demographic weakness: they have aging constituencies and have become, or are dangerously close to becoming, in Hadaway's phrase, "unstable destination denominations."[24] Large numbers of members who are only nominally committed and many who now are leaving the churches altogether make the liberal churches vulnerable as continuing vital religious institutions. With their lopsided age distributions, death rates are high and likely to become higher still unless the churches are able to replenish their ranks with younger people. Of all the major traditions, liberal Protestantism is suffering the most from the secular drift of the post-1960s. Lack of strong group cohesion means that many individuals either disaffiliate or simply become nominal members having little to do with congregational life. The greater religious voluntarism of modern life produces "alumni associations," or collectivities with vague ties to the churches. Even though many are attracted to a liberal stance of openness and pluralism, such traits tend not to generate strong institutional commitment.

Protestant conservatives, in contrast, fare better. Fewer of them are now switching to liberal denominations, and they hold on to more of their younger members. Their death rates are lower, and their birth rates higher—a winning combination in the game of religious growth. Compared with other Protestants, they gain the most committed converts, retain the most committed members, and lose those who are least likely to be regular participants and supporters. Loyalty to traditional doctrines runs deeper, and mechanisms of member commitment are stronger. Perhaps most important, conservative churches have stronger socioreligious group attachments, which play an important role in undergirding them as communities of belief. More emphasis upon the gathered community of believers and a sense of responsibility and accountability to one another serve as a "buffer" protecting the conservative churches more from the privatizing forces of modern society. Secular forces are strong, of course, and are propelling these churches in the direction of greater religious voluntarism, but relatively speaking they still enjoy greater social cohesiveness.

In some respects, Catholics and moderate Protestants have similar demographies. Neither are suffering from great decline in birth rates; death rates are about average; and both are losing increasing numbers of their members to the secular drift. Catholics choose, as Greeley says, "to go their own way," meaning that many now believe and practice in a manner in keeping with their personal preference and set their own conditions for religious belonging.[25] Traditional and rigid Catholic styles are giving way to a more voluntaristic style of "selective Catholicism"; many Catholics are functionally "unchurched," "nonpracticing," or "communal." Moderate Protestants, long a supplier of recruits to the liberal establishment, now lose members to liberal and conservative churches as well as many to the unchurched ranks. Both traditions enjoy a mainline status, which in recent years has become not just a mark of privilege but a burden as well—including the possibility of rejection and defection. Mainline Catholics and Protestants alike are feeling the effects of greater religious migration, or increasing numbers of persons moving in and out of the religious establishment on their own terms.

The American Jewish community, more self-contained and in some ways more removed from the trends toward greater voluntarism, suffers from a low birth rate and losses brought about by increased intermarriage and large numbers of "alternative families." Increased numbers of singles, intermarrieds, and divorcés contribute to a decline in Jewish ritual practices and communal loyalties. But this community also testifies to the fact that religious mobility can have positive effects. Many born-Gentile spouses of Jews convert to Judaism, and on average they are more religiously observant than the average born Jew. "Jews by choice," as the converts prefer to be called, often contribute a spirituality and piety that are rare among born Jews and thereby raise the religious consciousness of the community. Marginal Jews drop out and are replaced, so to speak, by those of another background who choose to be Jews. The result is what Milton Himmelfarb describes as a positive balance of trade: "Our imports," he says, "are better than our exports."[26]

The new voluntarism of which we speak is a significant aspect of the contemporary religious scene—whether Protestant, Catholic, or Jewish. Greater individualism as expressed in more diverse switching patterns suggests the growing importance of the migration analogy, or the possibility of easy movement from one tradition to another. Tocqueville recognized this potential in American religion more than a century ago, but it took the post-1960s period of religious and cultural disestablishment to bring these populist tendencies into clear focus. Tocqueville wrote: "If we examine it very closely, it will be perceived that religion itself holds sway there much less as a doctrine of revelation than as a commonly received opinion."[27]

Perhaps it should be said that the greater individualism as we have described it embodies both the best and the worst of religious trends today. By *worst* we mean simply that in the exercise of greater choice, individuals often become so cut loose from their groups that they lose the support needed for reinforcing institutional commitment. The plight of the liberal Protestant churches is an example: a lack of cohesion, too much openness and diffuseness, and absence of any clear sense of institutional identity. Those switching into these churches come already highly individualized and privatized in matters of faith, and many switch out into the ranks of the disaffiliated without much of a sense of having left any particular group. In this sense liberal Protestants are on the forefront of the confrontation with modernity, though hardly alone and distinct; increasingly Catholics and many conservative Protestants follow a similar path of enfranchising individuals with greater responsibility and choice in religious matters. Growing numbers of secular nonaffiliates drawn from all the major religious families is evidence enough of where the paths of greater individualism and privatism often lead.

Best refers to the enhancement of personal religious choice and emancipation of faith from ascriptive loyalties. The diverse types of switching we have described is a positive factor in shaping a more responsible, conscientious mode of religious commitment. Moral and ideological commitments play more of a role in determining religious loyalties today: people increasingly choose on the basis of their values and preferences whether to affiliate, and if so, with which church or tradition. This had led to the rise of a more self-conscious secular constituency but also to a better sense of religious alternatives. The boundaries of moral and religious communities have become more sharply distinguished and the range of life-style and belief systems expanded in a more genuinely pluralistic manner. America's many religious traditions and faith communities have taken on greater clarity in a market increasingly governed by individual choice and personal preference.

What all of this means—the changing demographies and greater voluntarism—for the future of American religion is a matter of no small significance. At stake is not just the shape of the changing religious establishment but the place of religion generally in public life. The new demographics and diversity of switching patterns have helped sharpen moral and cultural cleavages now so prominent within the religious mainline. The faiths have become more divided in the face of difficult and controversial issues, and it is to these new morally based divisions that we now turn.

Chapter Six

Mainline Morality

Not since the 1920s have political Fundamentalists been as well financed, visible, organized and effective. Deeply committed believers, working long and zealously, get tavern hours trimmed in Anchorage; disrupt school-board meetings in Hillsboro, Mo., as they demand to control curriculum; force doctors to stop performing abortions in Virginia Beach, Va., march in San Antonio streets to protest sex channels on cable TV. The shelves of religious bookstores are filled with their social protests, in which the buzz words "secular humanism" are used to cover anything and everything the authors disapprove of.

— TIME, SEPTEMBER 2, 1985

hile the issues and their proponents are of the 1980s, the moral strains of American religion have been dominant from the beginning: "Go into the churches," wrote Tocqueville, "you will hear morality preached, of dogma not a word." The emphasis on morality in American religion stems from the separation of church and state and the role forced upon the churches as guardians of public virtue in a free society. On matters of great public concern, it has fallen on the voluntary church to exercise persuasive power and to muster influence on behalf of social and ethical ideals. A pragmatic, this-worldly theology and folk piety prevails: concern is with what it does, with principle, with right and wrong far more than with other aspects of religion. As William Lee Miller writes, "In the main drift of religion in America the theological and liturgical and contemplative move into the background. . . . The penumbra of beyondness, absoluteness, and mystery fades

away, and leaves—as the core of what Americans think religion to be—the moral."[1]

That moral core persevered throughout most of American history, weathering even the 1920s and 1930s when Protestants were forced to accept Catholic and Jews as legitimate partners in the shaping of the nation's way of life. The major faiths might differ in their particulars but they shared a common morality and civil religious heritage. The consensus lasted into the 1960s when it began to erode as the nation entered a new period of moral and ideological pluralism. Now, with what appears to be a growing confrontation between religious traditionalists and secular humanists, America finds itself in a struggle over the shape of the new moral order. And nowhere is that struggle more intense than within grass-roots Protestantism. Jerry Falwell sees signs of a serious crisis resulting from America's fall from righteousness:

> We desperately need a genuine revival of spiritual righteousness in our land. America needs the healing touch of God because of her sins. *Legalized abortion* has claimed the lives of 15 million babies since the 1973 Supreme Court decision. The multi-billion dollar *pornography* industry is demeaning our women and destroying our children. *Secular Humanism* attempts to elevate man to a place where he has no need of God. Disallowing *prayer* in our public schools has cut our children off from the right to voluntarily pray to God during school hours. *Infanticide* and *euthanasia* are threatening both our children and our aged. The *drug epidemic* is sweeping our country and perverting our young people. *Homosexuality* is spreading everywhere, claiming our youth as its victims. The nearly 50 percent *divorce rate* threatens the very stability of our monogamous culture. America is in trouble and only God can save her.[2]

Another group of Protestant leaders, including heads or senior representatives of the United Presbyterian, United Church of Christ, American and Progressive National Baptist, and United and Christian Methodist churches are also concerned about the nation's moral agenda, but they see the issues facing the United States very differently:

On theological and ethical grounds, we object to the list of issues on which the religious right has identified as the moral
agenda facing our nation. We do not simply disagree with their
stance on particular items on their agenda; we find their selection of issues to be theologically and ethically inadequate. An
agenda identified by Christian believers ought to reflect God's
concern for the whole world. It ought to be consistent with
what God has revealed of Himself through the prophets and Jesus. It ought to be faithful to what Jesus called the "weightier
measures of the law." Our study of the biblical witness con-
vinces us that the God of the prophets and of Jesus calls the
people of God to work for peace and things that make for peace,
to seek justice for the poor, and to care for the created order.
What God wills for our common life is at heart a theological
question. We regard the theology of the religious right, expressed in their choice of issues for Christian concern, as un-
faithful to the fullness of biblical witness.[3]

The statements of Jerry Falwell and the group of religious leaders
reflect the depth of the moral chasm that divides the American religious communities. At a time when traditional *social* sources that
have divided religious groups are showing some signs of diminishing
significance, *moral* concerns are increasing in importance. At issue,
as the statement of the Protestant leaders suggests, is not only a particular position on a moral issue but the definition of what consti-
tutes morality itself. Lacking is any agreement over the fundamental link between religious and public morality. In this chapter we
"map" the moral struggles by looking at the growing tension between moral traditionalists and those advocating more libertarian,
freewill positions within the religious mainline. We deal first with
tolerance of nonconformists and racial minorities and later with
openness to changes in the roles of women and in personal morality.

Tolerance

The principle of religious freedom is implicit in the
notion of denominationalism. As Sidney E. Mead has emphasized,[4]
the principle itself owes its origin to a confluence of interests in the

eighteenth century between deistic intellectuals and evangelical Christians, the former concerned to protect the new American nation from the excesses of religious activism and the latter wanting freedom to "win the continent for Christ." Maintaining a balance between these two interests is essential to religious pluralism, and every period of the nation's history, at least from the early 1800s to the present, has reflected some mix of these themes.

In recent times this balance has undergone major shifts in ways that are both more and less progressive. On the one hand, the social and economic changes noted earlier, for example, the upward mobility of Catholics and secular nonaffiliates and their movement into the cultural mainstream and generally rising levels of education, have led to greater tolerance and have improved intergroup relations, particularly between whites and blacks and between Protestants and Catholics. Stereotypes and prejudices that once existed have declined. At the same time, the decline of liberal optimism and a turn to more conservative ideologies have aroused fears, polarized segments of the population, and opened new cleavages between religious traditionalists and secularists. The ideological shifts have brought about deep strains between liberals and conservatives in the religious establishment.

Civil Liberties

Along with freedom of speech, press and assembly, the right to petition one's government for grievances, and the right to bear arms, religious pluralism has stood historically as a hallmark of individual civil liberties. Acceptance of religious pluralism in principle has not always, of course, been lived out in practice; the majority culture's treatment of religious minorities has often fallen short of the ideals expressed in the Bill of Rights. Baptists, Quakers, Catholics, Jews, Mormons, Jehovah's Witnesses, Black Muslims, agnostics, and atheists have all, at one time or another, suffered harsh treatment at the hands of groups more convinced of the rightness of their own religious convictions than of the legitimacy of pluralism. Yet over the years there has been greater inclusion in American life as one group after another has been extended the core civil liberties enjoyed by the majority. With the reemergence of conservative evangelicalism as a social and religious force in American life, new attention is being given to the character and limits of religious pluralism. Upset by a sense that the culture is adrift from its moral foundations, groups that once felt themselves consigned to the periphery of American life have pressed for reconsideration of the philosophical and institutional bases on which pluralism rests.

One of the main battlegrounds in this debate is the legislative and judicial controversy over reinstitution of public prayer in the nation's schools. In a 1985 Supreme Court decision, Associate Justice John Paul Stephens, writing for the majority invalidating an Alabama "moment of silence" law, reasserted the link between individual freedom and religious voluntarism:

> Just as the right to speak and the right to refrain from speaking are complementary components of a broader concept of individual freedom, so also the individual's freedom to choose his own creed is the counterpart of his right to refrain from accepting the creed established by the majority. At one time it was thought that this right merely proscribed the preference of one Christian sect over another, but would not require equal respect for the conscience of the infidel, the atheist, or the adherent of a non-Christian faith such as Mohammadanism or Judaism. But when the underlying principle has been examined in the crucible of litigation, the Court has unambiguously concluded that the individual freedom of conscience protected by the First Amendment embraces the right to select any religious faith or none at all.
>
> This conclusion derives support not only from the interest in respecting the individual's freedom of conscience, but also from the conviction that religious beliefs worthy of respect are the product of free and voluntary choice by the faithful, and from recognition of the fact that the political interest in forestalling intolerance extends beyond intolerance among Christian sects, or even intolerance among "religions," to encompass intolerance of the disbeliever and the uncertain.[5]

Implicit in the Court's opinion is an appreciation of the dependence of both individuals and religious bodies on the protection of religious and nonreligious minorities from the tyranny of the majority. Religious and secular response to the Court's decision was decidedly mixed: some found comfort in the Court's reassertion of the principle of religious toleration; others saw the decision as "another exercise of raw judicial power by unelected federal judges."[6] Both the range of responses and depth of feelings expressed indicate how sensitive a person's right to pray—or not to pray—has become.

One of the most extensive empirical studies of Americans' views of civil liberties over time is by Clyde Nunn, Harry Crockett, and J. Allen Williams.[7] They have documented significantly increased support for civil liberties among both the general public and community leaders. Looking at a 1973 national survey of Americans and contrasting it with Samuel Stouffer's similar study of 1954, Nunn found an increase in the percentage (from 31 percent fo 55 percent) of the population with "more tolerant" scores on a scale measuring willingness to tolerate nonconformists. Increasing tolerance was shown for virtually all population subgroups. Both studies found differences in tolerance among religious groups. In 1973, 88 percent of Jews, 87 percent of nonaffiliates, 59 percent of Catholics, and 46 percent of Protestants had "more tolerant" scores on the scale. Without question, the general public today is more tolerant than in earlier decades.

The Nunn study shows clearly, however, that active religious participants have consistently lower tolerance scores than less active members. Religious persons, whether Protestant, Catholic, or Jewish, are more intolerant. Examining changes over two decades shows that gains in tolerance among inactive group members have been greater than among regular church attenders. Nunn and his colleagues find the evidence consistent and telling: "Americans, both rank and file and local leaders, who are 'religious' . . . may view themselves as decent people who are ready to extend constitutional freedom to their fellow citizens, but the evidence does not confirm their self-image. Instead, they must be counted among the most intolerant of our society."[8]

Granted that religious populations are less tolerant than nonreligious, but are there variations in attitudes for the religious families? This question is addressed in table 6-1, which shows responses to General Social Survey items dealing with the rights of a person who is against all churches and religions, who is a Communist, or who is a homosexual.[9] A slight majority are willing to grant rights to these individuals, especially the right to make a speech in their community; the public is more opposed to removing a book written by

TABLE 6-1
RELIGIOUS GROUP MEMBERS VIEW CIVIL LIBERTIES

	Atheists			Communists			Homosexuals		
	Favor Right to Speak	Favor Right to Teach	Oppose Removing Book	Favor Right to Speak	Favor Right to Teach	Oppose Removing Book	Favor Right to Speak	Favor Right to Teach	Oppose Removing Book
National	**64**	**43**	**61**	**57**	**58**	**58**	**66**	**55**	**57**
Liberal Protestants	**75**	**48**	**75**	**68**	**45**	**71**	**75**	**62**	**70**
Episcopalians	84	56	82	76	52	81	82	68	80
United Church of Christ	71	47	73	73	40	69	71	54	63
Presbyterians	72	44	72	63	43	67	72	61	66
Moderate Protestants	**63**	**38**	**60**	**53**	**37**	**55**	**64**	**51**	**55**
Methodists	62	37	61	51	36	56	64	50	55
Lutherans	68	41	63	59	41	62	69	57	62
Christians (Disciples of Christ)	56	27	51	51	29	49	60	43	43
Northern Baptists	63	38	53	49	35	48	59	46	47
Reformed	45	28	46	40	28	44	52	38	51
Black Protestants	**53**	**35**	**49**	**53**	**45**	**49**	**60**	**53**	**51**
Methodists	52	32	51	48	42	51	56	44	46
Northern Baptists	63	42	57	61	50	57	72	64	60
Southern Baptists	45	32	41	48	41	42	51	46	46

TABLE 6-1 (continued)
RELIGIOUS GROUP MEMBERS VIEW CIVIL LIBERTIES

	Atheists			Communists			Homosexuals		
	Favor Right to Speak	Favor Right to Teach	Oppose Removing Book	Favor Right to Speak	Favor Right to Teach	Oppose Removing Book	Favor Right to Speak	Favor Right to Teach	Oppose Removing Book
Conservative Protestants	45	26	39	37	26	37	44	30	36
Southern Baptists	45	24	38	36	25	36	44	30	35
Churches of Christ	53	29	47	40	27	44	48	33	42
Evangelicals/Fundamentalists	51	35	48	42	34	52	52	41	43
Nazarenes	46	23	39	46	23	39	50	28	33
Pentecostals/Holiness	41	27	40	35	32	39	41	33	35
Assemblies of God	36	21	36	31	22	28	41	23	31
Churches of God	30	15	29	30	20	29	35	15	26
Adventists	64	49	48	58	33	50	65	50	47
Catholics	70	49	67	61	46	63	73	62	63
Jews	80	65	84	81	61	82	86	84	79
Others									
Mormons	78	53	74	63	45	67	71	54	57
Jehovah's Witnesses	73	54	71	62	59	69	50	45	52
Christian Scientists	89	64	92	81	54	87	81	84	81
Unitarian-Universalists	93	89	96	89	70	100	96	96	91
No religious preference	87	75	86	82	69	82	84	78	80

an atheist than by a Communist or a homosexual. Americans are slightly less likely to support allowing controversial persons to teach in a college or university; majorities oppose the firing of a Communist or homosexual, but only a minority favor the right to teach of a person who is against all churches and religions.

At the same time there is considerable variation among the religious families. Persons with no religious preference and Jews are quite supportive of nonconformists' rights to speak, to teach, and to have their books remain in a public library. Catholics are also above average in supporting individual liberties, although majorities oppose the teaching rights of antireligionists and Communists. Catholics are more tolerant than most Protestants. Among Protestants there are marked differences along theological and racial lines. Black Protestants are more supportive of the rights of homosexuals and Communists than of antireligionists. Liberal and moderate Protestants are less supportive of Communists than of other nonconforming groups: the conservative Protestant family is consistently the least supportive of individual liberties; overall, majorities oppose the speaking, teaching, and library rights of each category of nonconformists by roughly similar proportions. Within this family there is variation, with Adventists tending to be more willing to grant civil liberties to others than most other conservative bodies. Jehovah's Witnesses and Mormons—often persecuted for their own religious views—are relatively supportive of others with unconventional views.

To get a summary measure of intergroup differences we combined three of the items in table 6-1 into a civil liberties scale. The items included in the scale are concerned with the rights of a person who is against all churches and religions. Views on these issues tend to parallel those regarding the rights of Communists and homosexuals. The scale was constructed by giving each person one point for each pro—civil liberties position taken regarding an atheist's rights. A person who favored allowing such an individual to make a speech in his or her community, opposed firing an antireligionist from a college teaching position, and opposed removing a book written by such a person from the pulic library would receive a score of three. A person who gave the negative response on each issue would receive a score of zero. These scores were then adjusted to give the public as

FIGURE 6-1.

RELIGIOUS GROUP SCORES ON THE CIVIL LIBERTIES SCALE.

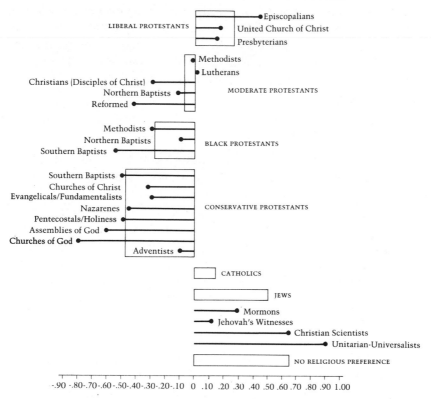

a whole a score of zero, with a range for most scores between plus and minus one.[10]

Figure 6-1 shows graphically the scores of families and individual denominations on the civil liberties scale. The scale is, in effect, a composite of member views of nonconformists, in this case some-one who is against all churches and religion.[11]

Four of the families have positive (pro–civil liberties) scores and three families have negative scores, indicating that members of the latter families are less supportive of nonconformists' rights than the general public. The secular nonaffiliates have the highest score, followed by Jews, liberal Protestants, and Catholics. The four smaller "other" groups also have positive scores; Unitarian-Universalists have the highest pro-tolerance score of any group. The moderate Protestant family score is slightly below the national mean, the black Protestant family is lower still, and the conservative Protestant family has the lowest score of all. Unquestionably there are significant differences among the major traditions of crucial importance to understanding the contemporary religious scene. The figure reveals as well some minor variation in support for civil liberties within the major families.

Racial Justice

While the formal rights of the nation's religious groups were established early in the nation's history, protection for legal rights of minority Americans was slower in coming. It took the nation "conceived in liberty, and dedicated to the proposition that all men are created equal" nearly one hundred years to eliminate slavery and another one hundred to translate the ideals of the Emancipation Proclamation into the Civil Rights Laws of 1964. Forced by the civil rights movement of the 1960s to face their own complicity in the denial of justice to minority citizens, America's churches and synagogues responded in various ways to what Niebuhr had noted three decades earlier:

> the sufficient reason for the frankness with which the color line has been drawn in the church is the fact that race discrimination is so respectable an attitude in America that it could be accepted by the church without subterfuge of any kind.[12]

From within their own midst, however, and from the outside—especially from leaders of the black churches—churches were forced to respond to new voices challenging the exclusion of persons from full participation in American life on the basis of the color of their skin. No voice was more persuasive than Martin Luther King, Jr's.:

> When we allow freedom to ring—when we let it ring from every city and every hamlet, from every state and every city, we will be able to speed up the day when all of God's children, black men and white men, Jews and Gentiles, Protestants and Catholics, will be able to join hands and sing in the words of the old Negro spiritual, "Free at last, Free at least, Great God Almighty, We are free at last."[13]

Though the separation of the races in the nation's churches continues, the climate of racial opinion has improved. Cultural attitudes have changed and discriminatory practices are less common. The mainline faiths are caught up in these changes, prompting us to ask: where do the various religious groups stand on issues facing blacks and other racial minorities?

The truth is that white America remains divided on matters of race. Seventy-three percent have no objection to black dinner guests in their home, 66 percent oppose laws prohibiting racial intermarriage, and 64 percent feel white homeowners have no right to exclude blacks from their neighborhoods (black respondents have been deleted from all tables dealing with minority rights). Only 40 percent, however, favor open housing laws that would guarantee blacks a right to purchase a home in a white neighborhood, and fully 70 percent agree with the statement that "blacks shouldn't push themselves where they're not wanted." Views vary depending on the specific racial issue. Table 6-2 shows these differences, both for the public at large and for religious groups.

Persons with no religious preference are the most supportive of black rights; a majority take a pro–civil rights position on every issue. Jews, Catholics, and liberal Protestants are also broadly supportive of blacks' rights, as are moderate Protestants by slightly smaller margins. Conservative Protestants are the least supportive. While many conservatives have no objection to black dinner guests in their homes, large majorities feel blacks should "not push themselves where they're not wanted," oppose open housing laws, and favor laws against interracial marriage. As seen earlier with respect to civil liberties, there is a tendency for groups that have themselves suffered persecution (Jews, Mormons, Catholics, Jehovah's Witnesses, and Adventists) to be supportive of rights for racial minorities.

Again we created a composite measure to show how groups vary in their commitment to racial justice. The scale was constructed of four items: acceptance of blacks as dinner guests, opposition to miscegenation laws, disagreement with the statement that blacks should not push for their rights, and support for open housing laws. Scores have been adjusted to give the sample as a whole a score of zero.[14]

Racial justice scores are shown graphically in figure 6-2 and fol-

TABLE 6-2

RELIGIOUS GROUP MEMBERS VIEW MINORITY RIGHTS

Religious Group	Blacks Shouldn't Push Where Not Wanted (disagree)	No Objection to Black Dinner Guest	Whites Have No Right to Exclude Blacks from Neighborhood	Opposed to Laws against Interracial Marriage	Favors Local Open Housing Laws
National	**30**	**73**	**64**	**66**	**40**
Liberal Protestants	**33**	**78**	**67**	**73**	**40**
Episcopalians	39	84	76	83	45
United Church of Christ	31	80	65	68	38
Presbyterians	31	75	64	69	38
Moderate Protestants	**26**	**72**	**65**	**60**	**38**
Methodists	24	69	63	57	36
Lutherans	30	74	68	67	36
Christians (Disciples of Christ)	22	74	66	58	41
Northern Baptists	25	74	67	56	43
Reformed	21	73	56	54	40

TABLE 6-2 (continued)
RELIGIOUS GROUP MEMBERS VIEW MINORITY RIGHTS

Religious Group	Blacks Shouldn't Push Where Not Wanted (disagree)	No Objection to Black Dinner Guest	Whites Have No Right to Exclude Blacks from Neighborhood	Opposed to Laws against Interracial Marriage	Favors Local Open Housing Laws
Conservative Protestants	**15**	**58**	**47**	**42**	**28**
Southern Baptists	14	52	45	37	23
Churches of Christ	17	64	60	54	29
Evangelicals/Fundamentalists	24	78	53	53	41
Nazarenes	23	60	55	45	44
Pentecostals/Holiness	15	68	44	51	40
Assemblies of God	17	77	51	54	33
Churches of God	15	56	41	34	29
Adventists	22	14	50	60	39
Catholics	**35**	**77**	**67**	**76**	**46**
Jews	**51**	**91**	**77**	**86**	**55**
Others					
Mormons	35	79	72	74	39
Jehovah's Witnesses	25	84	78	76	57
Christian Scientists	42	92	87	87	34
Unitarian-Universalists	68	100	80	93	54
No religious preference	52	85	78	84	56

FIGURE 6-2.

RELIGIOUS GROUP SCORES ON THE RACIAL JUSTICE SCALE.

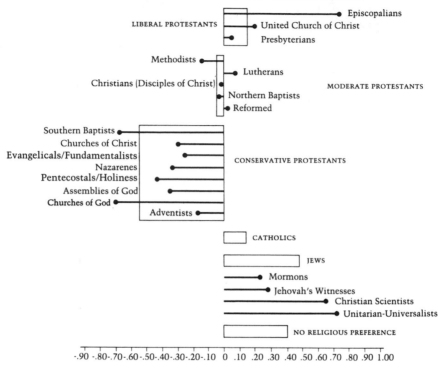

low the pattern for individual racial justice items: Jews and nonaffiliates are far above average in support of racial justice, liberal Protestants and Catholics are slightly above average, moderate Protestants score close to the national mean, and conservative Protestants are least supportive, with a score of -.56. Again, intrafamily variation is slight.

From our analysis it is evident that the major families of American religion are divided in their willingness to grant rights to ideological and racial minorities, and the divisions follow a consistent liberal-to-conservative spectrum:

Jews and nonaffiliates
Liberal Protestants

Catholics
Moderate Protestants
Black Protestants (in the case of civil liberties)
Conservative Protestants

Many factors influence a group's views on civil liberties and racial justice. Theological heritage is a factor, but important too are social background influences. Studies of civil liberties attitudes have shown fairly consistently, for example, that education, age, size of community, and region of the country are all associated with levels of tolerance for nonconformity. Three of these factors are among those cited by H. Richard Niebuhr as important "social sources" of denominationalism and continue to divide the nation's religious mainline. Given the close relationship between social and religious factors, one is led to ask whether the varying levels of tolerance are themselves a product of social backgrounds. For example, is the seeming insensitivity of conservative Protestants to civil liberties and racial justice a result of their members' low educational levels, concentration in the South, and rural residence? Conversely, does the greater liberalism of Jews follow from their higher levels of education, northern residence, and urban location?

To help answer this question we utilized a statistical procedure designed to sort out such possibilities.[15] While the technique is sophisticated, its purpose is simple. It asks what the scale score of a group would be if differences in social background were eliminated. In this case it "controls" for differences in years of education completed, regional concentration (South versus non-South), and size of community (in thousands of persons) among religious groups. To these we added age and gender, also shown in past studies to have a relationship to civil liberties and racial justice views.[16] Adjusted scores tell us whether group differences are essentially a product of varying social backgrounds or if they more truly reflect religious traditions.

In most cases the statistical adjustments bring civil liberties and racial justice scores closer to the national average. Table 6-3 shows that some of the variation found among the religious families results from differences in the social backgrounds of members. In the case of civil liberties, the greatest change is for nonaffiliates, whose average score moves 27 points closer to the national mean after con-

TABLE 6-3

CIVIL LIBERTIES AND RACIAL JUSTICE SCALE SCORES

	Civil Liberties		Racial Justice	
	Raw Score	Adjusted Score[a]	Raw Score	Adjusted Score[a]
Liberal Protestants	.26	.18	.17	.08
Moderate Protestants	−.06	−.04	−.03	−.03
Black Protestants	−.28	−.11	—	—
Conservative Protestants	−.48	−.31	−.56	−.26
Catholics	.14	07	.15	.09
Jews	.51	35	.47	.30
No religious preference	.65	38	.40	.20

[a] Adjusted for age, education, size of community, location in the South, and gender.

trols; this group's relative youth and high educational levels clearly contribute to its strong support for civil liberties. Similar change, although to a lesser degree, is seen for Jews. Adjusting for the social location of conservative and black Protestants also moves their scores toward the average. The low civil liberties scores of these two families are affected by their southern concentrations and low educational levels. With controls, they appear more supportive of civil liberties than without, although conservative Protestants remain by far the least open to the rights of nonconformists.

With racial justice scores, there is also movement of the families at the extremes toward the center, reflecting the more liberal racial views of younger persons, northerners, and those with more years of education. Conservative Protestants move 30 points toward the center (i.e., in a more liberal direction) on the racial justice scale, while those with no religious preference (20 points) and Jews (17 points) come closer to the national mean of zero from their pro–civil rights positions. Adjustments of the scores give some idea of how much a religious group's "contextual" characteristics contribute to its particular ideology or outlook.

Despite reductions in the amount of intergroup variation, sizable differences still remain. In this respect the adjusted scores are telling. Jews and nonaffiliates are the most tolerant, liberal Protestants and Catholics have above-average scores, moderate and black Protestants have scores slightly below average, and conservative Protestants are the least supportive of both civil liberties and racial justice.

Even with controls for social background characteristics, 49 points separate liberal and conservative Protestants in their civil liberties views, 37 points on racial justice. Religious subcultures differ markedly in their views aside from differences in their social backgrounds. The various constituencies, both religious and secular, foster among their members distinctive values, ethnocentric attitudes, and outlooks.

Morality

While levels of tolerance for nonconformists and minority groups have changed over time, the role of religion in maintaining respect for traditional understandings of family life and sexual behavior has remained fairly constant. In his classic study of symbolism in American culture, W. Lloyd Warner suggests that the reason lies in the close tie between religion and the family:

> If religious symbols are collective representations, reflecting at the supernatural level the collective realities of the group, most of those present in the sacred world to which Christians relate themselves are formed by, express, and reinforce the family structure. What the church is, Protestant or Catholic, its own self-conception, the image in which its members conceive themselves, as well as the sacred way of life which orders their relation to the church and to God—in short, the supernatural order of Christianity—is formed in, and nourished by, all or part of the family as a social and biological system. The church, its rites, beliefs and practices, would not exist if the family failed to survive.[17]

Beginning in the 1960s the ties between religion and traditional patterns of family life and personal moral values were increasingly challenged. In the society at large and in the churches, debate raged over one moral issue after another: more permissive sexual mores, homosexual rights, women's rights, abortion. It was a time, as Sydney Ahlstrom observed, of a "radical turn in theology and ethics,"[18] a period when the old foundations of moral traditionalism were awash. The debate came to center especially on the changing roles of women and the "new morality."

Women's Rights

The movement of women to secure equal rights was one of the most important developments in American society during the 1960s and 1970s. These decades saw sharp increases in the number of women graduating from colleges and universities, entering professions once thought to be the exclusive preserve of men, challenging male domination of decision-making structures in social institutions, and running in unprecedented numbers for public office. Congress passed an Equal Rights Amendment to the Constitution. Attitudes toward women entering into new roles improved. Throughout the country there was growing consciousness of new and expanding opportunities for women.

The drive for women's rights was not without opposition as women and men saw traditional sex roles challenged and traditional family life threatened. Nowhere was this opposition more obvious than in the fight against ratification of the Equal Rights Amendment by state legislatures. By the late 1970s battle lines had been drawn between feminists and a "profamily" movement dedicated to traditional relations between the sexes in the family and in society. Feminists stood not only for elimination of sex discrimination but also for the right to personal choice in matters of abortion and sexual preference. In contrast, "profamily" and "right-to-life" followers vigorously defended more conventional values of marriage, family life, and parental authority. For the New Christian Right, which surfaced during this period, the defense of the traditional family was seen as paramount and the key to a strong and moral America.

The churches were deeply affected by the women's movement and the controversies it generated. Several denominations that had prohibited the ordination of women (the Episcopal Church, American Lutheran bodies, the Reformed Church in America, and Reform and Conservative Judaism) reversed long-standing policies. Other churches saw dramatic increases in the number of women seeking ordination and professional placement. Women demanded representation on official boards at the parish and denominational levels and challenged sexist language in hymns and liturgies. Churches divided over the Equal Rights Amendment, with many groups affiliated with ecumenical bodies such as the National Council of Churches and the Catholic church supporting ratification and others, especially conservative Protestant evangelical and fundamentalist groups and Mormons, opposing it. Few issues sparked more heated debate in religious circles during this period.

That the women's movement would spark so much controversy within the churches is not surprising given the historic symbolic linkage between religious and family values. To the extent that the drive for equal rights and new roles for women was perceived as conflicting with attempts to restore the nuclear family to its central role in society, it would be a threat. Given the close relationship between family, religion, and nation and the threat, in the view of many, that the women's movement would change that symbolism, the debate over women's rights and roles continues to take on special importance within the religious communities.

Attitudes within churches are somewhat like those in the public at large. The American public is broadly supportive of women's efforts to attain equality in all aspects of social life. On some issues there is widespread consensus. Most people say they would vote for a woman nominated by their political party for president if she were qualified for the job, and they approve of the woman earning money in business even if she has a husband capable of supporting her. A majority also disagree with the statement that "Women should take care of running their own homes and leave running the country up to men." On these general issues there is broad support for greater opportunities for women.

On more specific issues the public is more divided. Forty-four percent believe that most men are better suited emotionally for politics than are most women, while 56 percent disagree. On abortion rights, an issue that has been important to many feminists, majorities favor a woman's right to obtain a legal abortion in some circumstances but oppose that right in others. Legal abortion is supported if a woman's health is seriously endangered, if there is a chance of a serious defect in the baby, if her pregnancy resulted from rape, and if low income prevents the family from being able to afford more children. It is opposed when the woman is not married and does not intend to marry the man, and when the woman is married but does not want more children.

The more specific the issue, the more the religious constituencies tend to be divided. Sizable majorities in each of the religious families say that they would support a woman candidate for president

TABLE 6-4
RELIGIOUS GROUP MEMBERS VIEW WOMEN'S RIGHTS

	Women Should Take Care of Home (disagree)	Both Women and Men Emotionally Fit for Politics	Approve Woman Working if Husband Can Support Her	Would Support Woman as Presidential Candidate	Favor Abortion in Case of Rape	Favor Abortion for Married Woman
National	**68**	**56**	**71**	**81**	**83**	**44**
Liberal Protestants	**78**	**61**	**79**	**83**	**95**	**62**
Episcopalians	80	68	85	86	95	68
United Church of Christ	80	64	82	86	95	60
Presbyterians	77	56	74	80	94	60
Moderate Protestants	**67**	**55**	**68**	**80**	**88**	**46**
Methodists	69	53	69	80	91	50
Lutherans	69	57	69	81	91	48
Christians (Disciples of Christ)	55	50	63	73	83	35
Northern Baptists	62	56	67	80	82	40
Reformed	48	49	58	80	71	27
Black Protestants	**62**	**53**	**69**	**82**	**77**	**35**
Methodists	60	47	68	81	73	33
Northern Baptists	71	58	71	83	81	46
Southern Baptists	56	52	67	81	60	28

TABLE 6-4 (continued)
RELIGIOUS GROUP MEMBERS VIEW WOMEN'S RIGHTS

	Women Should Take Care of Home (disagree)	Both Women and Men Emotionally Fit for Politics	Approve Woman Working if Husband Can Support Her	Would Support Woman as Presidential Candidate	Favor Abortion in Case of Rape	Favor Abortion for Married Woman
Conservative Protestants	**52**	**42**	**67**	**71**	**78**	**28**
Southern Baptists	54	40	70	70	82	32
Churches of Christ	56	51	60	73	82	25
Evangelicals/Fundamentalists	66	46	70	81	76	29
Nazarenes	49	53	63	78	82	26
Pentecostals/Holiness	43	44	57	71	57	18
Assemblies of God	49	33	69	60	74	16
Churches of God	49	30	67	72	63	21
Adventists	50	50	60	75	72	30
Catholics	**72**	**60**	**71**	**85**	**79**	**37**
Jews	**88**	**76**	**83**	**94**	**98**	**83**
Others						
Mormons	68	60	69	79	79	29
Jehovah's Witnesses	48	42	51	57	36	12
Christian Scientists	84	65	82	93	100	79
Unitarian-Universalists	94	75	91	100	100	94
No religious preference	**84**	**74**	**82**	**90**	**93**	**75**

and that they approve of women working outside the home and sharing in political leadership. Much the same pattern is seen at the level of "equality of opportunity"; it is fair to say that values and norms supporting women's rights are widely shared across the religious mainline. At the same time, less than half of the conservative and black Protestant family members, Jehovah's Witnesses, and Mormons believe women are as suited as men for political roles. Moderate Protestants, liberal Protestants, and Catholics are somewhat more likely to view women as emotionally qualified for public office; Jews and those with no religious preference are the most likely to give this response. This item, which concretely taps gender equality views, shows that responses vary along a conservative-to-liberal spectrum.

The greatest spread in responses is found on two abortion items —one is the case of a woman pregnant as a result of rape, the other a married woman who wants no more children. On the latter, especially, Americans are divided. Jews, nonaffiliates, and liberal Protestants favor abortion for a married woman not wanting more children; moderate Protestants tend not to favor such an abortion; Catholics, black Protestants, and conservative Protestants are strongly opposed. The divisions within Protestantism are strong, ranging from 62 percent of liberals favoring abortion rights in this instance to only 28 percent of conservatives. For a variety of cultural as well as theological reasons, the religious traditions are highly polarized over the abortion controversy. At present few issues evoke so strong and so divided a response among Americans.

Three of the items in table 6-4 were used to construct a scale tapping support for goals of the women's movement: approval of a woman working in business even if her husband is capable of supporting her; disagreement with the statement that men are better suited emotionally for politics than are women; and disagreement with the statement that women should take care of their homes and leave running the country to men. As with the other scales, the population as a whole has a score of zero and most scores range from one to minus one.[19]

Figure 6-3 shows Jews, nonaffiliates, and liberal Protestants to be more supportive of women's rights and new roles for women than the general public. Catholics, moderate Protestants, and black Protestants are close to the national average, with Catholics slightly more supportive and black Protestants less supportive. The conser-

FIGURE 6-3.
RELIGIOUS GROUP SCORES ON THE WOMEN'S RIGHTS SCALE.

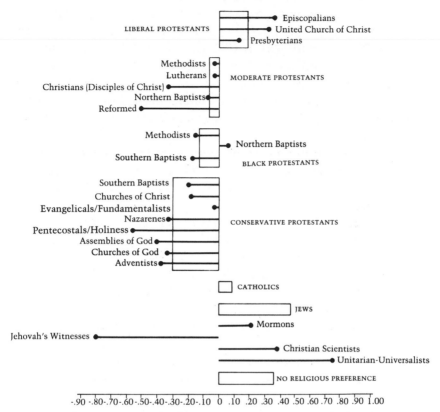

vative Protestant family is the least supportive of feminist goals. There are some intrafamily differences, but they tend not to be dramatic; far more important are the differences across families. The Protestant churches especially are divided, with liberal groups supportive, moderate and black Protestants occupying the middle ground, and conservative Protestants opposed to attempts to redefine women's traditional roles. Fully 52 points separate Protestant liberal and conservatives.

The New Morality

The women's movement is one important aspect of change that has aroused conservative religious concerns. Another concern is the alleged collapse of moral values and behavior, especially with respect to sexual practices. While Jerry Falwell's argument as reported at the beginning of this chapter may be overstated, there have been dramatic changes in sexual mores and practices. Examples abound. The number of legal abortions in the United States reached 1.6 million in 1981. A 1980 survey of 16,524 high school seniors found that 40 percent had experimented with marijuana or hashish more than once or twice; also the students viewed a man and woman living together without being married as "a worthwhile alternative life-style" (21 percent) or "doing their own thing and not affecting anyone else" (48 percent).[20] In 1980 the Census Bureau counted over 3.6 million persons living with persons of the opposite sex outside of marriage. Between 1960 and 1980 the divorce rate doubled. Sexual norms have changed markedly since the 1960s and diffused broadly in the culture.

Despite the changes in traditional moral views and the seeming inevitability of continued loosening of historic norms of personal behavior, it nonetheless came as a surprise to many Americans when the Moral Majority and other New Right groups emerged as a significant force in the 1980 and 1984 national elections. Historians will eventually look back on the 1980s and provide a perspective on the appearance of these grass-roots populist movements. Whether they appear in the body of the text as evidence of a major shift in the nation's moral consciousness and political structure or as mere footnotes alongside other ephemeral movemets in our national life is a question we cannot answer. What is clear is the extent to which the Moral Majority represents a direct challenge to the value and behavior changes that accompanied the baby-boom generation's transition to adulthood. With allies, they are engaged in a frontal attack on the "new morality" popularized by the post-1960s generation.

Table 6-5 shows six items that tap public sentiment regarding new morality issues. Various types of behavior having to do with greater personal freedom are described. Examination of national surveys since the mid-1960s shows that on these issues there has been a steady liberalization in outlook.[21]

Most Americans oppose each of the new morality positions described in the table. Support ranges from 24 percent who favor legalizing marijuana use to 37 percent who favor the unlimited right of a woman to obtain a legal abortion. Twenty-eight percent of the sample believe sexual relations involving a married person and someone

TABLE 6-5
RELIGIOUS GROUP MEMBERS VIEW MORAL AND SEXUAL ISSUES

Religious Group	Favor Abortion for Any Reason	Extramarital Sex Not Always Wrong	Premarital Sex Not Wrong	Homosexuality Not Always Wrong	Divorce Should Be Easier to Obtain	Marijuana Use Should Be Legalized
National	**37**	**28**	**35**	**27**	**29**	**24**
Liberal Protestants	**53**	**34**	**35**	**36**	**30**	**24**
Episcopalians	63	42	43	45	32	28
United Church of Christ	53	31	30	32	30	20
Presbyterians	48	31	33	31	28	24
Moderate Protestants	**37**	**23**	**29**	**23**	**20**	**20**
Methodists	41	25	27	23	21	18
Lutherans	38	25	32	26	21	21
Christians (Disciples of Christ)	31	16	23	18	19	16
Northern Baptists	34	22	28	21	20	22
Reformed	13	9	32	14	14	13
Black Protestants	**29**	**31**	**50**	**21**	**54**	**26**
Methodists	17	25	49	15	46	32
Northern Baptists	38	34	60	25	54	32
Southern Baptists	26	30	42	14	57	19

TABLE 6-5 (continued)
RELIGIOUS GROUP MEMBERS VIEW MORAL AND SEXUAL ISSUES

Religious Group	Favor Abortion for Any Reason	Extramarital Sex Not Always Wrong	Premarital Sex Not Wrong	Homosexuality Not Always Wrong	Divorce Should Be Easier to Obtain	Marijuana Use Should Be Legalized
Conservative Protestants	**21**	**14**	**19**	**11**	**21**	**12**
Southern Baptists	25	13	20	13	21	12
Churches of Christ	24	17	20	8	13	15
Evangelicals/Fundamentalists	24	14	22	10	28	16
Nazarenes	12	10	21	12	16	7
Pentecostals/Holiness	14	19	18	8	28	13
Assemblies of God	9	11	22	3	11	8
Churches of God	18	12	16	6	26	8
Adventists	27	10	21	12	22	10
Catholics	**32**	**30**	**36**	**31**	**26**	**25**
Jews	**76**	**51**	**56**	**64**	**40**	**42**
Others						
Mormons	25	12	25	15	20	14
Jehovah's Witnesses	11	12	16	5	18	13
Christian Scientists	75	38	44	54	20	47
Unitarian-Universalists	91	78	48	90	41	55
No religious preference	**68**	**59**	**66**	**60**	**52**	**57**

other than his or her spouse are acceptable under some circumstances; 35 percent view premarital sexual relations as acceptable; and 27 percent believe sexual relations between two adults of the same sex are not always wrong. About the same proportion believes divorce should be easier to obtain than it is now. As we might expect, however, there are sharp differences among religious groups on virtually every issue. On abortion rights, Unitarian-Universalists, Jews, Christian Scientists, and persons with no religious preference are the most supportive. Liberal Protestant family members support abortion rights, as do more than a third of moderate Protestants. While the Catholic church has been a strong opponent of abortion (a position with which a majority of lay Catholics agree), fully 32 percent of Catholic members approve of "abortion on demand."[22] Conservative and black Protestant family members are least supportive of such rights.

On the three sexuality items, views are consistent. Those with no religious preference, Jews, and Unitarian-Universalists are most open to extramarital, premarital, and homosexual sexual relations. Liberal Protestants are slightly more liberal on extramarital and homosexual relationships, while moderate Protestants generally resist new morality positions. Black Protestants tend to vary more than other groups on the three nontraditional patterns of sexual relationships. Members of black churches are more accepting of premarital and extramarital relationships but less accepting of homosexuality than the general public. Conservative Protestants are most resistant of all the groups, with only 19 percent finding premarital sex acceptable, 14 percent finding extramarital relations acceptable, and 11 percent viewing homosexuality as not always wrong. Black Protestants and religious nonaffiliates are the most likely to favor making divorce easier to obtain (as opposed to making divorce more difficult or leaving existing laws intact). Jews are also more likely than the general public to favor more lenient divorce laws. Liberal Protestants are close to the nation as a whole in their views on divorce laws, while moderate Protestants, Catholics, and conservative Protestants are less likely to favor changes. Most of the groups oppose by wide margins the legalization of marijuana, although a majority of those with no religious preference and Unitarian-Universalists favor decriminalization. Jews are more favorably disposed to legalization than other mainline groups; liberal and black Protestants are

FIGURE 6-4.

RELIGIOUS GROUP SCORES ON THE NEW MORALITY SCALE.

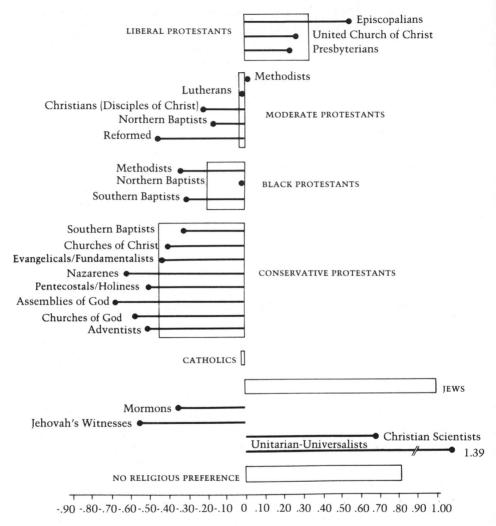

slightly more likely to favor legalization than moderate and conservative Protestants, who are strongly opposed.

The movement seeking a return to traditional moral norms has considerable support from a number of religious groups. The new morality has made its greatest inroads among those with no religious preference, Unitarian-Universalists, and Jews, and to a lesser extent among liberal Protestants, but the base of traditional morality remains strong within most mainline groups and especially among Protestant conservatives. Given the size of these collectivities and their commitment to conventional values and life-styles, there appears to be little evidence of a radical shift in the moral posture of middle America.

In constructing the new morality scale we used three items: support for unrestricted legal abortion; the view that a married person having sexual relations with someone other than the marriage partner is not always wrong; the view that sexual relations between two adults of the same sex is not always wrong. Scores were adjusted to give the population an average score of zero.[23]

Generally the scores follow the patterns observed earlier and underscore our conclusions. Unitarian-Universalists, those with no religious preference, and Jews have by far the highest scores. Liberal Protestants are the only other major family with a positive score; this family's three groups are all more liberal than the general public on issues of personal morality. Catholics and moderate Protestants have nearly identical scores, falling just below the mean. The base for traditional morality is stronger for black Protestants and conservative Protestants. By far those most opposed to new morality views are the predominantly white conservative Protestants, whose scores range from −.39 for Southern Baptists to −.66 for Assemblies of God members.

What about social background factors? Previously we noted that a religious group's position on ideological issues reflects a myriad of influences. Group differences on the civil liberties and racial justice scales lessened with statistical controls for age, education, community size, gender, and region of the country, although the basic patterns remained intact. Table 6-6 shows what happens when similar controls are introduced on the feminism and new morality scales. The family scores move closer to the national average score of zero as a result of statistical adjustments.

In the case of women's rights, adjusting for social background reduces the variation in feminist views, but the patterns among families remain essentially the same. Jews, nonaffiliates, and liberal Protestants remain the most supportive. The greatest change in score occurs for the nonaffiliates; it reduces from +.33 to +.10. This change reflects the youth, high educational levels, and regional

TABLE 6-6

WOMEN'S RIGHTS AND NEW MORALITY SCALE SCORES

	Women's Rights		New Morality	
	Raw Score	Adjusted Score[a]	Raw Score	Adjusted Score[a]
Liberal Protestants	.22	.13	.32	.26
Moderate Protestants	−.06	−.04	−.06	−.04
Black Protestants	−.10	.03	−.20	−.11
Conservative Protestants	−.30	−.16	−.45	−.33
Catholics	.09	.03	−.01	−.06
Jews	.47	.31	1.00	.82
No religious preference	.33	.10	.81	.66

[a] Adjusted for age, education, size of community, location in the South, and gender.

concentration outside the South of the "unchurched" population. Scores for Catholics, moderate Protestants, and black Protestants remain close to the national average. A considerable proportion of the low scores for black Protestants is accounted for by social background; after statistical controls, the negative score turns positive. Of the major families, Protestant conservatives remain the least supportive of women's rights. Although this constituency's score moves closer those of other groups, it remains negative. The patterns make clear the solid base of moderate-to-conservative opinion on this issue.

With new morality, in most cases the statistical controls bring the families' scores closer to the national mean by lowering high scores and raising those that are low. There are a few exceptions. Jews and nonaffiliates retain their very high scores. The Catholic score decreases slightly, from −.01 to −.06. Catholics are relatively young, urban, well educated, and located outside the South; the reduction in scores suggests that Catholics are less liberal in their personal moral views than others who share their social location. Most striking, however, are the differences among the Protestant families, even after controlling for the backgrounds of members. Fully 59 points separate the Protestant liberals and conservatives, with moderates remaining close to average and blacks slightly below average in acceptance of new moral views. The split within Protestantism is deeply rooted and mirrors the range of moral views now prevalent in the society.

If the Moral Majority and related movements are viewed as a reaction to the changing family and the loosening of traditional moral values that gained currency with the emergence of the postwar baby-boom generation during the 1960s and 1970s, the evidence reviewed here provides insight into the nature of the movement's institutional support base. Opposition to these changes is centered among those groups that have provided leadership and support to the Moral Majority and the new religious right: conservative Protestants, Mormons and, to a lesser extent, Catholics and members of black and moderate Protestant groups. Jews, some liberal Protestants, and the more secularized constituency of persons not having a religious preference are more open to value changes that have crystallized in the past two decades. Considering the depth of sentiment both favoring and opposing these changes in the general public, it is not surprising that they should emerge as important sources of division in the religious mainline in the 1980s.

Churched and Unchurched

Ever since Samuel Stouffer's widely read *Communism, Conformity, and Civil Liberties,* empirical research has demonstrated an inverse relationship between active religious involvement and tolerance. Going to church (or synagogue) in America is seen as conforming behavior often associated with conventional values and attitudes. As Gerhard Lenski has observed,[24] communal religious involvement tends to foster traditional views that are often parochial and narrow-minded. The question thus becomes: To what extent are the group attitudes on civil liberties, racial justice, women's rights, and new morality a reflection of differences in levels of religious involvement?

In chapter 3 we saw that the constituencies vary in institutional commitment and group attachments. Conservative Protestants, for example, go to church more frequently and are more involved in congregational activities than are liberals; Catholics are far more active than Jews. This being the case, we must examine separately the patterns for the "churched" and the "unchurched." As shown in table 6-7 and 6-8, churchgoers are generally more traditional in their attitudes than nonchurchgoers.

TABLE 6-7

ACTIVE AND NOMINAL MEMBERS ON CIVIL
LIBERTIES AND RACIAL JUSTICE

	Civil Liberties		Racial Justice	
	Active Members	Nominal Members	Active Members	Nominal Members
Total	−.15	.23	−.04	.04
Liberal Protestants	.20	.32	.19	.05
Moderate Protestants	−.15	.07	−.03	−.11
Black Protestants	−.33	−.17	—	—
Conservative Protestants	−.54	−.34	−.57	−.60
Catholics	.10	.34	.11	.20
Jews	.43	.55	.44	.47

Active church members differ in outlook from nominal members, but religious involvement by itself does not explain why the groups differ as they do. The religious families persist as carriers of distinctive cultural traditions. Usually the more active members exemplify best those values and norms, but not always. Patterns are far from uniform and thus call for specific comment.

Civil liberties scores, in general, are lower for active members than for the nominal members. While the churched, or regular worship attenders, are less tolerant than the unchurched (those attending services less often than once or twice a year), this does not account fully for civil liberties differences among families. Rank orders on tolerance are similar for actives and nominals. Among actives, Jews are the most tolerant, followed by Catholics and liberal Protestants. Moderate, black, and especially conservative Protestants are less tolerant. The ranking among inactives is similar, although nominal Catholics are somewhat more supportive of civil liberties than those who attend services regularly. Interfamily differences among nominal members are somewhat smaller than those among actives. Perhaps the most important finding in the table is the dramatic difference between active liberal and conservative Protestants: 74 points separate these two groups of active members.

Racial justice patterns are mixed. Active members are less tolerant than nonparticipants, but religious participation varies in its effects on racial justice. Church participation seems to contribute to support of minority rights for members of some groups, but is associated with more racist attitudes for others. Active members of the more liberal Protestant families appear less racist than inactive members. There are only slight differences between active and inactive Jews, but inactive Catholics are more supportive of blacks than are those who are active. Church activity makes no significant difference for conservative Protestants. The overall ranks for active and inactive family members follow what is now the familiar liberal-to-conservative spectrum. Again, over 70 points separate active liberal and conservative Protestants.

On the feminism scale, those who attend worship services regularly are less supportive of women's rights than those who do not attend. Once again there is wide variation among active Protestants. Fully 62 points separate liberal and conservative Protestant churchgoers; only 25 points separate the inactive members of the two groups. Active liberal Protestants are more supportive of women's rights than nominal members of this family, while active conservative Protestants are less supportive than nominal members. In both cases, active members best exemplify the views associated with the religious groups. They represent the ideological extremes in the contemporary moral and religious environment, while the differences are more blurred for the nominal members. In a sense this is not terribly surprising. The older mainline churches have been active and visible in support of the Equal Rights Amendment, abortion rights, and, in recent years, the ordination of women. Evangelical and fundamentalist Protestant bodies have tended to take opposing positions, viewing the feminist movement as a threat to the traditional family. To a considerable extent there is congruence between the public stances of organized religious groups and the views of their active constituents.

New morality differences are the greatest of the four clusters of issues examined here: actives tend to oppose unconventional moral positions with a score of $-.18$, while nominal family members are more supportive of nontraditional moral behavior, scoring a $+.33$. Recent studies of the reasons some Americans participate actively in religious groups while others do not have pointed to the importance of views on moral and life-style issues. The "churched" and "unchurched" differ on such issues more than on theological and doctrinal issues.[25]

In every family, new morality scores for nominal members are

TABLE 6-8
ACTIVE AND NOMINAL MEMBERS ON WOMEN'S
RIGHTS AND THE NEW MORALITY

| | Women's Rights | | New Morality | |
	Active Members	Nominal Members	Active Members	Nominal Members
Total	−.07	.12	−.18	.33
Liberal Protestants	.25	.15	.24	.42
Moderate Protestants	−.11	.02	−.16	.16
Black Protestants	−.14	.04	−.25	−.02
Conservative Protestants	−.37	−.10	−.52	−.24
Catholics	.07	.14	−.14	.31
Jews	.40	.47	.80	1.23

higher than those for active members. The differences in some instances are strong. Active moderate Protestants and Catholics have negative scale scores, while nominal members of the same families have positive scores; for moderates the difference is 32 points and for Catholics it is fully 45 points. These differences underscore the deep divisions on these issues within middle America's religious traditions. Because they occupy the nation's middle ground, the churches of the Protestant center as well as the Catholic church mirror to an unusual degree the strains and conflicts of the larger social order.

Generally the results point to the important role of religious traditions as subcultures. The churches are carriers of distinctive values and norms, the content of which depends in part on the social locations of their members. Even among those whose level of churchgoing is low and whose group attachments are weak, the traditions persist and sustain their own particular constellations of moral and cultural views. The relationship between religious involvement and the family subcultures is complex and ever changing. For the most part, such involvement reinforces group ideological divisions—the greatest being those between active liberal and conservative Protestants. Socioreligious involvement does not necessarily, however, result in a more conservative stance. Often it does, as with civil liberties and new morality views, but as we observed with racial views, involvement can also be a liberalizing influence. This is the case for

Protestant liberals—no doubt in large part because of the strong stand taken on civil rights by clergy and church leaders.

Switching and Morality

In our discussion of the changing demographics of the religious mainline we looked at recent patterns of denominational switching. To the extent that religious voluntarism has resulted in a sharpening of moral differences within the religious mainline, we might expect to observe differences among those who switch between religious families. To examine this possibility we looked at scores for switchers on the four scales introduced in this chapter. The results are revealing and for the most part point to movement toward ideological consistency among family members. "Converts" tend to reflect the social and moral views of their new family—no matter what their origins. Those who switch are more similar to the groups they switch to than to those they leave behind. As a result, switching contributes to the sharpening of moral and ideological divisions among the families of the American religious mainline.

The evidence of ideological switching is greatest among Protestants, and is observed in both liberal-to-conservative and conservative-to-liberal movement as well as in switching from the non-affiliated. We observe that the liberals differ significantly from the conservatives. The profiles for the two types of switchers are indeed quite striking.

On the new morality scale especially, the differences are marked: fully 88 points separate the two types of switchers in the movement among families (see table 6-9), and 103 points divide them among former nonaffiliates (see table 6-10). Apparently joiners are even more committed to the values of the new group than are those who have been part of the group from birth. For the most part liberal Protestant newcomers resemble persons raised in these groups; they tend to accentuate ideological and cultural styles. Not only on new morality values but on the other indexes as well, the views of the switchers are apparent. In many ways conservative Protestants are the liberals' mirror image. Persons joining conservative churches are

TABLE 6-9

SWITCHING TO LIBERAL AND CONSERVATIVE PROTESTANTISM

| | Switchers from Other Families to: | |
Scale	Liberal Protestantism	Conservative Protestantism
New morality	.37	− .51
Civil liberties	.27	− .51
Women's rights	.31	− .31
Racial justice	.14	− .39

consistently more conservative in moral views, civil liberties, women's rights, and racial views. For other families the differences are not so marked. There are fewer differences distinguishing those switching in or out of moderate Protestantism, whose scores tend to parallel those of the "average" American. Among Catholics, both "new" and "old" members have fairly similar views, although those switching in from other families to Catholics are slightly more liberal on feminist issues.

Equally revealing is the consistent liberalism of those switching to no religious preference (see table 6-11). Those who drop out are far more liberal than those who retain a religious affiliation. This is even true of conservative Protestant dropouts, who are less liberal than those other "former" members of other families, but considerably more liberal than those who retain a conservative connection. The contrasts between those who stay within the religious system and those who leave are sharpest on new morality views.

The switching patterns are striking, both in magnitude and consistency, and contribute to the emerging gulf between religious and

TABLE 6-10

SWITCHING FROM NO PREFERENCE TO LIBERAL
AND CONSERVATIVE PROTESTANTISM

| | Switchers from No Preference to: | |
Scale	Liberal Protestantism	Conservative Protestantism
New morality	.32	− .71
Civil liberties	.28	− .67
Women's rights	.74	− .50
Racial justice	.42	− .37

TABLE 6-11
THE NEW MORALITY SCALE AND SWITCHERS
TO NO RELIGIOUS PREFERENCE

Family	Nonswitchers	Switchers to No Religious Preference
Liberal Protestants	.28	1.06
Moderate Protestants	− .05	.83
Black Protestants	− .20	.22
Conservative Protestants	− .43	.32
Catholics	− .01	.96
Jews	1.02	1.37

secular cultures in contemporary American society. Those leaving the churches often feel hampered by the life-styles of church members and seek greater freedom in matters of personal behavior. Personal moral concerns may be paramount for this growing nonaffiliated sector of the population, but they are not the only issues: they overlap with other ideologically based nonconventional attitudes. Switching to nonaffiliation, for example, is also accompanied by greater support for civil liberties, women's rights, and racial justice. The church is a symbol of conventionality, and in a time when many have rebelled against conventionality, not surprisingly the church suffers from that rebellion.

A Mosaic of Moral Communities

In his provocative essay on moral philosophy, *After Virtue*, Alasdair MacIntyre argues that with the rise of modernity has come a fragmentation of meanings attached to moral concepts.[26] Moral discourse has become problematic because those who engage in it use different languages rooted in different notions of morality. Unitary conceptions have broken down, and increasingly participants in such discussions talk past one another. Moral philosophy, he argues, must therefore examine the contexts and uses of moral language: meanings vary depending on the situations out of which they arise and the interpretations given to them. Much the same can be said about the moral rhetoric of today's religious communities.

With the breakdown of the social and cultural consensus in the 1960s, moral values rooted in religious faith have become fragmented. Modern individualism fosters a view of moral judgments as expressions of *preference*, paralleling at the ethical level what is a fundamental conviction of Americans about religious faith itself. The resurgence of "old-fashioned" religion and morality and the sharpening of lines between faith and secularity in the past two decades have contributed to greater moral pluralism and a climate of confrontation. Indeed, faith presents itself to the modern world more often in moral language than in creed or doctrine. Moral concepts and symbols have become highly charged and expressive. To take a position on an emerging ethical issue is for many a religious act, a way of affirming what is in essence a deeply felt religious conviction about who they are and what they stand for.[27] Moral fragmentation suggests a deeper disjunction between culture and structure, between the traditional systems of meaning and actual realities of people's lives. Individual and group experiences are increasingly differentiated in a complex society, making it difficult for persons to agree on common meanings, much less to affirm them. Civil religious discourse becomes as much a source of division and discord than of cohesion; moral and religious rhetoric generally becomes pluralized and restricted to specific, essentially private, subcultures. The result is a "moral denominationalism," or religious communities distinguished by contrasting ethical styles and moral views.

At present, a mapping of the ideological spectrum of America's religious mainline looks something like this:

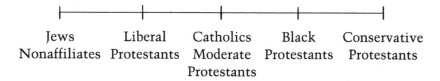

	Jews	Liberal	Catholics	Black	Conservative
Nonaffiliates		Protestants	Moderate	Protestants	Protestants
			Protestants		

On the left are Jews and persons with no religious preference. There are, of course, important differences among these constituencies, yet in social ideology and outlook on personal morality their positions are similar. Jews are internally divided along denominational lines and appear to have become more conservative in recent years; nonetheless they remain America's most consistently liberal religious or ethnic group. Jews are decidedly more liberal than other groups on a variety of issues, including, beyond those reviewed in this chapter, gun control, school prayer, tuition tax credits, the nuclear freeze, and defense spending.[28] Many sources of Jewish liberalism, both religious and historical, are identifiable, but none is more important than this family's efforts at integration into American society. American Jews, especially the liberal-to-moderate majority, have long held that integration would be fostered by advancing the tolerant pluralism of middle-class liberalism and adopting a universalistic ethic, allowing them at least nominal continued identification as Jews. Jews thus tend to be liberal in matters of civil liberties and personal morality, though less so where group interests are at stake, such as when affirmative action on behalf of blacks and other racial minorities is involved.

Nonaffiliates are also a diverse constituency, made up of secularists who claim no religion and others whose faith is so privatized that they retain little or no connection with organized religion. They are very liberal on issues of civil liberties, women's liberation, and personal morality. Quests for social and economic justice are important, as is openness in matters of personal moral behavior. Themes of self-fulfillment and sensitivity to interpersonal relationships appeal to a young, educated, middle-class clientele who, exposed to the idealism and expectation of the cultural changes of the 1960s, have had to face the realities of the "adult" world of bureaucratic constraints.[29] An expressive ethic and secular utilitarian values seem to fulfill many of the needs that others meet by more conventional moral and religious commitments. A cosmopolitan outlook, strong commitment to liberal causes, and weak ties to organized religion characterize nonaffiliates and Jews and thus contribute to their labeling by some as secular humanists.

At the opposite end of the spectrum are the conservative Protestants. Though hardly a religious or cultural monolith, they have been pulled together by a common enemy—secular humanism. As Carole Flake puts it: "For the fundamentalist crusader, secular humanism [has] become the source of all the sins of America, the multiformed beast of modern liberalism: the cold idol of godless science; the brazen serpent of pornography and homosexuality; the unpainted temptress of women's liberation; the meddling giant of big government."[30]

Moral rhetoric is for the conservatives a powerful and unifying force; secular concerns are translated into moral causes, and moral causes into political platforms. Recharging the old symbols of civil religion, conservatives have gone on the offensive in seeking to restore morality to the public realm and in a renewed commitment to a "Christian America." As the bearers of a tradition of personal moral purity, they have sought to overcome the excesses of privatism and the threats of unbridled pluralism. The fact that so many evangelicals and fundamentalists are now more securely positioned socially and economically adds to a sense of responsibility for the nation and furthers a view of themselves as the new moral custodians of the culture.

The middle consists primarily of Catholics and Protestant moderates. Being more at the center, both constituencies suffer from internal divisions; pluralism is very much a reality for them— theologically, culturally, morally. In many respects an "embattled middle," these families, roughly half the American population, are the folks whose sympathies are with neither the Moral Majority nor those who proclaim themselves members of the "Immoral Minority." These groups are deeply bound to the creed of middle America, to belief in the American Way of Life, and to the celebration of fundamental moral values that lean in a conservative direction on personal and life-style issues and in a more liberal direction on matters of social justice. Commitment to core values remains strong: "individual freedom, personal independence, human dignity, community responsibility, social and political democracy, sincerity, restraint in outward conduct, thrift . . . the uniqueness of the American order, and the great importance assigned to religion."[31] The culture prevails over religion in the sense that the normative faiths articulate and legitimate fundamental mainstream values and moral attitudes. Even among Catholics, whose institutional commitments and constraints are still stronger than those of Protestants, there seems to be little question about the direction American-style voluntarism is taking the church on moral issues. While Pope John Paul II may call for traditional norms in the areas of personal and sexual morality, few American bishops and priests appear to be attempting to "shape up" the laity to the point of realigning their beliefs and practices.

Two families must be seen at one side or the other of the cultural and religious middle: black and liberal Protestants. By virtue of its distinct racial experience, black Protestantism engenders a moral and religious style unlike that of any Protestant grouping. The ideology and praxis of this distinctive religious subculture champion the progressive religious tradition as the moral expression most favorable to black aspirations. Sometimes passive in mood, sometimes active, but always sensitive to the plight of its people, black Protestantism has provided the symbols and institutional structures for mounting a challenge to racial injustice. The disjunction between American ideals of equality and opportunity and the actual experience of blacks is the cauldron out of which moral passions continue to flame. On broad issues of civil liberties and personal morality, views of blacks tend to be conservative. A strong folk religious tradition and a more deprived social and economic base sustain its more moderate moral style.

Liberal Protestants are clearly left of center, but not as far left as Jews and secularists. This positioning helps account for strains currently evident in this community: it is "stretched" between the religious mainstream and elements of the secular, even more leftward culture. In ethical stance the liberal Protestant tradition still bears the legacy of its historical concern for social and political issues, making "the cure of souls" almost a lost art within the tradition.[32] As with the secular psychotherapies, personal autonomy and moral relativism are highly prized in personal life, though more for reasons having to do with a critique of middle-class conventionality than because of any positive theological ethic. But in public affairs the thrust is more activist and absolutist, motivated by strong reformist impulses. The result is a disjointed ethic, with the standards applied to social issues differing from the standards applied to private matters. Indeed, the private and public realms for liberal Protestantism have come so uncoupled that the tradition has lost much of its ability to mobilize personal energies on behalf of public causes.

In one way or another, all the religious communities mirror disjunctions between moral culture and the existential reality of contemporary life. The symbols, language, and forms of moral action abound, but lacking is any consistent moral and cultural cohesion. Specific groups and traditions use the symbols to frame, articulate, and legitimate their particular moral and political visions. Considerable energy is expended in the process of what is a rather fluid plu-ralistic "moral marketplace," each group competing with the others for the allegiance and support of freely opting individuals. And there is little doubt that moral pluralism of the sort described here will be around for a while. Prospects for a restored order or a newly inte-grated vision of public and private life, at least in the immediate fu-ture, seem slim. The forces of modernity leading to ever-greater plu-ralism and privatization of religious and moral life show few signs of abating, and those religious traditions most capable of providing an integrated cultural ethic are themselves lacking in the vision and vigor to do so.

Chapter Seven

The Future of the Mainline

My strategy is to consolidate the various name brands, even the strong flagship brands like Southern Baptist into one identifiable, Exxon-like entity. The target audience here is Mom, Dad, Butch and Sis—solid suburban Americans who want a little God in their life and a place to go before brunch. And after test-marketing various possibilities, I have decided upon the name Middle American Christian Church, or MacChurch for ad purposes. I will not be sure of MacChurch's theology until focus groups are run, but I plan on following the promotional path blazed so successfully by Holiday Inn. In other words, this will be your "no surprises" church. When Dad brings the family here, he can be sure that they will not be asked to speak in tongues, handle snakes, or give money to the Sandinistas.
                                                    —JACK CASHILL

Changes in the shape of the American religious mainline have stimulated new interest in its future. With tongue in cheek, Kansas City advertising executive Jack Cashill entertained readers of the *Wall Street Journal* with a "marketing plan" for revitalizing America's major religious faiths.[1] Among his proposals: for Judaism, a new denominational branch for baby-boomers; for Roman Catholicism, a "market segmentation" approach—RC Light for post–Vatican II liberals, RC Classic for traditionalists, and RC Free "for those more interested in liberation theology than in Papal Bulls." Protestantism, he says, presents marketers with special problems: "the individual churches will have to understand that there is just so much theological shelf space, that product differentiation is not viable for go-as-you-please Protestantism." Thus, the middle American Christian Church or "MacChurch."

Our intention in this final chapter is not to present an alternative marketing plan, but to offer some comments about the future of the American religious mainline. We look first at demographic trends in the nation's major religious families and at how the changes set in motion in this country since the 1960s will alter the religious and cultural scene in the years ahead. Second, we probe the changing composition and character of the "religious establishment." Finally, we examine the future of denominationalism in an age dominated by the new voluntarism in religion.

Demographic Projections

Our examination of the demographics of American religion shows six key trends underway.

1. The Catholic population of the United States has grown steadily throughout this century, both in absolute numbers (see fig. 7-1) and in "market share." Cohort succession and the high fertility of new immigrant groups have combined to ensure continued Catholic growth. Catholics made up only 19.4 percent of Americans born before 1907 but 28.7 percent of those born between 1958 and 1965.[2] Both demographics and relatively high levels of religious inheritance (staying with the religious family in which one was raised) suggest that Catholicism's share of the population will at least remain level and will probably rise.

Far more difficult to foretell is whether Catholic participation rates will increase along with "membership." American Catholicism's long-term ability to maintain strong communal bonds and high rates of participation is unclear in the face of continuing upward mobility, weakening ascriptive ties, and a laity that insists on unprecedented levels of personal religious freedom. The latter is recognized at the senior levels of the American Catholic hierarchy. Bishop James W. Malone, president of the National Conference of Catholic Bishops, notes the tension between church teachings and individual conscience in a report on the post-Vatican II church: "Confusion over moral issues has also been a recurring reality since Vatican II in the United States as elsewhere. This includes general questions like the role of conscience, the church's teaching authority with regard to morality, and the limits of dissent, as well as is-

FIGURE 7-1.
GROWTH OF MAJOR FAMILIES, 1926–1980

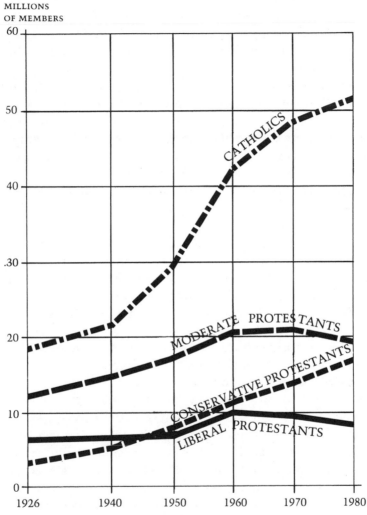

Sources: Yearbook of American and Canadian Churches, 1984 and 1926 Census of
Religious Bodies.

sues pertaining to specific moral norms."[3] Catholic leaders can take
some comfort in the American church's ability to adapt to external
changes and internal challenges. Today, wrestling with conflicting
social trends toward secularization on the one hand and a resurgent
traditionalism on the other, this church of "RC Classic," "RC

Light," and "RC Free" remains a witness to the power of a "universal faith" to encompass extraordinary diversity in the midst of a transcendent catholicity.

2. Judaism in America faces severe demographic challenges. Always a minority religious tradition in the United States, its low birth and conversion rates are a potentially serious threat. Concern for its long-term future and disillusionment with assimilation into American life have contributed to a "new survivalism" among many Jews. Stephen M. Cohen and Leonard J. Fein, who find fears for the future of American Jewry "unfounded," nonetheless see the 1960s as bringing about a discernable change in Jewish community priorities: "Jewish survival—that is, the survival of Jews as a distinct ethnic/religious group—has become a major priority of at least equal, and perhaps greater, concern to many Jews and, more particularly, to the agencies and institutions that determine the collective agenda of the Jewish community."[4]

From a demographic perspective, the challenges to Judaism appear to us to be quite real. Without a massive increase in rates of immigration or an unprecedented upturn in fertility, Jews seem likely to represent a steadily decreasing proportion of the U.S. population, albeit one that retains considerable social and religious significance. Though small in numbers, greater concern with survival rather than integration will likely bring renewed interest in the meanings and implications of the American Jewish experience.

3. Black Protestantism should continue to grow numerically and increase in importance as a societal force. Higher-than-average fertility plus strong communal bonds suggest continued growth for the nation's black Baptist and Methodist churches. Changes in white and black attitudes could contribute to accelerated movement of blacks into predominantly white churches, but we see this as unlikely for the reason discussed in chapter 4: race remains perhaps the most persistent "social source" of denominationalism.

The late twentieth century promises, moreover, to be an important period in the structural evolution of black Protestantism. Its organization beyond the local church level, like Judaism's, depends less on an ecclesiastical infrastructure than on a variety of paraparochial organizations united around both group interest and a common social vision rooted in biblical religion and historical experience. From time to time this reticulate structure has been of considerable importance, as in the civil rights movement in the 1960s. With upward mobility of black America, the influence of the black churches should grow. James M. Washington points to the 1980 presidential campaign of Jesse Jackson, in which black churches played a key role, as a breakthrough in black political achievement, but sees the need for its embodiment in lasting structures. "The politics of black spirituality, which are inherently symbolic and psychological," he writes, "must be embodied in church programs that recognize and resist the systemic nature of injustice lest they fall prey to the pitfalls of undisciplined subjectivism."[5]

Washington's proposal is no small challenge for a community of low, though rising, religiopolitical status. Whether black Protestantism can evolve lasting structures while retaining its strong community base as well as its vitality as a socioeconomic movement of the dispossessed is an important and unanswered question for the last decades of the twentieth century.

4. The churches of the Protestant establishment, long in a state of relative decline, will continue to lose ground both in numbers and in social power and influence. The proportion of the population that is Protestant will continue its gradual decline in the decades to come, and within Protestantism denominations and revitalization movements will continue their contest for power and influence. Throughout this century the balance of power within Protestantism has shifted back and forth—first from the conservative to the liberal and more recently from the liberal to the conservative wing. What we today call the liberal mainline churches (perhaps "old mainline" is more apt) have gradually lost ground to more conservative bodies. Membership trends, as shown in figure 7-1, illustrate this quite clearly. Liberal Protestant bodies grew until about 1960, then began declining. Moderate Protestant churches grew more rapidly, but they too had begun to decline by the 1970s. Conservative Protestant bodies continued to grow over the entire period, with the gap between the liberal and conservative theological camps widening in the decades after 1960. Even if total membership were to stabilize at current levels, it is clear that the Protestant community has rearranged itself along ideological lines and that its composition is more conservative now than only a few decades ago.

Birth cohorts tell the story. Most of the moderate-to-liberal denominations have lost ground among the recently born. Methodists, for example, often viewed as the most representative American religious group, made up 16 percent of all Americans born around the turn of the century but only 7.7 percent of those born between 1958 and 1965.[6] Despite the net growth of Methodism's churches during the twentieth century, its "market share" declined by about one-half. Similar shrinkage has occurred for Lutherans, Presbyterians, Episcopalians, the United Church of Christ, and the Unitarian-Universalists. The low birth rates of these groups are largely responsible for the declines. A small rate of natural growth combined with fewer gains from interdenominational switching in the post-1960s era have given them a weakened demographic base. Overall, the evidence seems irrefutable: the liberal branches of Protestantism are shrinking both as a proportion of Protestantism and of the general public.

Gradually, at times almost imperceptibly, over the decades, demographic trends have favored conservative Protestants over their more liberal counterparts. Among the generation born at the turn of the century, conservative Protestants made up 11.8 percent of the population. They dropped to 7.8 percent in the 1907–1923 cohort, but have increased since to a high of 12 percent in the 1958–1965 cohort. Sustained conservative growth over the period, combined with liberal shrinkage, casts light on the reasons for the significant shift in the balance of power within Protestantism. If numbers have any meaning for the future, they are on the side of conservative groups.

We see no reason to anticipate a fundamental change in this balance of power. Liberals will represent a smaller and smaller share of the Protestant movement. The age structure of liberal Protestantism suggests a rising death rate that, give the relatively few members of childbearing age, is unlikely to be offset by births. In the past, the liberal churches have offset their low natural rates of growth by favorable rates of switching. Since this is no longer true there is little reason to expect a return to the growth rates of the 1950s. Precisely the opposite is true for conservative Protestants, whose relative youthfulness portends lower death rates, continued above-average numbers of births, and, compared to liberals, favorable switching patterns among the younger population.

5. Given our emphasis here on mainline religion we have not said much about the "other" religious groups that also populate the

American religious scene. Taken individually, these groups are too small to make much of a dent in most national public opinion polls, but together they total about 4 percent of the nation's population. The "others" include members of the Orthodox churches, Buddhists, Muslims, Hindus, Zoroastrians, Sikhs, and small Protestant groups such as Quakers, Mennonites, and Brethren groups not easily classifiable into Protestant families.[7]

While we lack the kind of demographic data we have presented on other religious groups, the general patterns would seem to argue for continued expansion of the boundaries of American religious pluralism. The advent of the new religious voluntarism opens religious options hardly imagined even a generation ago. Recalling, for example, Will Herberg's comment that to profess oneself anything but a Protestant, Catholic, or Jew is "to imply being foreign," we would not argue that the religious traditions outside Christianity and Judaism have achieved "mainstream" status, but in a time when one's religious commitments are relegated to the "private" realm, neither do they render the individual automatically suspect. The normative climate in the future should be favorable to new religious and quasi-religious groups of many kinds.

Because the "other" families of American religion are so disparate, it is hard to generalize about their futures. For some, the diminishing strength of ethnic bonds may lead to difficult times. More than most religious traditions, for example, the Orthodox churches depend on the strength of ethnic ties; nationality remains an important continuing "social source of denominationalism" for these groups that tend to retain their national origin in their names, for example, the Patriarchal Parishes of the *Russian* Orthodox Church in America, the *Ukranian* Orthodox Church in the U.S.A., and the *Armenian* Orthodox Diocese of America.

At the same time, relatively high rates of immigration from Asia and the Middle East imply future growth among faith groups up to now not represented in large numbers in the United States. One scholar, for example, estimates that there are now about 3 million Muslims in the United States,[8] or as many Muslims as Episcopalians! While this estimate is overstated, an increase in the presence and influence of Asian and Middle Eastern faiths is likely. Generally we expect the "other" families to expand gradually over the next several decades.

6. The nonaffiliated sector of the population will probably continue to grow as well. This group accounted for about 3 percent of those born around the turn of the century, 11 percent of those born between 1941 and 1957, and 13 percent of the 1958–1965 cohort.[9] The number of Americans growing up outside the major religious traditions is increasing, which suggests the likelihood of an even larger, more distinct secular constituency in the future. A great deal depends on the baby-boom generation. If they return to the churches in large numbers, this will check somewhat the growth of a more self-conscious secular constituency. If they do not (and we see no signs of a massive return), we expect the chasm between "religious" and "secular" America to continue to deepen. As older cohorts die and more recent cohorts make up a larger share of the population, social divisions along religious and cultural lines may intensify.

The Changing Mainline

Demographics tell a great deal, but what they tell is only part of the story of the future of American religion. The relations between religion and culture are subtle; unexpected but profound shifts in institutional form and function occur. Already signs of emerging new alignments of religion and culture portend a religious future unlike that known in the past. The 1980s are a time of profound shifts and dislocations, a time of reappraisal and reposturing.

Throughout this book we have used the term *mainline* to refer to religious groups that identify with and contribute to the definition of the society's core values. To speak of a religious group as mainline is to acknowledge its place in the nation's religious establishment. Over time the mainline has changed in fairly dramatic ways that signal American religion's genius for adaptation and change in response to fluctuations in popular taste and sentiment. The colonial "big three," that is, Congregationalists, Presbyterians, and Episcopalians, were joined early on by the denominations of the nineteenth-century revivals and the settlement of the frontier— Methodists, Baptists (principally in the South), and Disciples of Christ. By the early decades of this century, not only had Lutherans and Reformed peoples joined the mainline, but the notion of an exclusively Protestant mainline was increasingly untenable. As Robert Handy and Will Herberg have argued, by midcentury Catholicism and Judaism had joined Protestantism at the spiritual center of the culture. With the civil rights movement, even the black churches could lay claim to mainline status.

Today the religious establishment is again caught up in widespread religious and cultural realignments. At one level, there is evidence of further integration into the religious mainline of groups once merely tolerated. This integration has occurred for the most part without severe ruptures in the normative order. For example, the Roman Catholic Church has moved ever more toward the center of American life over the past three decades. Partly because of the elevated social position of Catholics, partly because of changes following Vatican II, partly because of Protestantism's weakened hold on the culture, the American Catholic church has entered into a new and fuller involvement in national affairs. Always involved in "Catholic" issues (e.g., birth control, immigration policy, rights of working people), the new activism and visibility of Catholic bishops on issues of nuclear disarmament and economic justice signals a shift toward greater public participation in issues facing the entire national community. The Catholic church appears to us to be in its best position ever to assume a custodial role for American culture at large. Similarly, Judaism's place in the religious mainline is established. The prophetic strains in Judaism contribute to the shaping of the nation's common faith and remain an important source of national reflection and self-scrutiny. The New Religious Right's call for America to recapture its *Judeo*-Christian heritage is a powerful symbolic reminder of the inclusion of Judaism in the religious mainline. As important as these new developments are for Catholicism and Judaism, however, it is within Protestantism that the greatest changes are apparent in the relationship between religious collectivities and public life.

Conservative Protestantism: From the Margin to the Center?

The next several decades will be an important time of transition in the relationship between conservative Protestantism and the religious mainline. As sectarian religious groups achieved middle-class status in the past, they have tended to move toward the theological and political middle. In American religion, as in American politics, centripetal forces are strong and are likely to continue. Upward mobility and a broadened membership base predispose religious bodies to more middle-class values; sectarian and exclusivist stances lose out to more accommodating, less dogmatic religious styles. That same movement also generates strong counterreactions and has been an important social source of religious schism. Division will continue to occur in the conservative Protestant camp as successive reactionaries attempt to resist the trends toward greater accommodations.

As we have seen, conservative Protestants have made important gains in education, income, and occupational prestige in the postwar period. While retaining their membership base in the South and in small communities, conservative bodies are clearly moving into the socioeconomic and cultural mainstream. They are now positioned to exert considerable influence; but movement in this direction has also brought about new tensions within the conservative religious community.

The nation's largest Protestant denominational body, the Southern Baptist Convention, provides a contemporary case in point of the conservative Protestant struggle to retain distinctiveness along with social "respectability." For generations the convention has been an important guardian of cultural values in the South, but one perceived by its own members and the general public as a regional religious movement. Southern Baptists in recent years have become an important national force as well, more and more part of the nation's mainline. Symbolically, the election of Jimmy Carter in 1972 was a watershed no less important to the social standing of Southern Baptists than John Kennedy's election had been to Roman Catholics in 1960.

For many within the Southern Baptist Convention, however, the accommodation to national cultural values that comes with its new status comes at too high a price. Institutionally, despite its continued growth and the vitality of its mission programs, the convention faces internal challenges every bit as serious as those experienced by the historic mainline churches. Some see schism as a likely outcome of the continuing battle between fundamentalists and accommodationists. Southern Baptist church historian Bill J. Leonard, a moderate, sees the convention as engaged in a rear-guard struggle to recapture the nineteenth century. "For Southern Baptists," he writes, "the 19th century is finally over; the old securities of culture and denomination have given way and we are not sure what to do about it." Leonard sees Baptist fundamentalist leaders as attempting to redefine the convention along more explicitly ideological lines:

> Fundamentalists insist that ideological uniformity, not cultural and denominational coalition, has been and must remain the basis for denominational solidarity. This "new SBC," as sociologist Larry McSwain calls it, has reinterpreted what it means to be a Southern Baptist in order to promote an ideological version of the Baptist essence—hermaneutically, homiletically, socially and politically. The fundamentalists project a selective memory of the past as the unfulfillable model for the future. Ideologists project a fortress mentality as the only means for preserving the Baptist way of life from the onslaught of secularism, pluralism and diversity. This momentary success cannot recreate the 19th century, however. The world is not white, male, Protestant, or southern, and purging the denomination of so-called liberals will not keep the real problems of the 21st century from overtaking the SBC.[10]

The Southern Baptist struggle embodies tensions that are likely to become increasingly common within the conservative movement generally. Up to now that movement has been largely successful in maintaining its religious and ideological homogeneity. Given its position on the margins of American society, a degree of consensus was possible. Whether consensus is possible from its new position inside the "public square" is an open question. The experience of other religious groups in making this transition is testimony to the difficulties that lie ahead for what is, without question, an increasingly important force in the nation's religious and cultural life.

Liberal Protestantism: From the Center to the Margin?

For an extended period of American history, the groups we now think of as liberal Protestants were the mainline. One might say they established the rules of the American religious "game." With legal disestablishment, Congregationalists, Presbyterians, and Episcopalians were forced to admit other teams, but they continued to own the stadium. The second disestablishment further reduced their status to the not-unimportant role of umpire. Now for the first time in America, liberal Protestantism is on the field of play and forced to compete with other religious "teams." In the new religious environment, liberal Protestantism is a minority voice and one player among many in a more truly pluralistic modern context. Thus, while conservative Protestantism is facing new internal tensions owing to its new position closer to the center of American life, liberal Protestantism faces its own crisis of identity and purpose from a position closer to the margin.

Liberal Protestantism is unlikely to regain the dominant cultural position it once enjoyed, but we believe its distinctive traditions and emphases will hold up fairly well in the religious marketplace of the future. We agree with William R. Hutchison when he says that the challenge for liberal Protestantism is to conserve and appreciate its rich heritage. "To own, refurbish, and spiritually invigorate these distinctive features seems to me more important to the future of liberal Protestantism," writes Hutchison, "than the efforts, however worthy, to reach broader constituencies or to do something about the inadequate liberal birthrate."[11] Admittedly birth rates are a problem, but liberal Protestantism's greatest need at present is to regain a sense of pride and appreciation for its own heritage.

In their recent book, *Habits of the Heart*, Robert N. Bellah and associates observe that Americans speak two languages, both of which are derived in large part from the traditions that shaped the nation's early life: a rugged individualism and a commitment to community. They write: "if the language of the self-reliant individual is the first language of American moral life, the languages of tradition and commitment in communities of memory are "second languages" that most Americans know as well, and which they use when the language of the radically separate self does not seem adequate."[12] A community of memory is one that has a past to share through the telling of its stories and the celebration of its heritage; it is a carrier of traditions and values; it conveys a way of life and a sense of commitment to both self and others. Religious communities especially serve as communities of memory, offering a rich language of tradition and commitment.

For all their current difficulties, we see in the liberal churches a residual capacity to provide a vocabulary of symbols, beliefs, moral values, and feeling-responses for articulating a socially responsible individualism. As do other religious families, liberal churches have a common language informed by biblical religion and a group heritage kept alive through symbol, teachings, and ritual rehearsal of past events and future hopes. Their heritage as "bridging institutions"—concerned with public well-being and the larger social order—has given them an experience and sensitivity sorely missing in much religious rhetoric today. The task ahead will be to preserve this vital balance—to self and to community—and to affirm it in fresh and compelling ways.

In a 1984 book that generated a great deal of interest in scholarly and ecumenical religious circles, theologian George Lindbeck has proposed that only a reassertion of the particularities of the religious communities offers hope for "counteracting the acids of modernity." He writes:

> the viability of a unified world of the future may well depend on counteracting the acids of modernity. It may depend on communal enclaves that socialize their members into highly particular outlooks supportive of concern for others rather than for individual rights and entitlements, and of a sense of responsibility for the wider society rather than for personal fulfillment. It is at least an open question whether any religion will have the requisite toughness for this demanding task unless it at some point makes the claim that it is significantly true and unsurpassably true.[13]

A crucial challenge for liberal Protestantism is to recapture some sense of particularity as a community of memory and not merely as a custodian of generalized cultural values. This will require among other things a countering of the secular drift that has had a disproportionate impact on its traditional constituency. The liberal churches need their own particular language of faith to communicate with the "cultured despisers" of the modern world, in a manner that lays claim upon the self and the community.

This task will not be easy. As we have shown, in the past two decades the liberal churches have not lost members to the conservative churches, but to the ranks of the nonaffiliated and the "unchurched." Liberal Protestantism's "competition" is not the conservatives it has *spurned* but the secularists it has *spawned*. This latter group includes the most liberal segments of the population, people unlikely to join the ranks of the hard-line conservatives. Liberal Protestantism's future, we believe, lies not in a move toward the theological and ideological right, but in its becoming more self-consciously "liberal," if by that is meant an assertion of responsible individualism in a communal framework. If these churches are to reclaim the loyalties of persons lost to this secular-minded constituency, they will need to hold firm to their historic values and to testify to them in as direct and forceful manner as possible. Overcoming their organizational weaknesses and lack of solidarity, without sacrificing long-cherished values of toleration and the autonomy of the individual believer, will not be easy; achieving both of these ends at the same time has been the peculiar genius and contribution of this rich heritage.

Moderate Protestantism: Redefining the Center?

We have had much to say in this book about liberal and conservative Protestants, but less to say about the often embattled groups of the Protestant center. Methodists, Lutherans, ecumenically minded Baptists, and smaller groups such as the Disciples of Christ and the Reformed churches have much in common with the traditions to both their left and right. With liberal Protestants they tend to share an appreciation for the principle of intergroup toleration, an acceptance of the responsibility of Christians for social and economic justice for all, and a commitment to a continuing renewal of public life; with conservative Protestants they lean toward traditionalism in the realms of faith and moral values.

Few groups are more dependent on America's sense of self-understanding for their own sense of identity than these churches. The sharpening of liberal-conservative differences over moral and ideological issues puts moderate Protestantism, one of whose main distinctions has been the ability to adapt to an ever-shifting cultural and ideological center, in an increasingly difficult position. With the collapse of the religious center, the denominations of middle America, many of which are also losing their ethnic distinctiveness, face a new issue: where does a centrist religious tradition turn when the center seems no longer to hold?

Pressures on moderate Protestantism to move more sharply to the ideological left or right are considerable and may increase in the future. If this is the case, the decades ahead could be trying ones for moderate Protestantism. These are the folks who occupy the middle ground of American life—geographically, politically, and culturally—whose sympathies are not wholly with either the Moral Majority or the Immoral Minority, but who play a significant part in shaping the nation's future. In a very real way, the future of the nation's religious establishment rests with this constituency.

Moderate Protestantism has a disproportionate stake in the restoration of public faith and in the possibilities of what Martin E. Marty has called the "public church."[14] The public church, for Marty, includes segments of the old Protestant mainline churches, the contemporary Catholic church, and representatives of the evangelical churches. Its distinguishing features will be an enlivened sense of public responsibility and, without each tradition sacrificing its own integrity, a recognition that each has something important to contribute. In the terms of the previous section, these features amount to an ecumenism of communities of memory. Out of such intercommunity dialogue will come fresh articulations of the meanings of faith in personal and corporate experience.

If a revived public church is indeed on the horizon, moderate Protestantism will play a key role in bringing it into being. This will require forms and qualities of leadership that have seldom been forthcoming from the Protestant middle; a revitalized ecumenicity and new, bold theological affirmations are critical as well, especially a theology that resonates with and gives meaning to the experience of middle Americans. At the same time, by virtue of their size and heritage as well as their social position, the churches that represent this often-overlooked one-quarter of the population bring certain assets to the task, not the least of which is the considerable strength of their communal bonding. The moderate Protestant churches, with other groups at the center of the new American religious mainline—principally Catholics and black Protestants—could be in a position to forge anew a broadly based synthesis of belief and culture that has been missing in American life since the 1950s.

The New Denominationalism

What are the implications of the new religious voluntarism for denominationalism itself? Does the new emphasis on individualism in matters of faith and morals mean the death of denominationalism as we have known it? And what about the possibilities for public faith? Might we expect a broadly based synthesis of public and private dimensions of faith? These questions get at the very core of the changes in religion and culture we have discussed in this book, and it is appropriate that we address them in this concluding section.

Will Individualism Be the Death of Denominationalism?

To pose this question prompts, in good American fashion, speculation and intrigue. Consider the following hypothetical press release:

> Harvey Jackson announced today the formation of Denominations Aplenty, an organization committed to the idea that we need more denominations, not fewer. Eutychus interviewed Jackson at his Broken Arrow, Oklahoma headquarters.
> *Eutychus:* Why more denominations, Harv?
> *Jackson:* Every man's religion is a personal thing between him and God. Our goal for the eighties is for every family in the United States to have its own denomination. By the year 2000, we hope to extend that to a denomination for each and every family member. . . .
> *Eutychus:* What's your plan to carry out this mission?
> *Jackson:* We've put together a "Start Your Own Denomination" kit that sells for $29.95. Each kit includes a cassette tape of Jane Fonda singing "I've got to be me," a book of unregistered names for new denominations, and quicky incorporation papers for the state in which you register your denomination.[15]

Fanciful as this dialogue is, Eutychus drives home an important point: Americans are a highly individualistic people in matters of faith and practice. This notion is not altogether new; more than a century and a half ago Thomas Jefferson proclaimed "I am my own sect" and announced that if he could not go to heaven except with a group, he would prefer not to go at all. From the beginning, large numbers of Americans have held "privatized" or "individualized" understandings of faith that ultimately accept only the conscience as the final arbiter. Given the heritage of voluntarism, such expressions of personal faith are hardly surprising.

In the post–World War II period we have seen a reassertion of individualism in American religious life that, with demographic and other cultural changes, has reshaped the nation's religious groups and relations among them. No longer restricted to the fringes of American religious life, religious individualism has come to occupy a position at its center. Almost imperceptibly, the notion of religious voluntarism, long affirmed in principle for religious collectivities, has been extended to individuals as well. This new voluntarism is now a part of the culture; it will take on features as yet unknown but will not go away.

Already national denominational structures have receded in importance as culture-shaping institutions. The major religious bodies that gave shape to so much of the country's way of life—that founded colleges, hospitals, and social service agencies, supplied the energy for social movements from abolition to temperance to civil rights, delivered votes in an urban ward or in the halls of a state legislature or the Congress—now seem distant entities. There is a vague awareness that Jimmy Carter is a born-again Southern Baptist, Marie Osmond a Mormon, and Michael Jackson a Jehovah's Witness, but these affiliations seem to mean little more than personal idiosyncracies, interesting raw material for *People* magazine feature articles. Religion, after all, is personal, a matter of one's opinion, a private matter with which neither state nor church is empowered to interfere. Popular religion as found in the cities and towns across the country is highly subjective and experiential, ranging in its expressions from Robert H. Schuller's "possibility thinking," to the "new charismatics," from *est* and yoga on the human potential front to born-again Christianity among the more traditionally religious.

Viewing the American scene circa the mid-1980s, then, one could make a case for the triumph of what Ernst Troeltsch in 1911 called mysticism, that radically individualistic form of religion that "envisions a new situation altogether, in which it will no longer become necessary to connect religion with the decaying churches."[16] Troeltsch went on:

> [Mysticism] creates no community, since it possesses neither the sense of solidarity nor the faith in authority which this requires, nor the no less necessary fanaticism and desire for uniformity. It lives in and thrives on communities which have been brought into existence by other ruder energies; it tends to transform these groups from confessional unities into organizations for administration, offering a home to varying minds and energies. It is opposed to ecclesiastical spirit by its tolerance, its subjectivism and symbolism, its emphasis upon the ethical and religious inwardness of temper, its lack of stable norms and authorities.[17]

There are elements of Troeltsch's mysticism in American religion, and his discussion of it provides helpful perspective on the growing proportion of the population who proclaim no religious preference. As a general characterization of the American religious scene, however, it falls short. America produces religious individualists in great numbers, but few real mystics in any classical sense. Seeing only the individual dimension, mysticism ignores the communal and group dimensions of religion which continue to find expression in congregational and other forms of organized religious life. Religion as most Americans know it involves both dimensions —the mountaintop and the pew, the personal as well as the social. Americans, as Bellah and associates have noted, are "bilingual": they speak both the language of individualism (in its religious and secular forms) and that of tradition and commitment in communities of memory.

Despite the radical religious individualism of some sectors of the society, the denominational traditions have exhibited surprising staying power. The denominational community incorporates elements of mysticism, just as it has traits of Troeltsch's better known "church" and "sect." Mainline religious communities are characterized by puzzling paradoxes: they are individualistic, but incurably social; they are strong and empowering, but also accommodating and vulnerable. The durability of the denominational community in the face of wrenching social and cultural change has been and remains one of its fundamental features. A peculiarly American socioreligious form, it has proved to be an amazingly resilient institution and has flourished in a nation whose "all-pervasive religiousness" and "persistent secularity" is similarly paradoxical.[18]

The great genius of denominationalism as a religious form has been its adaptability, its capacity to adjust to a changing context of voluntary faith. Consequently, religion in America has not followed the pattern seen in other developed nations. Despite increased privatization of faith, renunciation of religious identity remains relatively rare. The dominant theme is not so much radical separation as what Thomas Luckmann describes as "secularization from within"—privatization within a context of continuing religious loyalties. So viewed, the threat of religious individualism lies not so much in a militant anti-institutional sentiment as in growing subjectivism of religious belief and practice. For many people, bonds to churches and synagogues may be weak and definitions of religious reality may have undergone changes, but still they retain a positive stance toward religion as an institution; they may seem indifferent to organized religion, "unchurched" in terms of meaningful contact or participation, but "their" church remains "their" church, continuing to provide a "second language" when the "first language" of radical individualism fails.

Will individualism be the death of denominationalism? We think not, but it will change it. It already has. Ultimately, denominationalism will survive to the extent it is able to do in the future what it has done in the past: to provide members with a sense of who they are as participants in a reality that extends beyond the self.

There is much concern today about religious renewal and rediscovery of religious traditions. The breaking down of old ascriptive loyalties has brought on identity crises and related outbursts of new energies and quests. Over the past quarter century a vast number of religious reform movements have emerged, focusing on spiritual renewal as well as other aspects of renewal such as evangelism, scripture, doctrine, social ministry, and liturgy.[19] Some of the movements transcend institutional boundaries, yet many are denominational and are having an impact on particular groups. For example, movements such as the Forum for Scriptural Christianity among Methodists and the Evangelical and Catholic Mission in the Episcopal church—established in 1966 and 1977 respectively—have arisen among clergy and laity calling for a return to historic beliefs and practices. Both the number of reform movements and the scope of such reforms are evidence to the depth of spiritual currents now flowing and of efforts at "reconstructing" religious traditions. In the years ahead we may see more such efforts at reshaping existing institutions.

This flurry of renewal movements partly reflects a search for institutional identity and revitalization, but also it has been brought on by concerns over how to interpret the religious traditions to the disaffected, more secular sectors. Large numbers of religious dropouts and persons marginally involved in churches and synagogues are prompting unusual efforts at recruiting "their own people" and communicating to them basic teachings and practices. Judaism provides a case in point. Synagogues have generally been very traditional institutions serving those who come to them, but now they are reaching out more, trying to bring secular Jews back into the community of faith.[20] The publication of "Jewish Catalogues," as distilled versions of the traditions of Judaism, the offering of crash courses in the Bible and the Talmud, and the use of "mitzvah vans" to encourage observance of rituals in many cities are examples of efforts to make Judaism and the synagogue more accessible and to extend their orbit of influence.

By the turn of the century, many religious groups may have a clearer religious and cultural identity than they now have. Reform movements have the potential of redirecting institutional policies and renewing commitment to selected aspects of denominational histories and traditions. Broader trends in the society as well may augur in favor of more distinct boundaries for major groupings. More voluntary patterns of religious switching in the future will contribute to more homogeneous orientational and behavioral styles. As church affiliation ceases to fulfill a vaguely perceived social obligation, and as the choice of a church ceases to express one's social standing and cultural background, individuals will "sort themselves out" more on the basis of personal preference. As a result, ideological differences between the churches could become more pronounced. A growing secular constituency, too, should mean that boundaries between the more traditionally religious and the disaffected "unchurched" will become more apparent. Already this cleavage is fairly evident in the western states, by all counts the most secular region of the nation, and we would expect the boundaries to intensify elsewhere in the years ahead.[21]

More distinct boundaries between faiths, however, need not mean diminished religious differences within traditions and churches. We would expect a growing diversity of spiritual and religious styles —some people stressing doctrinal or ecclesiastical authority, others more concerned with the experiential dimension of faith, still others caught up in specialized ministries, but all relating to the same faith community. The sovereignty of the individual in matters spiritual virtually assures internal institutional pluralism, or "religious populism."[22] Populism implies fluid standards, diversity in ideas and styles, changing definitions of common beliefs, and core practices that can unify and integrate the largest majority. Diversity and fluidity in personal commitment and organizational structures, in response to popular will, most certainly will characterize major Protestant, Catholic, and Jewish bodies as they seek to accommodate themes of religious individualism that are deeply rooted in middle-class, mainstream culture.

Denominations will persist as organizations but they will be less able to command permanent loyalty. Both religious leaders and rank-and-file lay members know this; they also know that change is a reality of the modern world—in religious life as in other realms. Gary Wills points out that the great revelation of Vatican Council II to members of the Roman Catholic Church was that "the Church" *can change.*[23] Catholics who had thought of the church as eternal and nonchanging suddenly discovered otherwise. Now in the aftermath of the 1960s there is greater awareness that religious institutions are fragile and malleable structures. The challenge for the churches and synagogues will be to adapt to this new milieu and to find ways to inspire commitment in a doubtful, not-so-awestruck world.

A Restored Public Faith?

Today there is a loud clamor of religious voices throughout the land—often highly charged in moral and symbolic content. The voices have taken on new public significance, reflecting in a deeper sense the lack of a genuine religious presence in the broader public arena. One can speak of a rediscovery of religious groups (and religious traditions more generally) as "communities of memory" with their own distinctive versions of reality. Perhaps more now than at any time since the 1950s, religion is in the public eye and developments have forced to the forefront the question of religious America—if, and in what way, can the country be conceived of as a sacred enterprise.

Whether these communities of memory have the requisite resources—the symbols, the language, the conviction—to restore a broadly based public faith appears unlikely, at least in the manner we knew it prior to the 1960s. The forces of modern individualism have become far too powerful, and the dislocations in religion and culture far too great. But we can expect more limited, and no doubt more fragile, consensuses to emerge, forged out of practical and pragmatic more than dogmatic solutions to moral and societal issues. In an era of moral pluralism, we can expect a continuing struggle of groups and forces, both religious and secular, seeking to shape the normative order. This will generate conflicts and tensions but also compromises, which may in turn ward off serious moral divisions that would be threatening to the nation. Pluralism generates a moderating influence on all forces, secular as well as religious, and encourages shifting alignments and constituencies organized around one issue or another.

But moral crusading will no doubt continue, and it may even intensify. The polarization into religious and ideological camps has heightened awareness of the nation's many religious heritages and of competing visions of personal and corporate life. With the decline of a religious and cultural center, the country now confronts a new and wider range of individual and communal possibilities and the very real likelihood of a continuing "uneasy" period of coexistence and shifting configurations for some time to come. Here we have looked at some of the contours of this continuing struggle, but we have no special insight into its likely developments. What is clear is that the religious context of the country is much different now than at any time in the past. It may well be that a new stage in the evolution of religious pluralism is upon us—a stage that is inherently unstable and impossible to predict.

Whatever the future may bring, the concerns of lasting significance are not really the changing demographics, the shifting configurations of groups and ideologies, or even the survival of specific institutions. Far more important are the well-being of the people themselves and the perpetuation of a culture that sustains the life of the spirit as well as that of the body. We are impressed by the fact that the voices now calling for a reinvigorated public life—be they Catholic, conservative Protestant or black Protestant—all have and draw upon strong communal experiences. The faiths most capable of galvanizing a new and vital American center are those most deeply rooted in the lives of the people. Debate over religion's role in American life will continue, and no doubt new alliances and counteralliances will emerge, but it is hardly imaginable that the historic faiths and traditions that have helped shape American life will not continue to inform its future.

Appendix

The General Social Survey and the Religious Groupings

The General Social Survey (GSS) is an annual survey of a representative sample of approximately 1,500 noninstitutionalized English-speaking persons living in the continental United States.[1] Surveys were conducted annually from 1972 to 1978, 1980, and 1982 to 1984 and made available in computer-readable form as a resource for social scientists by the National Opinion Research Center with support from the National Science Foundation. For this book we have combined eleven independent surveys (including a 1982 oversample of black Americans) to yield a total of 17,052 individual cases.

The high quality of the General Social Survey makes it a valuable resource for students of contemporary American life. Most of the items asked in individual surveys are repeated on a regular cycle, making it possible to combine surveys to examine views of small social groups and to examine trends over time. While the surveys contain few items dealing with religion per se, they provide extensive demographic and attitudinal data on the American population.

Thoughout this book we have made extensive use of data on religious denominations and families derived from the General Social Survey computer files. A word of explanation is needed on the way we have constructed these groups. The General Social Survey asks respondents several questions about their religious preference. It begins with the following: "What is your religious preference? Is it Protestant, Catholic, Jewish, some other religion, or no religion?" Of those who give a Protestant preference an additional question is asked: "What specific denomination is that, if any?" The interviewer records Baptist, Methodist, Lutheran, Presbyterian, Episcopalian, and "No Denomination or Non-Denominational Church" responses on the questionnaire itself. For those reporting an "other" group, the group named is recorded verbatim and later coded by National Opinion Research Center staff. The result is a list of over 130 individual religious groups.[2]

The 26 denominational groupings referred to in this book were assembled for computer analysis as follows:

Catholics, Jews, No Religious Preference: All persons giving these responses to the general GSS religious preference item.

Episcopalians, Presbyterians, Lutherans, Churches of God, Churches of Christ, Jehovah's Witnesses: All respondents giving these groups as their denominational preference.

Methodists: Persons whose race is black, religion is Protestant, and denominational preference is Methodist are classified as *black Methodists.* Methodists of all other races are included in the general *Methodist* category.

Baptists: Baptists were separated first by race (blacks and all others) and then by U.S. census region (South and non-South), yielding four categories: *white* (nonblack) *Northern Baptists, black Northern Baptists, white Southern Baptists, black Southern Baptists.*

United Church of Christ: Persons giving their denominational preference as Congregationalist, Evangelical and Reformed, Reformed United Church of Christ, United Church of Christ.

Christian (Disciples of Christ): Christian Disciples, Christian, Central Christian, Disciples of Christ, First Christian.

Reformed: Hungarian Reformed, Christian Reform, Dutch Reformed, First Reformed, Reformed, Grace Reformed.

Miscellaneous Evangelicals/Fundamentalists: Evangelical Congregational, Independent Bible, New Testament Christian, Christian and Missionary Alliance, Eden Evangelist, Plymouth Brethren, United Brethren, United Brethren in Christ, Christ in Christian Union, Open Bible, Covenant, Evangelical, Evangelist, Evangelist Free Church, Salvation Army, Wesleyan, Wesleyan Methodist—Pilgrim, Evangelical Covenant, Mission Covenant, Swedish Mission, Fundamentalists.

Nazarenes: Holiness (Nazarene), Nazarenes.

Miscellaneous Pentecostals/Holiness: Church of Prophecy, Apostolic Faith, Witness Holiness, Church of God in Christ, Church of God in Christ Holiness, Full Gospel, Four Square Gospel, Holy Roller, Holiness, Church of Holiness, Pilgrim Holiness, Pentecostal

TABLE A-1

THE SAMPLE

Religious Group	Total	Percent of Total
National	17,052	100.0
Liberal Protestants	1,482	8.7
Episcopalians	439	2.6
United Church of Christ	257	1.5
Presbyterians	786	4.6
Moderate Protestants	4,128	24.2
Methodists	1,745	10.2
Lutherans	1,322	7.8
Christians (Disciples of Christ)	249	1.5
Northern Baptists	735	4.3
Reformed	77	0.5
Black Protestants	1,549	9.1
Methodists	279	1.6
Northern Baptists	562	3.3
Southern Baptists	708	4.2
Conservative Protestants	2,696	15.8
Southern Baptists	1,569	9.2
Churches of Christ	209	1.2
Evangelicals/Fundamentalists	121	0.7
Nazarenes	78	0.5
Pentecostals/Holiness	418	2.5
Assemblies of God	101	0.6
Churches of God	122	0.7
Adventists	78	0.5
Catholics	4,262	25.0
Jews	394	2.3
Others	1,361	8.0
Mormons	176	1.0
Jehovah's Witnesses	99	0.6
Christian Scientists	48	0.3
Unitarian-Universalists	36	0.2
Miscellaneous	1,002	5.9
No religious preference	1,180	6.9

Church of God, Pentecostal, Pentecostal Holiness, Holiness Pentecostal, Sanctified, Sanctification, United Holiness.

Assemblies of God: Assembly of God, Pentecostal Assembly of God.

Adventists: Advent Christian, Seventh-Day Adventist.

Mormons: LDS, LDS-Mormon, LDS-Reorganized, LDS–Jesus Christ, Church of Jesus Christ of the Latter-Day Saints, Mormon.

Christian Scientists: Christian Science, Religious Science.

Unitarian-Universalists: Unitarians, Universalists, Unitarian-Universalists.

Groups Not Classified: Among those we did not classify into a denominational grouping are the following:[3] Enkakar, Church of God, Saint and Christ, Moravian, Spiritualist, Church of the Brethren, Christadelphians, Church of the Living God, Community Church, First Church, Friends, Mennonites, Quakers, Reformed Church of Christ, Mind Science, Unity Church, Zion Union, Disciples of God, United Church of Christianity, Federated Church, Muslim, Orthodox Christian, etc.

Table A-1 shows the number and percentage of the combined General Social Survey sample we have included in each religious family and denomination.

The same procedures were followed with respect to religious preference at age sixteen.

Notes

INTRODUCTION

1. Martin E. Marty, *A Nation of Behavers* (Chicago: University of Chicago Press, 1976), 18.

2. Quoted in the "Preface," in *The Lively Experiment: The Shaping of Christianity in America,* by Sidney E. Mead (New York: Harper and Row, 1963).

3. J. Gordon Melton, ed., *Encyclopedia of American Religions* (Wilmington, N.C.: McGrath, 1978).

4. Harvey Cox, *Religion in the Secular City* (New York: Simon and Schuster, 1984); and William G. McLoughlin, *Revivals, Awakenings, and Reform* (Chicago: University of Chicago Press, 1978).

5. Michael Harrington, *The Politics at God's Funeral* (New York: Penguin Books, 1983).

CHAPTER 1. THE LEGACY OF THE SIXTIES

1. Sydney E. Ahlstrom, *A Religious History of the American People* (New Haven: Yale University Press, 1972), 1080.

2. John Cogley, *Catholic America* (Garden City, N.Y.: Doubleday, 1974), 95.

3. Jeffrey K. Hadden, *The Gathering Storm in the Churches* (Garden City, N.Y.: Doubleday, 1969).

4. See Martin E. Marty's "Foreword," in *Understanding Church Growth and Decline, 1950–1978,* ed. Dean R. Hoge and David A. Roozen (New York: Pilgrim Press, 1979), 10.

5. See *Religion in America, 1977–1978,* Gallup Opinion Index, Report No. 145, for summaries of these trends during the 1960s. Weekly church attendance dropped from 47 percent in 1960 to 42 percent in 1970. Thirty-one percent of Americans thought religion was losing influence in 1962 compared to 75 percent in 1970. Data on the importance of religion in one's life are reported in *Religion in America, 1984,* Gallup Opinion Index, Report No. 222. Seventy-five percent of Americans said religion was "very important" to them in 1952, 70 percent in 1965, and 52 percent in 1978.

6. Will Herberg, *Protestant—Catholic—Jew* (Garden City, N.Y.: Doubleday Anchor, 1960), 56.

7. Ibid., 257–258.

8. Ibid., 234.

9. See Robert T. Handy, *A Christian America: Protestant Hopes and Historical Realities* (New York: Oxford University Press, 1984), 185–210.

10. *Religion in America, 1984,* 54–55. Many who identify themselves as church members are essentially uninvolved in religious institutions. Using a more rigorous definition of religious participation, a 1978 study identified 41 percent of the U.S. adult population as "unchurched" and 59 percent as "churched." (The unchurched were those who reported not being a church or synagogue member or who had not attended a religious service in the past six months apart from weddings, funerals, or special holidays such as Christmas, Easter, or Yom Kippur.) See *The Unchurched American* (Princeton: Princeton Religion Research Center and the Gallup Organization, Inc., 1978).

11. Aside from *The Unchurched American,* see J. Russell Hale, *The Unchurched: Who They Are and Why They Stay Away* (New York: Harper and Row, 1980); and David A. Roozen, *The Churched and the Unchurched in America* (Washington: Glenmary Research Center, 1978).

12. See George Gallup, Jr., "U.S. in Early Stage of Religious Revival?" *Journal of Current Social Issues* (Spring 1977), 50–52.

13. See David A. Roozen, "What Hath the 1970s Wrought?: Religion in America," in *Yearbook of American and Canadian Churches, 1984* (Nashville: Abingdon Press, 1984). Roozen reports data showing similar patterns in Eastern and charismatic faiths for 1978 and 1979.

14. "Playboy Interview: Steven Jobs," *Playboy* 32 (February 1985).

15. Dean M. Kelley, *Why Conservative Churches Are Growing* (New York: Harper and Row, 1972), 88–90.

16. See Dean R. Hoge and David A. Roozen, *Understanding Church Growth and Decline, 1950–1978* (New York: Pilgrim Press, 1979).

17. Dean R. Hoge, "A Test of Theories of Denominational Growth and Decline," in Hoge and Roozen, *Church Growth and Decline.*

18. *Religion in America, 1984,* 57.

19. Marty, *Nation of Behavers,* 71.

20. Sydney E. Ahlstrom, "The Radical Turn in Theology and Ethics: Why It Occurred in the 1960s," *Annals of the American Academy of Political and Social Science* 387 (January 1970), 1–13.

21. See Kelley, *Conservative Churches Are Growing;* and Phillip B. Jones, "An Examination of the Statistical Growth of the Southern Baptist Convention," in Hoge and Roozen, *Church Growth and Decline.* Between 1971 and 1981 alone there was a 47 percent increase in the number of Protestant private schools, a 95 percent increase in the number of students enrolled, and a 116 percent increase in teachers. See U.S. Bureau of the Census, *Statistical Abstract of the United States, 1981,* 102d ed., no. 242, Washington, D.C., 1981.

22. *Religion in America, 1977–1978,* 19.

23. See Gallup, "U.S. in Early Stage of Religious Revival?"

24. John C. Pollock, Peter Finn, Adam Snyder, Sam Kingsley, Michael Wolk, Kathy Bloomgarden, and Arthur Pfenning, *The Connecticut Mutual Life Report on American Values in the 1980s: The Impact of Belief* (Hartford: Connecticut Mutual Life Insurance Company, 1981), 17.

25. See Samuel C. Heilman, "Constructing Orthodoxy," in *In Gods We*

Trust, ed. Thomas Robbins and Dick Anthony (New Brunswick, N.J.: Transaction Books, 1981), 141–157; and Harold S. Himmelfarb and R. Michael Loar, "National Trends in Jewish Ethnicity: A Test of the Polarization Hypothesis," *Journal for the Scientific Study of Religion* 23 (June 1984), 140–154. Also see Natalie Gittelson, "American Jews Rediscover Orthodoxy," *New York Times Magazine,* September 30, 1984.

26. Reported in the *Los Angeles Times,* February 25, 1980. Also see Jeffrey K. Hadden and Charles E. Swann, *Prime Time Preachers: The Rising Power of Televangelism* (Reading, Mass.: Addison-Wesley Publishing, 1981).

27. *Religion and Television: A Research by the Annenberg School of Communication, University of Pennsylvania and the Gallup Organization, Inc.* (Philadelphia: Annenberg School of Communication, April 1984).

28. Marabell Morgan, *The Total Woman* (Tappan, N.J.: Fleming H. Revell, 1973).

29. According to a New York Times/CBS News poll, 81 percent of white, born-again Protestants voted for the Reagan-Bush ticket in 1984 compared to 58 percent of white Catholics, 69 percent of other Protestants, and 32 percent of Jews. See *New York Times,* November 15, 1984.

30. Sidney E. Mead elaborates on Chesterton's quotation in "A Nation with the Soul of a Church," *Church History* 36 (September 1967), 1–22.

31. Lowell D. Streiker and Gerald S. Strober, *Religion and the New Majority: Billy Graham, Middle America, and the Politics of the 70s* (New York: Association Press, 1972), 23.

32. Herberg, *Protestant—Catholic—Jew,* 78–79.

33. Robert N. Bellah, *The Broken Covenant* (New York: Seabury Press, 1975), 142.

34. See Bellah's essay "Religion and Legitimation in the American Republic," in Robbins and Anthony, *In God We Trust,* 48.

35. Daniel Bell, *The Cultural Contradictions of Capitalism* (New York: Basic Books, 1976).

36. *Emerging Trends* (Princeton: Princeton Religion Research Center), May 1980.

37. For writings on the quest for self-fulfillment in the 1960s and 1970s, see Peter Clecak, *America's Quest for the Ideal Self* (New York: Oxford University Press, 1983); Christopher Lasch, *The Culture of Narcissism* (New York: Norton, 1979); Philip Rieff, *The Triumph of the Therapeutic: Uses of Faith after Freud* (New York: Harper and Row, 1966); Joseph Veroff, Elizabeth Douvan, and Richard A. Kulka, *The Inner American: A Self-Portrait from 1957 to 1976* (New York: Basic Books, 1981). Some commentators point to a distinct break between these two decades, the sixties being a period of protest and the seventies a time of turning more deeply inward; others like Clecak argue in favor of the continuities over this span of time. We hold to the latter position.

38. Richard J. Neuhaus, *The Naked Public Square: Religion and Democracy in America* (Grand Rapids, Mich.: William B. Eerdmans Publishing, 1984).

39. Richard M. Merelman, *Making Something of Ourselves: On Culture*

and Politics in the United States (Berkeley: University of California Press, 1984).

40. John M. Cuddihy, *No Offense: Civil Religion and Protestant Taste* (New York: Seabury Press, 1978), 7.

41. Handy, *Christian America*, 159–184.

42. James Davidson Hunter, *American Evangelicalism: Conservative Religion and the Quandary of Modernity* (New Brunswick, N.J.: Rutgers University Press, 1983), 107ff.

43. Peter L. Berger, *The Sacred Canopy* (Garden City, N.Y.: Doubleday, 1967), 132–133.

44. Ibid., 133.

CHAPTER 2. THE NEW VOLUNTARISM

1. For details surrounding this debate, see coverage in *Newsweek*, August 6, 1984. A more extended discussion of the moral rhetoric in the campaign is provided by Steven M. Tipton, "Piety and Presidential Politics," *Christian Century* 101 (October 31, 1984).

2. James Wilcox, *Modern Baptists* (New York: Penguin, 1983), 97.

3. Robert Bellah, Richard Madsen, William Sullivan, Ann Swidler, and Steven Tipton, *Habits of the Heart* (Berkeley: University of California Press, 1985), 221.

4. See Winthrop Hudson, *The Great Tradition of the American Churches* (New York: Harper and Row, 1953).

5. Mead, *Lively Experiment*, 104.

6. Henry K. Rowe, *History of Religion in the United States* (New York: Macmillan, 1924), 54.

7. Clecak, *America's Quest for the Ideal Self*, 9.

8. Daniel Yankelovich, *New Rules: Searching for Self-Fulfillment in a World Turned Upside Down* (New York: Random House, 1981), chap. 5.

9. Ibid., 90.

10. This is Clecak's phrase. See *America's Quest for the Ideal Self*, chap. 11.

11. Steven M. Tipton, *Getting Saved from the Sixties* (Berkeley: University of California Press, 1982).

12. See Carl S. Dudley's discussion in *Where Have All Our People Gone?: New Choices for Old Churches* (New York: Pilgrim Press, 1979).

13. James Davidson Hunter, "Conservative Protestantism," in *The Sacred in a Secular Age*, ed. Phillip E. Hammond (Berkeley: University of California Press, 1985), 160.

14. Andrew M. Greeley, William C. McCready, and Kathleen McCourt, *Catholic Schools in a Declining Church* (Kansas City: Sheed and Ward, Inc., 1976), 304. For a general review of the "erosion of authority" problem, see Patrick H. McNamara, "American Catholicism in the Mid-80s: Pluralism and Conflict in a Changing Church," *Annals of the American Academy of Political and Social Science* 480 (July 1985), 63–74.

15. Dean R. Hoge discusses issues of concern to Catholic "dropouts" in *Converts, Dropouts, Returnees: A Study of Religious Change Among Catholics* (New York: Pilgrim Press, 1981). He notes that those leaving the church discussed moral teachings, when interviewed, much more than doctrinal ones. Most salient in their minds were teachings concerning marriage and sexuality. Also see Elaine Sciolino, "American Catholics: A Time For Challenge," *New York Times Magazine*, November 4, 1984. She examines Catholics' changing attitudes toward abortion, divorce, and homosexuality and the growing trends toward independence from Rome on such matters.

16. See Andrew M. Greeley, *The American Catholic: A Social Portrait* (New York: Basic Books, 1977), chap. 14.

17. The data are from U.S. Bureau of the Census, *Statistical Abstract of the United States, 1981*, 96 102d ed., no. 34, Washington, D.C., 1981.

18. Widick Schroeder, "Age Cohorts, the Family Life Cycle, and Participation in the Voluntary Church in America: Implications for Membership Patterns, 1950–2000," *Chicago Theological Seminary Register* 65 (Fall 1975), 18.

19. See Ruth T. Doyle and Sheila M. Kelly, "Comparison of Trends in Ten Denominations, 1950–1975," in Hoge and Roozen, *Church Growth and Decline*, chap. 6.

20. Robert Wuthnow, *Experimentation in American Religion* (Berkeley: University of California Press, 1978). His treatment of the counterculture as a "generational unit" is especially illuminating. He examines the effects of age, exposure to trends, life cycle, and countercultural involvement in religious commitment and finds in his Bay Area sample that countercultural involvement was a critical intervening variable accounting for life-cycle effects on religiosity.

21. Also see the conclusions of Hoge and Roozen, *Church Growth and Decline*, chap. 14. This study offers a comparison of institutional and contextual influences on the churches during this period across denominations.

22. *U.S. News and World Report*, November 5, 1984, 68.

23. See "Values: Generations Apart," compiled by Everett C. Ladd in *Public Opinion*, December–January 1984, 21–40.

24. This is the thesis found in H. Richard Niebuhr, *The Social Sources of Denominationalism* (New York: Henry Holt, 1929). We examine his argument further in chap. 4.

25. Andrew Greeley, *The Denominational Society* (Glenview, Ill.: Scott, Foresman, 1972).

26. See William McKinney and Wade Clark Roof, "A Social Profile of American Religious Groups," in *Yearbook of American and Canadian Churches, 1982* (Nashville: Abingdon Press, 1982), 267–273.

27. Vance Packard, *A Nation of Strangers* (New York: David McKay, 1972).

28. For an extended discussion of "locals" and "cosmopolitans" and the relation of these groups to religion, see Wade Clark Roof, *Community and Commitment: Religious Plausibility in a Liberal Protestant Church* (New York: Elsevier North-Holland, 1978).

29. J. Milton Yinger, *Sociology Looks at Religion* (New York: Macmillan, 1963), 90.

30. Cuddihy, *No Offense*, 16.

31. Talcott Parsons, "Christianity and Modern Industrial Society," in *Sociological Theory and Modern Society* (New York: Free Press, 1967), 413.

32. Peter L. Berger, *The Heretical Imperative* (Garden City, N.Y.: Doubleday, 1980).

33. Parsons, "Christianity and Modern Industrial Society," 416.

34. These data are reported in Phillip E. Hammond, "The Extravasation of the Sacred and the Crisis in Liberal Protestantism," in *Liberal Protestantism: Realities and Prospects*, ed. Robert Michaelsen and Wade Clark Roof (New York: Pilgrim Press, 1986).

35. Greeley, *American Catholic*, 28.

36. Peter H. Rossi, as reported in Andrew Greeley, "American Catholics: Going Their Own Way," *New York Times Magazine*, October 10, 1982.

37. The term is Greeley's. See his "American Catholics."

CHAPTER 3. THE FRAGMENTED MAINLINE

1. Edwin Scott Gaustad, "Did the Fundamentalists Win?" in *Religion and America*, ed. Mary Douglas and Steven M. Tipton (Boston: Beacon Press, 1982), 175.

2. See Elwyn Smith, "Voluntary Establishment of Religion," in *The Religion of the Republic*, ed. Elwyn A. Smith (Philadelphia: Fortress Press, 1971), 154–182.

3. Neuhaus, *Naked Public Square*, 202.

4. Dorothy C. Bass, "Faith and Pluralism in the United States," *On the Way*, vol. 3, no. 1 (September 1985), 12ff.

5. Streiker and Strober, *Religion and the New Majority*, 173.

6. Marty distinguishes among six major groupings: the mainline, evangelicalism and fundamentalism, Pentecostal-charismatic, the new religions, ethnic religion, and civil religion. His is an excellent overview of behaviorally based trends in American religion.

7. Herberg, *Protestant—Catholic—Jew*, 4.

8. Gerhard Lenski, *The Religious Factor* (Garden City, N.Y.: Doubleday, 1961).

9. Greeley, *Denominational Society*.

10. Michael Novak, "The Communal Catholic," *Commonweal* 17 (January 1975), 321.

11. Marty, *Nation of Behavers*, 75–76.

12. For a classification system based on distinctions between transplanted European and indigenous American faiths, see Milton V. Backman, Jr., *Christian Churches of America* (New York: Charles Scribner's Sons, 1976). A typology of the major religious traditions can be found in the *World Christian Encyclopedia*, ed. David B. Barrett (Oxford: Oxford University Press,

1982), 714–715. An ambitious, comprehensive typology of American faiths is proposed in J. Gordon Melton, *A Dictionary of Religious Bodies in the United States* (New York: Garland Publishing, 1977). Life-style, thought world, and heritage are considered, resulting in a listing of 1,275 distinct religious groups and 17 family groupings.

13. Charles Y. Glock and Rodney Stark, *Religion and Society in Tension* (Chicago: Rand McNally, 1965), chap. 5.

14. Martin E. Marty, *Righteous Empire: The Protestant Experience in America* (New York: Harper Torchbooks, 1970).

15. Rodney Stark and Charles Y. Glock, *American Piety: The Nature of Religious Commitment* (Berkeley: University of California Press, 1968), chap. 8.

16. Kit Konolige and Frederica Konolige, *The Power of Their Glory* (New York: Wyden Books, 1978), 27.

17. See Albert Menendez, *Religion at the Polls* (Philadelphia: Westminster Press, 1977). The appendix to this volume carries the religious affiliations of members of Congress, 1961–1977. For a similar breakdown for members of the Ninety-ninth Congress, see *Christianity Today*, January 18, 1985.

18. Quote in Winthrop S. Hudson, *American Protestantism* (Chicago: University of Chicago Press, 1961), 128.

19. Quoted in F. E. Mayer, *The Religious Bodies of America* (Concordia Press, 1954), 310.

20. See the ratings of the various denominations by independent judges in Dean R. Hoge, "A Test of Denominational Growth and Decline," in Hoge and Roozen, *Church Growth and Decline.* A survey on beliefs (belief that it is necessary to accept Jesus to be saved, and belief in the Devil) shows that only 7 percent of Episcopalians, 13 percent of Congregationalists, and 13 percent of Presbyterians agree to both. Figures are considerably higher for moderate Protestants: 25 percent for Methodists, 29 percent for American Lutherans, 19 percent for Disciples of Christ, 30 percent for American Baptists. Data are from the Anti-Semitism in the United States Survey, conducted in 1974 by the National Opinion Research Center.

21. According to the General Social Surveys, 84 percent of blacks are Protestant and 71 percent are Baptist or Methodist. We have included only blacks of Methodist or Baptist background in this grouping. Blacks giving their religious preferences as other than Baptist or Methodist are included in the non–racially based grouping with which they identify.

22. See David Bromley's account of the place of the black church in the lives of its people in "Portrait of a Small Black Church," *New York Times Magazine*, June 30, 1985.

23. Martin E. Marty, "The Career of Pluralism in America," in *Religion in America: 1950 to the Present*, ed. Jackson W. Carroll, Douglas W. Johnson, and Martin E. Marty (New York: Harper and Row, 1979), 53.

24. These data are reported in Hunter, *American Evangelicalism*, chap. 5.

25. George M. Marsden, "Preachers of Paradox: The Religious New Right

in Historical Perspective," in Douglas and Tipton, *Religion and America*, 165.

26. Greeley, "American Catholics," 29.

27. Reported in ibid.

28. Quoted in *Religion in America, 1979–80* (Princeton: Princeton Religious Research Center), 75.

29. Charles E. Silberman, *A Certain People: American Jews and Their Lives Today* (New York: Summit Books, 1985), 24.

30. For an early descriptive piece on nonaffiliates, see Glenn M. Vernon, "The Religious 'Nones': A Neglected Category," *Journal for the Scientific Study of Religion* 7 (1968). Rodney Stark and William Bainbridge report that the "nones" today, though they have no religious affiliation, express considerable belief in the mystical and supernatural and are hardly irreligious, in *The Future of Religion* (Berkeley: University of California Press, 1985), 47–48.

31. This distinction comes from John G. Condran and Joseph B. Tamney, "Religious 'Nones': 1957 to 1982," *Sociological Analysis* 46 (Winter 1985), 415–423. Structural nones refer to religious outsiders, because of their marginal and isolated social position. In contrast, cultural nones are a product of value changes and shifting worldviews.

32. See Peter L. Berger's description of a "plausibility structure" and its functions, in *Sacred Canopy*, especially 45ff.

CHAPTER 4. THE SOCIAL SOURCES OF DENOMINATIONALISM REVISITED

1. John Wilson, *Religion in American Society: The Effective Presence* (Englewood Cliffs, N.J.: Prentice-Hall, 1978), 141.

2. The earlier profile is taken from Herbert Wallace Schneider, *Religion in Twentieth Century America* (Cambridge: Harvard University Press, 1952), Appendix A, table 1. His data are from the Office of Public Opinion Research at Princeton University and are based upon more than twelve thousand cases from four surveys in 1945 and 1946. For an earlier study, see Hadley Cantril, "Educational and Economic Composition of Religious Groups," *American Journal of Sociology* 47 (March 1943), 574–579. For a ranking based on data from 1957–1958, see Bernard Lazerwitz, "A Comparison of Major United States Religious Groups," *Journal of the American Statistical Association* 56 (September 1961), 568–579. Also see Liston Pope, "Religion and the Class Structure," *Annals of the American Academy of Political and Social Science* 256 (March 1948), 84–91. The current profile represents a rank order based on the average (mean) of the three rankings for education, occupational status, and income as taken from the General Social Surveys shown in table 4-2.

3. See Lazerwitz, "Major United States Religious Groups," for the 1957 data and the General Social Surveys for the later standings.

4. Greeley's research shows that Catholic gains are greater in income

than in education or occupation. He also argues that today Catholics rank above elite Protestants, most notably Episcopalians and Presbyterians, in the nation's income elite; however, that conclusion does not follow from our analysis of the General Social Surveys. See Greeley's *Ethnicity, Denomination and Inequality* (Beverly Hills: Sage, 1976) as well as the response by Wade Clark Roof, "Socioeconomic Differentials among White Socioreligious Groups in the United States," *Social Forces* 58 (September 1979), 280–289.

5. John H. Hendricks, "Religious and Political Fundamentalism," Ph.D. diss., University of Michigan, 1977.

6. Vance Packard, *The Status Seekers* (New York: David McKay Co., 1959).

7. For discussion of the class-based conflict in contemporary religion, see Peter L. Berger, "The Class Struggle in American Religion," *Christian Century*, February 25, 1981. For broader discussions of the "new class," see Irving Horowitz, "On the Expansion of New Theories and the Withering Away of Old Classes," *Society* 16 (2), 55–62; also see Hunter, *American Evangelicalism*, 107–119.

8. Neuhaus, *Naked Public Square*, 240–241.

9. These estimates are based upon General Social Survey data.

10. Taken from the U.S. Bureau of the Census, *Religious Bodies, 1916*, part 2, Washington, D.C., 1919.

11. Based on the General Social Surveys of 1972–1975, reported in Mary T. Hanna, *Catholics and American Politics* (Cambridge: Harvard University Press, 1979), 103.

12. Greeley, *American Catholic*, 38.

13. The literature on Catholic ethnicity is extensive but see Andrew Greeley's "Ethnic Variations in Religious Commitment," in *The Religious Dimension: New Directions in Quantitative Research*, ed. Robert Wuthnow (New York: Academic Press, 1979), 113–134; and Harold Abramson, *Ethnic Diversity in Catholic America* (New York: John Wiley, 1973).

14. Charles H. Anderson, *White Protestant Americans: From National Origins to Religious Group* (Englewood Cliffs, N.J.: Prentice-Hall, 1970), 173.

15. Reported in *Christianity Today*, April 4, 1986.

16. See Samuel S. Hill, Jr., "Religion and Region in America," in *Annals of the American Academy of Political and Social Science* 480 (July 1985), 132–141. He reviews evidence showing that regional religious styles persist in America.

17. See the historical accounts of William W. Sweet, *The Story of Religion in America* (New York: Harper and Brothers, 1950), and Edwin S. Gaustad, *A Religious History of America* (New York: Harper and Row, 1966).

18. See *Emerging Trends*, October 1981, which carries as a headline "Third of Westerners 'Never' Attend Church." This compares with only 13 percent of southerners, 14 percent of persons living in the Midwest, and 19 percent of easterners who say they *never* attend church.

19. See the discussion in Kenneth K. Bailey, *Southern White Protestantism in the Twentieth Century* (New York: Harper and Row).

20. See Samuel S. Hill, Jr., *Southern Churches in Crisis* (New York: Holt, Rinehart and Winston, 1966). Another insightful analysis of southern religion is found in John Shelton Reed, *The Enduring South* (Chapel Hill: University of North Carolina, 1974), chap. 6.

21. Roger Stump, "Regional Migration and Religious Commitment in the United States," *Journal for the Scientific Study of Religion* 23 (September 1984), 292–303.

22. On Southern Baptists see Phillip Barron Jones, "An Examination of the Statistical Growth of the Southern Baptist Convention," in Hoge and Roozen, *Church Growth and Decline*, chap. 7.

23. This argument is put forth cogently by Grant Wacker in "Uneasy in Zion: Evangelicals in Postmodern Society," in *Evangelicalism and Modern America*, ed. George Marsden (Grand Rapids: William B. Eerdman, 1984), 17–28. He notes the growing coalescence of mainstream and southern evangelical outlooks as evidenced by the acceptance of southern-born evangelical preachers on television, southern religion's historic involvement in secular politics, and the uncanny resemblance of the South's Cult of the Lost Cause to the myth of sacred American origins and divine plans. Also see Lewis M. Killian, *White Southerners* (New York: Random House, 1970), chap. 5.

24. Rodney Stark and William Bainbridge argue that there is an "Unchurched Belt" extending from the Mexican border through Alaska. Church membership is weak but not necessarily other more personal forms of religiosity. See *Future of Religion*, chap. 4.

25. Gibson Winter is credited with the saying in *The Suburban Captivity of the Churches* (Garden City, N.Y.: Doubleday, 1962), 30.

26. Membership figures are taken from Sydney E. Ahlstrom, "The Rise of the Black Churches," in *Religious History of the American People*, 698–714.

27. Niebuhr, *Social Sources of Denominationalism*, 259.

28. See Liston Pope, "The Negro and Religion in America," in *The Sociology of Religion: An Anthology*, ed. Richard D. Knudten (New York: Appleton-Century-Crofts, 1967).

29. These results are reported in C. Kirk Hadaway, David G. Hackett, and James F. Miller, "The Most Segregated Institution: Correlates of Interracial Church Participation," *Review of Religious Research* 25 (March 1984), 204–219.

CHAPTER 5. THE DEMOGRAPHY OF RELIGIOUS CHANGE

1. Henry P. Van Dusen, "The Third Force's Lessons for Others," *Life* 44 (June 9, 1958), 122–123. Also see William G. McLoughlin, "Is There a Third Force in Christendom?" *Daedalus* 96 (Winter 1967), 43–68.

2. Throughout the period from the 1920s to the 1960s, conservative churches were growing at a rapid rate, sometimes as much as 100 percent per decade. By comparison, the more liberal churches grew on an average of 19.2 percent per decade. See William R. Hutchison, "Does Liberal Protestantism Have an American Future?" in Michaelsen and Roof, *Liberal Protestantism: Realities and Prospects*, 65–82.

3. The 1985 *Yearbook of American and Canadian Churches* is the best source of these institutional statistics. Also see Hutchison, "Does Liberal Protestantism Have an American Future?"

4. Robert Lynn and Helen Lynn, *Middletown in Transition: A Study in Cultural Conflicts* (New York: Harcourt and Brace, 1937), 298.

5. Theodore Caplow, Howard M. Bahr, and Bruce A. Chadwick, *All Faithful People: Change and Continuity in Middletown's Religion* (Minneapolis: University of Minnesota Press, 1983), 77.

6. The 1957–1958 data are taken from Lazerwitz, "Major United States Religious Groups," table 2. More recent data on age composition can be found in the Gallup report *Religion in America, 1984* Report No. 22.

7. See Benton Johnson, "Liberal Protestantism: End of the Road?" in *Annals of the American Academy of Political and Social Science* 480 (July 1985), 39–52.

8. These data are taken from William V. D'Antonio and Joan Aldous, eds., *Families and Religions: Conflict and Change in Modern Society* (Beverly Hills: Sage Publications, 1983), p. 81ff.

9. Taken from William V. D'Antonio, "Family Life, Religion, and Societal Values and Structures," in D'Antonio and Aldous, *Families and Religions*, 106.

10. John Scanzoni, *Sex Roles, Life Styles, and Childbearing: Changing Patterns in Marriage and the Family* (New York: Free Press), 87.

11. Dennison Nash, "A Little Child Shall Lead Them: A Statistical Test of the Hypothesis That Children Were the Source of the American 'Religious Revival,'" *Journal for the Scientific Study of Religion* 7:238–240.

12. Reported in Leo Rosten, *Religions of America: Ferment and Faith in an Age of Crisis* (New York: Simon and Schuster 1975), 393.

13. Reported in Wilson, *Religion in American Society*, 252.

14. These patterns were evident in the special Census Bureau study, conducted in March 1957. See U.S. Bureau of the Census, *Statistical Abstract of the United States, 1958*, 79th ed., no. 40, Washington, D.C., 1958. Differences in birth rates among Protestant denominations were greater than those between Protestants and Catholics.

15. Sydney E. Ahlstrom draws this observation. See *Religious History of the American People*, 847.

16. Peter L. Berger, *The Precarious Vision* (Garden City, N.Y.: Doubleday, 1961), 74.

17. N. J. Demerath III, *Social Class in American Protestantism* (Chicago: Rand McNally, 1965), 71n.

18. Stark and Glock, *American Piety*, 10.

19. Reported in *Emerging Trends*, June 1980.

20. Much research confirms this estimate for Protestants. Stark and Glock's earlier study reported 46 percent switching in their California sample and slightly more than 40 percent nationally. Comparable estimates are found in more recent research. See Frank Newport, "The Religious Switcher in the United States," *American Sociological Review* 44 (August 1979), 528–552; and Wade Clark Roof and C. Kirk Hadaway, "Denominational Switching in the Seventies: Going Beyond Stark and Glock," *Journal for the Scientific Study of Religion* 18 (December 1979), 363–377. Switching for Catholics and Jews is much lower.

21. This is also the argument of Steven Bruce in "A Sociological Account of Liberal Protestantism," *Religious Studies* 20, no. 3 (September 1984), 414.

22. Stark and Glock, *American Piety*, 203.

23. Kirk Hadaway, "Changing Brands: Denominational Switching and Membership Change," in *Yearbook of American and Canadian Churches, 1983* (Nashville: Abingdon Press, 1983), 262–268.

24. Ibid.

25. Greeley, "American Catholics," 28ff.

26. Reported in Silberman, *A Certain People*, 299. Also see Silberman's chapter "Jews by Choice."

27. Alexis de Tocqueville, *Democracy in America*, vol. 2 (New York: Vintage Books, 1945), 12.

CHAPTER 6. MAINLINE MORALITY

1. William Lee Miller, "American Religion and American Political Attitudes," in *Religious Perspectives in American Culture*, ed. James Ward Smith and A. Leland Jamison (Princeton: Princeton University Press, 1961), 94.

2. Jerry Falwell, "Government Has Role in Advancing Religion," *USA Today*, June 7, 1985, 12A. Falwell adds: "What is it about God that so infuriates liberals? Don't they realize that it has been our collective escape from God and godly principles that has contributed to the numerous social problems we now face?"

3. "Christian Theological Observations on the Religious Right Movement," October 21, 1980. Reprinted in Peggy L. Shriver, *The Bible Vote* (New York: Pilgrim Press, 1981), 107–111.

4. Mead, *The Lively Experiment*, esp. chap. 3.

5. Quoted from the *New York Times*, June 5, 1985, B5.

6. Jerry Falwell, "A Master Plan to Save America," *update* (Lynchburg, Va.: Jerry Falwell Ministries), September 1984, p. 1. Falwell attributes these problems to liberal religious groups: "Bible-believing Christians have remained silent too long while the religious Liberals and Secular Humanists have dominated the political scene. They have expelled God from our

schools, legalized abortion, promoted pornography, and brought about the general moral breakdown of society."

7. Clyde Nunn, Harry J. Crockett, and J. Allen Williams, *Tolerance for Nonconformity* (San Francisco: Jossey-Bass, 1978).

8. Ibid., 131.

9. The items are introduced with the statement, "There are always some people whose ideas are considered dangerous by other people," followed by a particular case: "For example, somebody who is against all churches and religion." The respondent is then asked whether he or she would permit such a person to make a speech in the community, to teach in a college or university, and whether, if some people in the community suggested that a book he wrote should be taken out of the public library, they would be opposed to its removal.

10. This procedure is a common one in the social sciences and is followed for each of the issues examined in this chapter. It makes it possible to compare scores on the civil liberties scale with others that follow.

11. To validate the civil liberties scales we looked at scores of persons taking positive and negative positions on other civil liberties items not included in the construction of the scales themselves. The results suggest that the civil liberties scale is a fairly good indicator of general positions on civil liberties for nonconformists. Representative examples: sample members supporting a Communist's right to make a speech have a score of .53, those opposing that right −.68; those favoring removal of a library book written by a Communist have a scale score of −.72, those opposing removal .54; those favoring a homosexual's right to teach have a score of .43, those opposing a score of −.74.

12. H. Richard Niebuhr, *The Social Sources of Denominationalism* (New York: Meridian Books, 1957), 236.

13. Martin Luther King, Jr., *I Have a Dream* (Los Angeles: John Henry and Mary Louise Dunn Bryant Foundation, 1963).

14. Racial justice scale scores were examined using two validity items. Sample members who feel a homeowner should have the right to refuse to sell a home to blacks score −.48; those opposing this right score .28. Those who say they would vote for a black presidential candidate score .98; those who say they would not vote for a black score −.22.

15. The technique is multiple classification analysis, which is described in Norman H. Nie, C. Hadlai Hull, Jean G. Jenkins, Karin Steinbrenner, and Dale H. Brent, *SPSS: Statistical Package for the Social Sciences*, 2d ed. (New York: McGraw Hill, 1975).

16. The scale scores were "adjusted" by the amount of their deviation from the sample average score that is due to the intercorrelation between each background variable and the two scales.

17. W. Lloyd Warner, *The Family of God* (New Haven: Yale University Press, 1959), 265–266.

18. Sydney E. Ahlstrom, "The Radical Turn in Theology: Why It Oc-

curred in the 1960s," *Annals of the American Academy of Political and Social Science* 387 (1970).

19. Two items were examined to validate the women's rights scale. Those who feel women and men are equally suited emotionally for political office score .45; those viewing women as less well suited score −.56. Those favoring a woman's unqualified right to an abortion score .34; those opposing it score −.11.

20. Jerald G. Bachman, Lloyd D. Johnson, and Patrick M. O'Malley, *Monitoring the Future—1980* (Ann Arbor: Survey Research Center, University of Michigan, 1981).

21. D. Garth Taylor and Tom W. Smith, "Public Opinion Regarding Various Forms of Sexual Behavior," GSS Technical Report No. 10, National Opinion Research Center, 1978.

22. Official Catholic teaching opposes abortion under almost all circumstances. As observed in the prior section, lay Catholics take a much more qualified position: 79 percent favor abortion in the case of rape, 37 percent in the case of a married woman who chooses to have no more children. See table 6-3.

23. We looked at three additional items to validate the new morality scale. Persons viewing premarital sex as not wrong at all have a scale score of .44, while those viewing premarital sex as always wrong have a score of −.65. Persons who favor making divorce easier to obtain score .40; those feeling divorce should be more difficult to obtain score −.31. Those favoring sex education in the public schools score .12; those opposed score −.52.

24. Gerhard Lenski, *The Religious Factor*, rev. ed. (Garden City, N.Y.: Doubleday Anchor, 1963), 328ff.

25. *Unchurched American, passim.*

26. Alasdair MacIntyre, *After Virtue: A Study in Moral Theory* (Notre Dame, Ind.: University of Notre Dame Press, 1981).

27. For an examination of this theme with respect to religious institutions, especially churches and synagogues, at the local level see David A. Roozen, William McKinney, and Jackson W. Carroll, *Varieties of Religious Presence: Mission in Public Life* (New York: Pilgrim Press, 1984).

28. See Stephen M. Cohen and Leonard J. Fein, "From Integration to Survival: American Jewish Anxieties in Transition," *Annals of the American Academy of Political and Social Science* 480 (July 1985), 75–88. Also Stephen M. Cohen, *American Modernity and Jewish Identity* (New York: Tavistock Publications, 1983).

29. Erhardt Seminars Training (*est*), for example, gives people a "rule-egoism," helping them to find self-fulfillment in a highly bureaucratized order by means of "following the rules and keeping your agreements." See Tipton, *Getting Saved from the Sixties*, chap. 4.

30. Carol Flake, *Redemptorama: Culture, Politics, and the New Evangelicalism* (Garden City, N.Y.: Doubleday, 1984), 218.

31. Herberg, *Protestant—Catholic—Jew*, 80.

32. Benton Johnson attributes what he sees as a disproportionate empha-

sis on social and political issues in liberal Protestantism to the legacy of Reinhold Niebuhr's thought. See Johnson's "Liberal Protestantism," 39–52.

CHAPTER 7. THE FUTURE OF THE MAINLINE

1. Jack Cashill, "Marketing Revelation Could Save Religions," *Wall Street Journal*, July 30, 1985, 30.

2. Tom W. Smith, "America's Religious Mosaic," *American Demographics*, June 1984, 19–23.

3. *New York Times*, September 16, 1985, A12.

4. Stephen M. Cohen and Leonard J. Fein, "From Integration to Survival: American Jewish Anxieties in Transition," *Annals of the American Academy of Political and Social Science* 480 (July 1985), 76.

5. James Melvin Washington, "Jesse Jackson and the Symbolic Politics of Black Christendom," *Annals of the American Academy of Political and Social Science* 480 (July 1985), 105.

6. Smith, "America's Religious Demographics," 19–23.

7. The Orthodox are probably the largest of these groups. For reasons we do not fully understand, Gallup consistently records about 1 percent of the population as Orthodox Christians. The National Opinion Research Center total is far lower. Orthodox Christians total only 59 of the 15,439 persons interviewed for the General Social Survey between 1973 and 1984, or 0.4 percent of those interviewed. The difference may lie in the differing ways the two organizations' religious preference question is posed. Gallup includes Orthodox as a response option along with Protestant, Catholic, Jewish, Some Other Religion, and No Religion, while NORC asks simply "What is your religious preference?"

8. Yvonne Y. Haddad, "The Muslim Experience in the United States," *The Link* 12, no. 4 (September/October 1979), 3.

9. Smith, "America's Religious Demographics," 19–23.

10. Bill J. Leonard, "Southern Baptists: In Search of a Century," *Christian Century*, July 17–24, 1985, 683–684.

11. William R. Hutchison, "Past Imperfect: History and Its Prospect for Liberalism" in Michaelsen and Roof, *Liberal Protestantism*.

12. Bellah, Madsen, Sullivan, Swindler, and Tipton, *Habits of the Heart*, 154.

13. George A. Lindbeck, *The Nature of Doctrine: Religion and Theology in a Post Liberal Age* (Philadelphia: Westminster Press, 1984), 127.

14. Martin E. Marty, *The Public Church* (New York: Crossroad, 1981).

15. "Eutychus and His Kin," *Christianity Today*, December 14, 1984.

16. Colin Campbell has made this case with respect to religion in Western culture. See "The Secret Religion of the Educated Classes," *Sociological Analysis* 39 (1978), 146–156.

17. Ernst Troeltsch, *The Social Teachings of the Christian Churches*, trans. Olive Wyon (New York: Harper and Row, 1931), 2:796.

18. Seymour Martin Lipset, *The First New Nation* (Garden City, N.Y.: Doubleday, 1967), chap. 4.

19. See, for example, Robert Wuthnow, "The Growth of Religious Reform Movements," *Annals of the American Academy of Political and Social Science* 480 (July 1985), 106–116.

20. *New York Times*, September 29, 1985, 54.

21. *Unchurched American*, 64.

22. Robert Wuthnow, *Experimentation in American Religion* (Berkeley: University of California Press, 1978), 196. For Wuthnow the distinguishing characteristics of religious populism are: (1) a primary belief in the "intrinsic and immediate validity of the popular will," (2) fluid standards subject to fads and crazes, (3) diversity in ideas and organization (sometimes known as the Janus character of populism), (4) resentment of elites and elite intellectuals, and (5) organizations that treat people as members of a mass audience or market.

23. Gary Wills, *Bare Ruined Choirs: Doubt, Prophecy, and Radical Religion* (Garden City, N.Y.: Doubleday, 1972), 21.

APPENDIX

1. For a detailed introduction to the General Social Survey see James A. Davis, *General Social Surveys, 1972–1984* (Chicago: National Opinion Research Center, 1984). General Social Survey data reported throughout this book come from Davis, *General Social Surveys, 1972–1984*, machine-readable data file. Principal Investigator, James A. Davis; Associate Study Director, Tom W. Smith; Research Assistant, C. Bruce Stephenson.

2. In 1984 the General Social Survey probed further to seek the specific Baptist, Methodist, Lutheran, and Presbyterian denomination with which persons are affiliated. In future years this change will give researchers more precise data on members of these groups than has heretofore been available. Given the small number of persons affected by the 1984 changes, we have not made use of them here.

3. This is a representative list of "other" groups. For the full list see Davis, *General Social Survey, 1972–1984*, Appendix J.

Index